The European Journal of Applied Linguistics and TEFL

Diversity and Representation in the ELT Classroom

2022 · VOLUME 11 · NUMBER 2

The European Journal of Applied Linguistics and TEFL
Volume 11 Number 2

Special Issue: Diversity and Representation in the ELT Classroom

Editors: Andrzej Cirocki and Heiko Motschenbacher

Proofreader: James Chantry

ISSN: 2192-1032

ISBN: 978-1-911369-95-0

eISBN: 978-1-911369-96-7

First edition 2022

Journal website: http://theeuropeanjournal.eu

Article submissions: editors@theeuropeanjournal.eu

Subscription enquiries: info@linguabooks.com

A CIP catalogue record for this publication is available from the British Library.

LinguaBooks
Elsie Whiteley Innovation Centre
Hopwood Lane, Halifax HX1 5ER
www.linguabooks.com

We wish to sincerely thank all the contributors for their valuable input to this issue. We are also deeply grateful to the Editorial Board for meticulously reviewing all of the manuscripts, despite their other numerous commitments. Special thanks go to James Chantry, who proofread the articles.

Editorial   **1**

1. **VILMA HUERTA CORDOVA, MARIO E. LOPEZ-GOPAR AND WILLIAM M. SUGHRUA, BENITO JUAREZ AUTONOMOUS UNIVERSITY OF OAXACA, MEXICO**

   Cultures in Contact: University Students and Speakers of Indigenous Languages .. **3**

2. **MOHAMMED ATEEK, UNIVERSITY OF LEICESTER, UK**

   Refugee Foreign Language Learning: Trauma and the Use of Translanguaging Space as a Vehicle for Psycho-Social Support **21**

3. **KATHRYN DEPIETRO, STEVENSON COLLEGE, USA, DENIZ ORTACTEPE HART, UNIVERSITY OF GLASGOW, UK, AND XINXIN LIU, YU MING CHARTER SCHOOL, USA**

   Harvesting Digital Spaces for Emergent Bilinguals: Culturally-Sustaining MALL Pedagogies for Migrant Children **43**

4. **VIVIANE LOHE, UNIVERSITY OF ERFURT, GERMANY**

   "We Are All Equal?!" – Gender, Gender Awareness and Attitudes towards Gender in Foreign Language Teaching and Learning **63**

5. **BENEDICT J. L. ROWLETT, HONG KONG BAPTIST UNIVERSITY, HONG KONG**

   Thinking Queerly: Implications for Transformative Teacher Practice in the English Language Classroom **85**

6. **JAYSON PARBA, UNIVERSITY OF HAWAI'I AT MANOA, USA, AND IRISH FERNANDEZ-DALONA, MINDANAO STATE UNIVERSITY-ILIGAN INSTITUTE OF TECHNOLOGY, PHILIPPINES**

   Disrupting English Hegemony and Promoting Critical Language Pedagogy in Philippine ELT **103**

7. **JENNIFER YPHANTIDES, SOKA UNIVERSITY, JAPAN**

   EFL Teachers' Experiences with Neurodiverse Students and Self-Efficacy for Inclusive Practice in Japanese Universities **125**

8. **BIMALI INDRARATHNE, UNIVERSITY OF YORK, UK**

   Using the Multisensory Structured Teaching Approach to Help Learners with Dyslexia in Acquiring a Second/Additional Language **141**

The European Journal of Applied Linguistics and TEFL is a refereed scholarly publication that aims to disseminate information, knowledge and expertise in the broad area of Applied Linguistics. A strong preference is given to contributions relating to second language acquisition, foreign language pedagogy, teacher education and classroom innovation.

This special issue consists of ten articles focusing on different aspects of *Diversity and Representation in the ELT Classroom*. Viewed in total, the contributions evidence the multitude of dimensions that can shape learning and teaching experiences, and thus call for the implementation of specific measures if it is our aim to increase inclusivity levels. Among the relevant dimensions discussed, there are heterogeneous aspects that can lead to a person's social and, by extension, educational marginalisation, such as L1, ethnicity, gender identity, sexual identification, neurodiversity, personality type, cognitive style, aptitude as well as being a refugee, living in a migrant family, and having dyslexia. Furthermore, the articles highlight that the complexity of social inclusion in educational contexts necessitates shifts away from more traditional teaching practices towards aspects that have started to shape language education more recently, such as intercultural awareness as a learning goal, translanguaging as a legitimate linguistic practice, mobile-assisted language learning, the questioning of traditional and stereotypical gender and sexuality discourses, critical language pedagogy, attending to learners with disabilities, multisensory language teaching, virtual simulation of educational contexts, and inclusive pedagogies.

Across the various articles, this special issue provides the ELT community with a thorough overview of current theory, research and practice surrounding the concepts of diversity and representation in English language education, including contributions from Mexico, the UK, the USA, Germany, Hong Kong, the Philippines and Japan.

We are thankful to the contributors to this volume for sharing their experiences and research on several important aspects of inclusive education. We hope that their views, practices and empirical findings will not only inspire English language teacher educators and practitioners to enrich their own professional practice, but also ensure that inclusive classrooms are widely promoted in their contexts, and all students are treated fairly and receive equal opportunities.

Heiko Motschenbacher
Guest Editor

Andrzej Cirocki
Editor

1

CULTURES IN CONTACT: UNIVERSITY STUDENTS AND SPEAKERS OF INDIGENOUS LANGUAGES

Vilma Huerta Cordova, Mario E. López-Gopar and William M. Sughrua
Benito Juarez Autonomous University of Oaxaca, Mexico

ABSTRACT

This research took place in the state of Oaxaca, Mexico: home to 16 officially recognised Indigenous languages, whose speakers have been represented as primitive, backward and in need of help due to Mexico's colonial history. In order to raise awareness of the diversity of Oaxaca and the need to develop inclusive pedagogies, the study presented in this article was carried out at the Faculty of Languages of the University of Oaxaca (FL-UABJO), with the participation of two groups: a group of Indigenous speakers of Oaxacan languages at risk of disappearance and a group of mestizo university students enrolled in the BA programme in language teaching at FL-UABJO. Utilising a peer tutoring scenario, employing qualitative methodology, and including theory on diversity, intercultural education and representation, this article explores the perspectives of the FL-UABJO students on diversity and inclusion. Based on the recursive and iterative analysis of the data, three emergent themes are discussed: (1) interculturality: attending a congress of cultures, (2) reconfiguring oneself and others, and (3) awareness of the collective agency of Indigenous language speakers.

KEYWORDS

Indigenous languages, peer tutoring, future language teachers, Mexico.

1. INTRODUCTION

This research took place in the state of Oaxaca, located in southern Mexico. Oaxacan inhabitants face high rates of poverty and marginalisation, especially minoritised groups such as the Indigenous population (López-Gopar, 2016). Oaxaca is home to 16 officially recognised Indigenous languages, most of which are experiencing language shift and some of which, like *Chontal, Chocholteco* and *Ixcateco,* are currently at the highest risk of disappearance (García Vargas, 2018). Not only are these Indigenous languages in danger, but also their speakers are represented as primitive, backward and in need of help due to Mexico's colonial history (Maldonado Alvaro, 2002; Mignolo, 2000). The high presence of Indigenous groups in Oaxaca has made Oaxacan classrooms and schooling institutions culturally and linguistically diverse in terms of language as well as such issues as gender, sexual orientation, (dis)ability, social class, and religion. Approaching this diversity and representation from a cultural-ethnic and linguistic lens, this research, set in Oaxaca, specifically centres on the Faculty of Languages (FL) of the

Universidad Autónoma Benito Juárez de Oaxaca (UABJO), the largest public university in the state.

Each academic year, the UABJO receives students from different communities in the state of Oaxaca: young people of Indigenous origin, mestizos, Afro-Mexicans and returnees from the United States. This diversity is also present in the FL and its BA degree programme focused on the development of language teachers, especially in English and Spanish, but also in other languages such as Italian, Portuguese, Japanese, Zapotec and Mixe (these last two being Indigenous languages from Oaxaca). In order to raise awareness of the diversity of the state of Oaxaca and the need to develop inclusive pedagogies, the study presented in this article was carried out at the FL, with the participation of two groups: a group of Indigenous speakers of Oaxacan languages at risk of disappearance and a group of mestizo university students, future teachers of English, Chinese, and French from the BA programme at FL-UABJO. Utilising a peer tutoring scenario, conceptualised as a pedagogical approach, based on the creation of pairs of participants who take turns at teaching and learning from each other (Durán & Vidal, 2004), the FL-UABJO university students prepared lessons to teach a foreign language to Indigenous speakers, and then the Indigenous speakers designed lessons to teach their native language to these future teachers. Reporting on this experience, while employing a qualitative methodology (Flick, 2015) and including theory on diversity, intercultural education and representation, this article explores the perspectives of the FL university students on diversity and inclusion. In the sections to follow, the context, the theoretical framework, the process of the project, and the methodology are discussed. Then, based on the recursive and iterative analysis of the data, three emergent themes are discussed: (1) interculturality: attending a congress of cultures; (2) reconfiguring oneself and others; and (3) awareness of the collective agency of Indigenous language speakers. Finally, conclusions will be offered.

2. OAXACA, THE FACULTY OF LANGUAGES, AND THE BA PROGRAMME

The state of Oaxaca, as indicated previously, is the most culturally and linguistically diverse state of Mexico. Oaxaca has the highest percentage of Indigenous people in Mexico, representing 16.3 per cent of the national total population of over seven million (*Instituto Nacional de Geografía e Informática* [National Institute of Geography and Information of Mexico], 2020). In addition, Oaxaca has the highest population of speakers of Indigenous languages in Mexico. However, Barabas (1999) argues that the number of Indigenous people is or should be much higher and that the exaggerated proportion of the so-called non-Indigenous (*mestizo*) population is the result of cultural elements tied to Indigenous languages: "speaking a 'dialect' [pejorative term to refer to Indigenous languages] is considered a custom of Indians, associated with an inferior identity" (p. 164, our translation). Being an Oaxacan is equated with being an Indigenous and formally uneducated person in other states of Mexico. Hence, "many Indigenous peoples deny their ethnicity, language and culture" (López Hernández, 2002, p. 5, our translation).

Besides facing discrimination, Indigenous peoples struggle financially and educationally. According to Vásquez Parra and Campos-Rivas (2016), Mexico is considered the country in the

4

world with the second highest poverty rate among the Indigenous groups (eight out of ten living in poverty), which results in low educational achievement and low-paying jobs. The average level of schooling for the Indigenous population of Oaxaca is 5.4 years, which implies that the majority do not complete the elementary school level. Also, health services in Indigenous communities are precarious (García Vargas, 2018). Despite this hardship, Indigenous groups have resisted. It is important to acknowledge that many Indigenous teachers working in rural areas are making enormous efforts to provide culturally appropriate and responsive education that respects and promotes diversity and multilingualism (López-Gopar, 2016).

As previously mentioned, the FL at UABJO mirrors the cultural and linguistic diversity present in Oaxaca. Nevertheless, the BA programme in teaching languages started with a sole focus on English language teaching. French was also promoted as the only elective language when the BA programme started in 1992. In 2001, the BA programme was reformed to focus on wider educational issues, but it did not prioritise or make room for Indigenous languages. It was not until 2013, when the BA programme underwent another curricular reform, that the BA programme included two Indigenous languages as part of their language electives. One can say that it took 20 years for the FL to realise that it was seated in the most culturally and linguistically diverse state of the country and that its BA programme should prepare language teachers who work in favour of the multilingual and intercultural groups present in Mexico. The next section focuses on theories that frame this study and that have found their way, albeit recently, into the BA programme of the FL at UABJO.

3. CRITICAL INCLUSION, INTERCULTURAL EDUCATION AND REPRESENTATION

Diversity is the norm in educational spaces, as evident in the different ways of being, knowing and speaking of the students in the classroom. Diversity in the classroom can be ignored or recognised as a problem or as a strength/richness (Hamel, 2000). Diversity, when understood as a strength/richness, implies maintaining a positive attitude and appreciation for what is different and offering a high-quality education to *all* students. On the other hand, when diversity is ignored or regarded as a problem, highly exclusive practices are developed. One example is justifying a watered-down curriculum for a certain group of students because their academic performance is limited (Rockwell, 2004). Diversity thus can bring out inclusion or exclusion, both being problematic, depending on how they are approached. Diversity encompasses many different identities in the classroom, and because of that, when teachers design educational strategies that are too narrowly focused on a specific student identity, there is a risk of excluding other important intersectional understandings of students within the classroom. Educational strategies should be sought, so that all students are participants in collaborative learning.

In terms of inclusion, Estermann (2014) warns that an inclusionary discourse has the potential to make invisible structures of asymmetry and hegemony that are characteristic of colonial societies imposing their culture over another. Abramowski (2014) argues that apparently positive narratives of inclusion can hide asymmetric and vertical intentions, as in the case of beneficence or charity. Beneficence creates unequal and antagonistic positions whereby the giver is understood as the guardian of the recipient, positioning the recipient as inferior, lacking and needy. The recipient of beneficence is placed in a status of subordination, dependence and eternal gratefulness. This can be problematic because in the name of compassion, people such as teachers may create exclusionary acts, which position the recipients such as students in constant need or codependence whereby the giver benefits by feeling good, needed or generous while the student remains dependent on these actions. One alternative to beneficence is interdependence, which involves mutual negations about giving and taking as well as reciprocity challenging problematic political and power situations. Another alternative is to maintain a critical stance that reveals situations where, in the name of the appreciation of difference, acts of exclusion are exercised. This critical stance, according to Aizencang and Bendersky (2013), must be applied to educational practices since these practices respond to epistemological assumptions and representations produced in a specific situation. It is therefore necessary to denaturalise the contexts, challenge exclusionary practices, understand them from a historical perspective, and hence unveil the assumptions that built and sustain them; this enables the emergence of new meanings. Continuing along this line of thought, Estermann (2014) states that seeking decolonisation and trying to stop the segregation of certain vulnerable, marginalised and minority groups entails a series of processes, always open and inconclusive, that demand a long-term historical and a utopian effort. In other words, the fight against exclusion and the false appreciation for diversity (e.g., race, gender, culture, ethnicity, linguistic, social class, (dis)ability) demands from teachers and other educational actors a state of permanent reflection, actions of cognitive, personal, and social efforts, and a high dose of hope. One of the educational options that can result in the appreciation of diversity and inclusion is intercultural education.

Intercultural education and critical inclusion have multiple connections that can and should guide educational practice (Arroyo González, 2013). According to McLaren (2005), in order to pursue critical inclusion, educators need to develop dialectical thinking in order to grasp the contradictions of everyday life. Using this statement as a foundation, critical inclusion can be thought of as meaning being aware that, when in attempting to be inclusive, highly exclusive and discriminatory acts may be inadvertently performed or the concept may be assumed superficially. Jordán (1994) says that it is important not to conceive these types of critical concepts such as inclusion in a simple way, and that there should be an attempt to understand these concepts more deeply because they are significant to understanding the role of education for school and society. Education from an intercultural perspective not only responds to cultural diversity from a respectful understanding, but also values cultural pluralism as inherent and enriching to current societies. Focusing on linguistic diversity within spaces where different languages combine (e.g., foreign and Indigenous languages both being used within one class activity), this intercultural approach becomes even more relevant. Morales Saavedra et al. (2018, p. 57, our translation) state:

> The intercultural educational approach seeks to improve the quality of teaching and learning in relation to Indigenous-Western knowledge and vice versa, as mutual learning, in order to generate a [pluri]universality of ways of knowing and knowledge. Through this approach, an education that values and respects difference is promoted, assuming

difference as an opportunity to enrich the teaching-learning processes. This process allows us to build more humane, and understanding relationship systems, capable of recognising differences, advantages and disadvantages, configuring an alternative paradigm of critical interculturality.

For Díaz Aguado (2013), intercultural education, which in this case does not refer to a school subject but rather to an approach at all educative levels that emphasises that all *cultural* groups can learn from one another, provides a way to fight against exclusion, by adapting education to the diversity that characterises students, and thereby ensuring that equal opportunities are guaranteed. In addition, Díaz Aguado (2013) argues that part of the intercultural approach is to respect the right to one's own identity: "For this it is necessary to carry out profound transformations in a school system until now monocultural in which the only possibility of integration was assimilation to the mainstream identity" (Díaz Aguado, 2013, p. 20, our translation). From this point of view, the promotion and distribution of leadership is sought, ensuring that all participants experience a relevant role in educational activities, collaborating from a status of equality with shared objectives (Díaz Aguado, 2013). Hence, the relationship between the different groups should aim for mutual recognition by being horizontally-symmetrical rather than vertically-asymmetrical.

In a horizontally-symmetrical framework of relationships, fostered in this case by intercultural education, the cultures in contact have greater possibilities to recognise each other and establish a more egalitarian dialogue (Elboj Saso et al., 2013). This involves recognising and valuing the knowledge that we all share as a source of learning. Nevertheless, we must keep in mind that tensions and conflicts emerge at different intensities at any time and should not be seen as something negative, but rather as a condition inherent in every intercultural process. Elboj Saso et al. (2103) believe that in order to build a learning community through a project of social and cultural transformation whereby all learners are successful in the current information society, dialogic learning is necessary. For Elboj Saso et al. (2013), an egalitarian dialogue occurs when the contributions of each participant are recognised and valued by considering the validity of the arguments presented in the interaction. According to Fisher (Fisher, 2013), "[d]ialogue involves two or more people who listen to each other, share ideas and take into account different points of view. In a dialogue, those who participate try to reach an understanding, although it does not necessarily end in agreement" (p. 21, our translation). The intercultural educational approach proposes, then, to establish more horizontally-symmetrical frameworks that allow people to position themselves in a more equitable way, not forgetting, as Corona Berkin and Kaltmeier (2012) point out, that some cultures are more powerful than others (e.g., mestizos versus Indigenous groups of Mexico; certain Indigenous groups versus other Indigenous groups). The Indigenous languages in this article, for example, are those in greatest danger of disappearing as contrasted with other Indigenous languages in a better position to survive. The highest risk of disappearance of Chocholteco, Chontal and Ixcateco, the languages presented in this article, is connected with greater poverty and marginalisation of the communities where these languages are spoken. This, in turn, is connected to issues of representation: how these languages and their speakers are seen or positioned by the mainstream society. This leads us to theories of representation in connection to horizontal/vertical relationships.

The problem of the representation of *others* from the perspective of a dominant culture has led to deficient and fixed perceptions of the people who do not fully belong to these cultures. Freire (2013) shows the construction that is made of students from vertical and exclusive positions of power, where students are configured as ignorant, lacking voice and discipline. Rudduck and Flutter (2007) make the point that the apparently minimal participation of children and young people in the processes of dialogue and decision making in school life is perhaps the result of them being considered as participants who do not have the capacity to make initiatives and reflections on the situations that affect them in institutions. Maddonni (2014) believes that school failure should not be blamed solely and exclusively on the subject (so-called personal deficits) and their environment (so-called cultural deficits), since this would lead to labelling and stigmatising people negatively, thus hiding deep structural inequalities. In addition, the supremacy of Western knowledge has generated an epistemological violence that affects thousands of subjects who do not fit in with the dominant narratives.

Connecting issues of representation to intercultural encounters, Riaño (2012) argues that there are obstacles that should be considered when two culturally different groups meet: barriers of imaginary, social and spatial hierarchy. The barrier of imaginaries has to do with the perception that one has of the *other*, and in vertical relationships there is a tendency to perceive only the weaknesses of the other, obscuring the differences and richness within the groups (Riaño, 2012). The barriers of social hierarchy, on the other hand, do not allow us to recognise the different types of knowledge that the subjects possess. This reduces the knowledge that does not fit within the dominant paradigm at the lower levels of the hierarchy (Riaño, 2012). Spatial barriers also play their part in the subordination of some and the recognition of others. For example, in terms of research, researchers may go to the space of *others* to collect information, getting to know these spaces quite well. However, that information is processed and disseminated in academic spaces which the investigated subjects can rarely access. Thus, it is important that subordinated groups can also have access to spaces usually reserved only for academics (e.g., universities, research centres) in order to tell their own stories and engage in respectful dialogic encounters (Riaño, 2012). In our case, we believe that contact between people is a good beginning to demystify what we believe about ourselves and about others. A true intercultural education that breaks down barriers of imaginary and social hierarchy must essentially have exchanges between people. The next section details the methodology of the Mexican project that brought together the university students and Indigenous speakers.

4. METHODOLOGY

The methodology used for the study is qualitative. In general terms, qualitative methodology "starts from the notion of the social construction of the realities under study and is interested in the perspectives of the participants in the daily practices and in the daily knowledge that refers to the question studied" (Flick, 2015, p. 15, our translation). In order to explore the perspectives on diversity and inclusion of the FL university students from a qualitative perspective, different methods were used (Hesse-Biber, 2017). In this research, the methods used were photograph analysis and ethnographic field notes taken by the researchers, reflective notes written by the FL university students, and an audio-recorded focus group discussion with FL university students (Kitzinger & Barbour, 1999). This study, however, directly refers only to the data generated by the focus group discussion. To prepare for the focus group discussion, the researchers utilised the photographs and field notes, while the students utilised their reflective notes taken during the process leading up to the focus group session. Because the photographs, field notes and reflective notes thus had an operative role in the realisation of the focus group, and because the focus group was the main and culminating method, this article does not make further mention of the photographs, field notes and reflective notes, instead relying exclusively on the audio-recordings of the focus group, by way of a qualitative content analysis (Hesse-Biber, 2017), in order to allow those themes with relevance to the research purpose to emerge from the focus group data.

For this study, six pairs were formed to teach an Indigenous or foreign language to one another. As previously mentioned, the six students from the FL were mestizo and Spanish-speaking people. In other words, none of them spoke an Indigenous language. They were all born and raised in the city of Oaxaca and were enrolled in the sixth semester of their 8-semester BA programme in language teaching at FI-UABJO. The six Indigenous language speakers lived in different Indigenous communities of Oaxaca. Two were primary school teachers and four were subsistence farmers with basic schooling. All six were activists in the preservation of their Indigenous language. The following table shows the composition of the pairs, and specifically the language the FL university students taught and the Indigenous language they learnt from the Indigenous speaker (Table 1). Hence, the FL university students played the roles of both tutor (teacher) and tutee (student).

Table 1

Languages Taught and learnt by the FL University Students

FL University Student Transcription Code	Foreign Language Taught	Indigenous Language Learnt
FLUS1	Chinese	Ixcateco
FLUS2	English	Chocholteco
FLUS3	English	Chocholteco
FLUS4	French	Chontal
FLUS5	English	Chocholteco
FLUS6	English	Chontal

The implementation of the peer tutoring experience between the two groups of participants consisted of the following five stages:

1. ***Development of communication skills and sharing personal knowledge.*** Peer tutoring is a way of teaching and learning that involves contact between people and dialogue. Therefore, it is essential that time be allocated for participants to get to know each other

and to develop or to polish their communication skills to improve the interactions when practising peer tutoring. For these reasons, an 8-hour workshop course was designed in which the participants reviewed topics such as physical and verbal attention as well as active listening. Using hands-on activities, they practised what active listening accompanied by physical gestures, position and eye contact looks and feels like (e.g., talking to someone who is not looking at you). During this stage, the participants in the pairs spent a lot of time sharing information about themselves.

2. ***Training of participants on peer tutoring and basic lesson planning elements***. As a second step, a 6-hour workshop course was carried out, so that the participants would have information about what peer tutoring is and how it is used. They also went over basic guidelines to plan the peer-tutoring activities; in other words, basic lesson planning elements.

3. ***Planning of peer tutoring activities.*** The next step was to design the planning of the peer tutoring sessions. The participants spent a couple of hours planning their tutoring sessions. The planning contemplated the objective of the lesson, the sequence of tasks, the selection or construction of the teaching materials, and the evaluation activities.

4. ***Peer tutoring practice.*** As previously mentioned, the peer-tutoring practice in this study consisted of the participants teaching the Indigenous or foreign language to the other person. The peer-tutoring sessions were monitored by us, as the researchers. Each session lasted around one hour (two hours in total for the peer-tutoring practice).

5. ***Reflection on peer tutoring practice.*** As a whole group, and with our facilitation, the six pairs reflected on the peer-tutoring session and on all the stages described above.

A few days after this peer-tutoring experience, and as previously mentioned, a focus group interview with the six FL university students was conducted. This event was conducted in Spanish and audio recorded. Some of the questions that guided the focus group conversation were: (1) Before this experience, what did you know about the Indigenous communities, peoples and languages? (2) What did you learn as a tutor of a foreign language and a tutee/learner of an Indigenous language? (3) What did you learn about Indigenous communities/peoples from this experience? For the analysis, the focus group interview/discussion was transcribed and iteratively analysed by the three of us, in search of emerging themes connected with the issues of diversity and inclusion. The following section presents the three emergent themes, intertwined with our discussion.

5. INTERCULTURALITY: ATTENDING A CONGRESS OF CULTURES

Schools, classrooms, and community spaces are places characterised by diversity. One can find differences in gender, culture, ethnicity, sexual diversity, and language, among others. One FL university student (FLUS, followed by a number to distinguish between participants, henceforth) put it this way:

This experience was an interaction of cultures; we shared a lot. I did not know, before this experience, about these people and their communities. I did not know what they did, where they worked, what language they spoke. For me, it was a discovery. (FLUS1, our translation)

This peer-tutoring experience, according to this university student, opened a space for the interaction of cultures and the discovery that the participants came from different environments with their own characteristics. Before the experience, this information was non-existent and would have been hidden if the stories had not been shared. Being face-to-face and building a dialogic space opened the window to difference and knowledge. Another FL university student commented: *"This experience was quite enriching. I can be a teacher of people who speak another language and who have another culture. If I do not know the students, we will lose a lot"* (FLUS2, our translation). This university student, projecting this experience to her future practice as a teacher, realises the importance of knowing and valuing the students' culture; not doing so, would be a loss for herself as a teacher and for the group. When the teacher has a deeper personal knowledge of the students, the teacher can then see the cultural richness that characterises each student (Díaz Aguado, 2013). If the teacher has a positive appreciation of diversity, it can be a source of richness and not a problem (Hamel, 2000).

Based on this experience, the FL university students began to acknowledge and appreciate the diversity present on campus, in terms of the students, teachers, administrators, counsellors, cafeteria workers, and cleaning staff. One FL university student mentioned: *"Now I think that in the school there are people who come from many places and have a different culture; a teacher at the school speaks Zapotec"* (FLUS1, our translation). Another FL university student added:

The woman who sells food at the entrance of the university speaks Mixteco [an Indigenous language from Oaxaca]. *So, I think that there are many people who walk around the school who are not students and who have, as my partner says, a different culture and different knowledge.* (FLUS5, our translation)

Educational institutions are broad. They encompass different social, ethnic and linguistic groups. When investigating, there will surely be as many other features that increase diversity, which are not as visible and perhaps hidden. Hence, the underlying idea is that the entire school community is diverse. This FL university student refers to constructing educational policies and practices that favour the valuing and appreciation of difference. This is especially important because, according to Díaz Aguado (2013), schools start from a vision of a dominant and hegemonic culture that leaves little space for difference.

In addition to positively viewing the community as culturally diverse, the FL university students concluded that teachers must acknowledge interculturality; that is, a teacher must not only appreciate diversity, but also engage in certain practices in order to demonstrate this appreciation. One FL university student commented: *"I think that you shouldn't just say that people from other places have a lot of richness, and then not do anything concrete, just words and no changes"* (FLUS5, our translation). In similar terms, Jordán (1994) highlights the importance of teachers putting interculturality into practice on a daily basis. Jordán (1994) explains that it is important for teachers to understand the intercultural approach and to think of it not only as something theoretically attractive, but also, and above all, as an indispensable condition for school success and good relationships among students. Therefore, future teachers, through this experience of meeting with Indigenous language speakers, built a valuable idea of diversity, while highlighting the congruence between theory and practice. By trying to explore the concept of interculturality in greater depth, another university student revealed what she means by the term:

> That relationship or interaction that we had, where we both shared, I take that as interculturality. I understand interculturality as a congress of different people, different cultures, different social environments. I think the key is to interact and share experiences. (FLUS5, our translation)

This FL university student conceptualises interculturality as a congress of different people, where difference becomes the positive motive and the central objective of the meeting. For the student, difference allowed the congregation of people and the dialogue between them.

Interculturality, as a congress of different peoples, also permitted an educative dialogue way beyond simply learning another language. In this dialogue, different points of view, knowledge and experiences were exposed, and thus learning was achieved, as indicated by an FL university student:

> The woman I had to work with told me where she came from and who her family members are. We shared many things: how we behave at home, the way we speak. [She told me about] the tone of voice in her language. Then, what happens is an exchange of cultures. I think she learned a little bit from me, and I learnt something from her. (FLUS3, our translation)

Language learning was enriched by sharing the way the participants behave at home, the way they speak and their tone of voice. It was about not only the structure of the language, but also the participants' daily life. This gives language learning/teaching a personal touch full of warmth and humanity. It also leads to a change of how one views oneself and the other, as can be seen in the next emergent theme.

6. RECONFIGURING ONESELF AND OTHERS

The peer-tutoring experience led to an understanding of interculturality and cultural (ex)changes as well as new visions the FL university students had about themselves and Indigenous peoples. One FL university student mentioned:

> While he talks to me, I'm going to his culture. I left mine for a little while, and then I think about mine again. We both change. We go from one place to another; that's why I say: "change of cultures." Changing your culture is interesting; you learn a lot. (FLUS4, our translation)

The peer-tutoring experience allowed "change of cultures," as indicated here. The FL university students abandoned their own cultural configurations for a little while, changed by interacting with the new culture, and then came back to embrace their own culture and knowledge. Consequently, through their interaction with other people, their identity became more flexible, rearranged and enriched with the interaction and the gaze of the other. After many significant encounters, one is not the same, by the influence of the other. That is, we do not construct ourselves alone; we construct ourselves by interacting with the presence and words of others and by leaving our culture momentarily and appreciating other cultures, as expressed by the FL university students.

During the peer tutoring experience, the FL university students challenged the barriers created by misconceptions. One FL student stated:

> *It is important that differences do not separate us, but they should unite us. For example, I speak English and she speaks Chontal, and those differences can cause us to distance from one another, especially if I have preconceptions about the other person* [However,]...[t]*alking* face-to-face helps us to get to know each other, learn, and also helps us to appreciate each other. (FLUS4, our translation)

This university student centres the discussion on how difference and the way in which we imagine others can build a barrier preventing learning from one another. Working from the notion of linguistic barrier, which covers a "varied range of potentially exclusionary phenomena in language and language use," Motschenbacher (2016) argues that "full inclusion can only be reached when the included identities are positively represented in classroom materials and talk" (pp. 166–167). In addition to the linguistic barrier, certain barriers of the imaginary (Riaño, 2012) can emerge through our preconceptions, as suggested by the same FL university student elaborating on mainstream peoples' misconceptions: *That the* [Indigenous language] *Chontal is not important; that in the Indigenous communities they are backward; that in the city we are selfish, that we are only competitive."* (FLSU4, our translation) These deficit appreciations can be reinforced when there is no interaction among cultural groups. There is a superficial look at the other and no time is devoted to getting to know the students and the members of that cultural group. From deficit and superficial views, students and other minoritised groups such as Indigenous communities are not seen as valuable and capable of achieving academic, personal and social goals (Freire, 2013; Rudduck & Flutter, 2007). Nevertheless, as believed by the previous FL university student, the best way to build a positive vision of people is through contact and the exchange of knowledge.

This peer-tutoring experience positioned Indigenous speakers as valuable, bringing down the existing social hierarchy barrier (Riaño, 2012). An FL student commented:

> *My partner who speaks an Indigenous language told me: "Because I wear different shoes, because I don't dress like someone in the city or because I don't have something that some people from the city do, that doesn't mean I don't have the ability to learn or teach." He*

taught me his language. He was my teacher and I learnt [from him]. (FLUS2, our translation)

This university student elaborated on how her peer-tutoring partner, an Indigenous language speaker, clearly pointed out to her a constant narrative of overvaluation of cities over Indigenous territories and communities; this refers to a barrier of social hierarchy (Riaño, 2012), built and maintained by vertical and colonialist structures. In this peer-tutoring experience, the Indigenous language speaker positioned himself as a subject with a valuable identity, with the ability to teach and learn, which was recognised and valued by the FL university student: *"He taught me his language. He was my teacher."* This in turn generated a recognition of knowledge and caused both parties to identify themselves as valuable and diverse. Similarly, Riaño (2012) argues "[t]hat is why we propose that the relationship be built on the basis of a relationship equivalent to a society where both parties are considered as experts, contribute different types of knowledge, and work as research partners" (p. 143, our translation). Negative appraisals can condition our teaching, which may lead to a reduction in the quality of the pedagogical practices that we offer, further affecting the groups that we consider disadvantaged. These educational deficit beliefs are not natural or fixed. Thus, there are opportunities to question and to change them. According to Corona Berkin and Kaltmeier (2012), school culture is built by establishing meeting spaces that invite dialogue: taking turns, as speakers and as listeners. The class, from this point of view, becomes a communication space, where interactions flow in multiple directions (e.g., student-student, student-teacher, teacher-student, teacher-teacher) and not just in one direction. Therefore, the dynamic flow of the interactions helps not to fix positions that later prevent the actors from being valued and represented from a non-deficit vision.

7. AWARENESS OF THE COLLECTIVE AGENCY OF INDIGENOUS LANGUAGE SPEAKERS

Through the peer tutoring experience, FL university students not only started to change their perceptions regarding Indigenous speakers, but they also recognised their activism and agency in defence of their Indigenous languages. One FL university student commented:

> *We hardly ever hear about the Indigenous languages and the efforts to preserve them, and never from the real voice* [of an Indigenous person]. *With my partner that changed, because he told me that in his language, he grows avocados* [and] *produces mezcal and that these activities help him to live.* (FLUS1, our translation)

This FL university student realised that Indigenous languages are part of people's daily lives and activities. At times, Indigenous languages are seen as organisms which can be "pickled in formaldehyde" (Holm, 2006, p. 10). However, through this peer-tutoring experience, languages came to life as vehicles for economic activities. FL university students' awareness arose when they were face-to-face with an Indigenous language speaker. In this encounter, there were also conditions of openness, appreciation and trust that facilitated the exploration of the daily, economic, social and political life that constitutes the person.

FL university students recognised the political activism performed by the Indigenous speakers to preserve their Indigenous language. Focusing on political activism, one university student stated:

> *My partner told me that he moves in the political arena. He talks to organisations to obtain support from the government. They always seek to obtain support to carry out activities to preserve their language. They go from one place to another. If they want their language to stay alive, they cannot stop. They must keep fighting.* (FLUS6, our translation)

Similarly, another FL student stated:

> *My partner is a cultural activist, and he does not want his language to get lost. I would not like his language to disappear. In his community, they are trying to teach the young people the language. They organise themselves to rescue their language.* (FLUS2, our translation)

Both comments show actions taken by the Indigenous speakers to preserve their language, one seeking support from the government and the other through the organisation of the communities themselves. People who speak an Indigenous language, who want their language to remain alive, cannot stop. They must continue fighting; passivity is not an option for them. They must raise their voices and knock at doors, sometimes successfully and other times not. Their going from one place to another generates hope.

The awareness of the FL university students about Indigenous peoples' activism made them realise that the preservation of Indigenous languages should be a collective effort in which all of us should be involved. One FL university student spoke about the collective responsibility to preserve Indigenous languages:

> *Many of us here have gone to talks about the preservation of languages, or they have told us, we must preserve languages. But, really, none at that time stopped and went to look for a speaker of an Indigenous language to learn it. We also have the responsibility of taking care of those languages. I feel responsible for learning and also teaching what I know; we have to act.* (FLUS3, our translation)

To be preserved, Indigenous languages need the responsibility, commitment and praxis (reflection plus action) of their speakers, but the mainstream groups must get involved. In this way, efforts could be increased, generating solidarity with the arduous task of revitalising Indigenous languages. In the same line of reflection, another FL university student commented:

> *With this experience, I also realise that the comrades of the* [Indigenous] *communities have been activists for a long time. We are slow; the teacher told us that it took the university 20 years to realise that we must focus on Indigenous languages. It is the first time these Indigenous peoples are physically at our university, when they have knowledge of Indigenous languages.* (FLUS2, our translation)

This student's comment showed a critical stance, questioning the slowness with which public organisations (in this case, universities) respond to the preservation of Indigenous languages. It also showed how higher-level educational spaces maintain a physical and social hierarchy over speakers of Indigenous languages. Another FL university student commented:

> *My partner told me that he was a revolutionary of his language, because the most important events were of people rising up. He had never been to the university, but the meeting filled us with hope. I remember his words a lot: "We never imagined that we were going to be at the university, and now here we are, as teachers and students."* (FLUS5, our translation)

The preservation of endangered languages is an activity that cannot occur within comfort zones. It is necessary to be a revolutionary who denounces the structural barriers that limit certain languages and favour others (Abramowski, 2014; Estermann, 2014; Riaño, 2012). It takes people rising up and doing something as a collective effort.

Being aware of the political and praxis-oriented effort necessary to foster and preserve languages from minoritised groups made FL university students realise the complicit roles universities play while valuing certain groups over others, including the languages they speak. Universities can be exclusionary spaces if only students, teachers or researchers have a place in these educational spaces. Universities should make room for other actors, as there are people with other "non-educational" profiles who can teach and learn. Teaching and learning should not be the private property of educational institutions. Other actors can also be a source of knowledge (Freire, 2013). This peer-tutoring experience allowed students, as future language teachers, to understand that teaching and learning have political, historical, economic and social dimensions that is often hidden by traditional views focusing mainly on content and seeing educational practices as neutral and fixed. This view eliminates the possibility of people taking action with respect to the contexts in which they operate. Along this line, one FL university student commented:

> *My tutor commented, he is moving in the political area, talking to different actors to generate support: He is acting on the matter, so I think, what do we, who will be language teachers, have to do to support their effort? ...Well, getting together was the first step, and as my classmates say, we have to get more involved in language preservation projects, [and] invite more people to teach us. I think there are many things to do.* (FLUS6, our translation)

FL university students, through this experience, started seeing themselves as subjects who become socially responsible by facing diversity. Friere (2013) conceives human beings as "historical beings that are made and remade socially" (p. 27, our translation). As Freire states, "[i]t is the social experience that ultimately makes us, the one that constitutes us as the way we are" (2013, p. 27, our translation). Being face-to-face with the other reveals the circumstances that configure each person from different angles: personal, historical, economic and social. Therefore, education should be a collective experience in which we can engage with other people when we invite them to teach, as commented by the above student. With this approach, we can transform our reality, which, in this case, may lead to the disappearance of both a language and a culture.

8. CONCLUSION

The main purpose of this article, as mentioned previously, was to explore the perspectives of the FL university students on diversity and inclusion as emergent from their participation in a peer tutoring experience with speakers of endangered Indigenous languages. The way in which the peer-tutoring experience was structured led to a greater symmetrical and horizontal exchange between the participants and their respective knowledge, avoiding fixed roles and the prevalence of misconceptions especially about Indigenous peoples. Both FL university students and the speakers of Indigenous languages had something valuable to contribute: their language and their life experiences. Focusing on foreign languages (e.g., Chinese, English and French) as well as Indigenous languages (Chocholteco, Chontal and Ixcateco), both the FI university students and Oaxacan Indigenous speakers were the object of teaching and learning. This generated greater symmetry between these languages, challenging the idea that only prestigious, so-called "modern" languages should be learnt.

In this peer-tutoring experience, inclusion, respect, appreciation and mutual recognition were generated, demonstrating that all these elements are favoured when those involved work cooperatively and when time is allocated for mutual understanding and the sharing of knowledge. Through this peer-tutoring experience, the participants went beyond the linguistic domain. The FL university students put a face on the Indigenous languages. These concrete faces have life stories that enrich the learning and teaching of languages. Through this experience, everyday life practices were recognised. The FL university students viewed Indigenous peoples, along with their native languages, from a non-deficient perspective, recognising that Indigenous language speakers have a great depth of knowledge and take collective actions in favour of the recognition and revitalisation of their endangered languages. Consequently, it is important for teachers of language courses (e.g., English) and content courses (e.g., didactics, sociolinguistics) to approach diversity from a personal stance rather than accepting stereotypical or false preconceptions that usually stem from deficit discourses. The challenge is to create spaces within universities for minoritised group members to act as teachers. Once this is done, critical inclusion and enriching diversity might be possible. Finally, we should also say that in future studies, the ideological, political, social and personal tensions that might arise when two cultural groups come together should be explored in greater depth in order to avoid the romanticisation of intercultural cooperation and practices.

This study has important implications. First of all, contexts such as Oaxaca are plurilingual, which means that teachers need to develop an appreciation for diversity, in this case, linguistic diversity. Taking this diversity into consideration, students can integrate their linguistic knowledge into their class activities, and this knowledge can thus be seen as something positive and not as an obstacle to teaching. Secondly, it is important to create education spaces where Indigenous languages such as Zapotec and "modern languages" such as English can interact in a more horizontal relationship. Thirdly, the use of inclusive methodologies is an effective pedagogical strategy to put into practice in the TESOL classroom, where all students are included in the learning process.

REFERENCES

Abramowski, A. (2014). *Maneras de querer: Los afectos docentes en las relaciones pedagógicas* [*Ways of wanting: The effects of teaching on pedagogical relations*]. Buenos Aires: Paidós Cuestiones de Educación.

Aizencang, N., & Bendersky, B. (2013). *Escuelas y prácticas inclusivas: Intervenciones psicoeducativas que posibilitan* [*Schools and inclusive practices: Psychoeducational interventions that enable*]. Buenos Aires: Ediciones Manantial SRL.

Arroyo González, J. (2013). La educación intercultural: Un camino hacia la inclusión educativa. [Intercultural education: The road to inclusive education]. *Revista de Educación Inclusiva, 6*(2), 144–159.

Barabas, A. M. (1999). Los rru ngigua o gente de idioma: El grupo etnolingüístico chocholteco [The *rru ngigua* or language people: The Chocholteco ethnolinguistic group]. In A. M. Barabas & M. A. Bartolomé (Eds.), *Configuraciones étnicas en Oaxaca: Perspectivas etnográficas para las autonomías* [*Ethnic configurations in Oaxaca: Ethnographic perspectives for the autonomous regions* (pp. 159–189). México, D.F.: Conaculta-Inah.

Corona Berkin, S., & Kaltmeier, O. (2012). Introducción: En diálogo: Metodologías horizontales en ciencias sociales [Introduction: In dialogue: Horizontal methodologies in the social sciences]. In S. Corona Berkin & O. Kaltmeier (Eds.), *En diálogo: Metodologías horizontales en ciencias sociales* [*In dialogue: Horizontal methodologies in the social sciences*] (pp. 11–21). Barcelona: Gedisa.

Díaz Aguado, M. (2013). *Educación intercultural y aprendizaje cooperativo* [*Intercultural education and cooperative learning*]. Madrid: Ediciones Pirámide (Grupo Anaya, S.A).

Duran, D., & Vidal, V. (2004). *Tutoría entre iguales: de la teoría a la práctica* [*Peer tutoring: From theory to practice*]. Barcelona: Editorial GRAÓ, de IRIF, S.L.

Elboj Saso, C., Puigdellivol Aguade, I., Soler Gallart, M., & Valls Carol, R. (2013). *Comunidades de aprendizaje: Transformar la educación* [*Learning communities: Transforming education*]. Barcelona: Graó.

Estermann, J. (2014). Colonialidad, descolonización e interculturalidad [Coloniality, decolonisation and interculturality]. *Polis, 38*(13), 1–18.

Fisher, R. (2013). *Diálogo creativo: Hablar para pensar en el aula* [*Creative dialogue: Speaking in order to think in the classroom*] (P. Manzano, Trans.). Madrid: Editorial Morata, S. L.

Flick, U. (2015). *El diseño de la investigación cualitativa* [*Designing qualitative research*]. Madrid: Editorial Morata, S. L.

Freire, P. (2013). *Pedagogía del Oprimido* [*Pedagogy of the oppressed*]. (J. Mellado, Trans.). Mexico, D. F.: Siglo XXI Editores.

García Vargas, L. (2018). Radiografía demográfica de la población indígena en Oaxaca [Radiographic demography of the Indigenous population of Oaxaca]. *Nueva Época, 41*, 7–22.

Hamel, R. E. (2000). Políticas de lenguaje y estrategias culturales en la educación indígena [Politics of language and cultural strategies in Indigenous education]. In IEEPO (Ed.),

Inclusión y diversidad: Discusiones recientes sobre la educación indígena en México [*Inclusion and diversity: Recent discussions about Indigenous education in Mexico*] (pp. 130–167). Oaxaca: IEEPO.

Hesse-Biber, S. (2017). *The practice of qualitative research.* Los Angeles, CA: Sage.

Holm, W. (2006). The "Goodness" of bilingual education for native American children. In T. McCarty & O. Zepeda (Eds.), *One voice, many voices – Recreating Indigenous language communities* (pp. 1–46). Tempe and Tucson: Arizona State University Center for Indian Education.

Instituto Nacional de Geografía e Informática [National Institute of Geography and Information]. (2020). *Hablantes de lenguas indígenas en México* [*Indigenous language speakers in Mexico*]. Retrieved from https://cuentame.inegi.org.mx/poblacion/lindigena.aspx

Jordán, J. (1994). *La escuela multicultural: Un reto para el profesorado* [*The multicultural school: A challenge for teachers*]. Barcelona: Editorial Paidós Ibérica.

Kitzinger, J., & Barbour, R. (1999). Introduction: The challenge and promise of focus groups. In R. S. Barbour & J. Kitzinger (Eds.), *Developing focus group research: Politics, theory and practice* (pp. 1–20). London: Sage.

López Hernández, F. (2002). Lengua y migración [Language and immigration]. In Coordinación Estatal de Atención al Migrante Oaxaqueño [State Coordination Office Giving Attention to the Oaxacan Migrant] (Ed.), *Memoria: Ciclo de conferencias sobre migración* [*Conference Proceedings: Series of conferences on immigration*] (pp. 1–8). Oaxaca: Gobierno Constitucional del Estado de Oaxaca.

López-Gopar, M. E. (2016). *Decolonizing primary English language teaching.* Bristol: Multilingual Matters.

Maddonni, P. (2014). *El estigma del fracaso escolar: Nuevos formatos para la inclusión y democratización de la educación* [*The stigma of academic failure: New formats for inclusion and democratisation in education*]. Buenos Aires: Paidós.

Maldonado Alvarado, B. (2002). *Los indios en las aulas: Dinámicas de dominación y resistencia en Oaxaca* [*Indians in the classrooms: Dynamics of domination and resistance in Oaxaca*]. Mexico, D. F.: INAH.

McLaren, P. (2005). *La vida en las escuelas: Una introducción a la pedagogía crítica en los fundamentos de la educación* [*Life in schools: An introduction to critical pedagogy in the foundations of education*] (S. Guardado, Trans). México, D. F.: Siglo XXI Editores.

Mignolo, W. (2000). *Local histories/global designs: Coloniality, subaltern knowledges, and border thinking.* Princeton, NJ: Princeton University Press.

Morales-Saavedra, S., Quintriqueo-Millán, S., Uribe-Sepúlveda, P. A., & Arias-Ortega, K. (2018). Interculturalidad en educación superior: Experiencia en educación inicial en La Araucanía, Chile [Interculturality in higher education: Experience in initial education in La Araucanía, Chile]. *Convergencia, 25*(77), 55–76.

Motschenbacher, H. (2016). Inclusion and foreign language education: What linguistics can contribute. *ITL - International Journal of Applied Linguistics, 167*(2), 159–189.

Riaño, Y. (2012). La producción del conocimiento como "minga" y las barreras a la equidad en el proceso investigativo [Knowledge production as "*minga*" and the barriers to equality in the research process]. In S. Corona Berkin & O. Kaltmeier (Eds.), *En diálogo: Metodologías horizontales en ciencias sociales* [*In dialogue: Horizontal methodologies in the social sciences*] (pp. 137–159). Barcelona: Gedisa.

Rockwell, E. (2004). Herencias y contradicciones de la educación en las regiones indígenas [Inheritance and contradictions of education in Indigenous regions]. In L. Meyer, B. Maldonado, R. Carina & V. Garcia (Eds.), *Entre la normatividad y la comunalidad: Experiencias educativas innovadoras del Oaxaca indígena actual* [*Between normativity and communality: Innovative educational experiences of current Indigenous Oaxaca* (pp. 3–23). Oaxaca: IEEPO.

Rudduck, J., & Flutter, J. (2007). *Cómo mejorar tu centro escolar dando la voz al alumnado* [*How to improve your school by giving voice to the students*]. (P. Manzano, Trans.) Madrid: Morata.

Vásquez Parra, J., & Campos-Rivas, C. (2016). Discriminación laboral indígena: Una aproximación desde el imaginario colonial y la teoría elsteriana [Indigenous work discrimination: An approach from the colonial Imaginary and Elsterian Theory]. *Saber, 28*(4), 828–837.

THE EUROPEAN JOURNAL OF APPLIED LINGUISTICS AND TEFL

2

REFUGEE FOREIGN LANGUAGE LEARNING: TRAUMA AND THE USE OF TRANSLANGUAGING SPACE AS A VEHICLE FOR PSYCHO-SOCIAL SUPPORT

Mohammed Ateek, University of Leicester, UK

ABSTRACT

Refugee language learners have traumatic experiences that could hinder their language learning and negatively impact on their academic achievement. Literature on the effects of trauma on refugee foreign language learning is still modest even with unprecedented numbers of refugees. This article investigates the effects of trauma on refugee education in English-as-a-foreign-language settings and draws on the translanguaging practices of refugees, internally displaced and host community learners. I do so by reviewing the relevant literature and applying the concept of translanguaging using an ethnographic study in a non-profit organisation in the Kurdistan region of Iraq. Interviews, observations and fieldnotes were used to record translanguaging practices employed by coaches and beneficiaries of the non-profit organisation, not only to maximise communication and learning, but also to create safe spaces for learning. The article concludes with a set of pedagogical implications and recommendations for English language teachers regarding how to implement translanguaging as a vehicle for psycho-social support in refugee settings.

KEYWORDS

Refugees, trauma, translanguaging, EFL classroom.

1. INTRODUCTION

According to the United Nations High Commissioner for Refugees (UNHCR, 2021), the number of people forcibly displaced as a result of persecution, conflict, violence, human rights violations or events seriously disturbing public order worldwide amounted to 82.4 million at the end of 2020. Out of this number, 48 million are internally displaced people and more than 30 million are refugees and asylum seekers. Forced migration includes refugees, asylum-seekers, internal displacement, trafficking, development-induced displacement, and exile (Castles, De Haas, & Miller, 2013). Most displaced people are located in the Global South "where there are fewer unified systems for dealing with asylum and refugee protection" (Capstick, 2020, p. 218). For example, Syrians fleeing the war in their country make up a fifth of the population of neighbouring Lebanon. These unprecedented numbers have posed great challenges to different countries, especially those with limited resources. These challenges include the provision of education, employment, health, public funds, and other services. Similarly, refugees and asylum seekers experience culture shock, adaptation and an uneasy process of socialisation (Demirdjian, 2011).

Socioeconomic hierarchy, social inequality, linguistic discrimination, and monolingual bias are issues that coexist with huge waves of migration, and refugees are at the forefront to deal with them. For example, refugees are perceived as powerless, unskilled and illiterate because their language(s), semiotic repertoires and cultural practices differ from those of the host community. These ideologies and perceptions often result in refugees experiencing social exclusion, low self-esteem and cultural inequality (Blommaert, 2010). Central to this discussion is the importance of communication and second/foreign language (L2/FL) learning. In refugee settings, this importance is boosted by the need to communicate in the host community language or a shared language for numerous purposes (e.g., employment, education, accessing services, etc.). In a globalised world, flows of commodities, cultures, ideas and languages go hand in hand with the mobility of people that transcend national borders. Therefore, it becomes pressing for vulnerable people such as refugees to learn a foreign language in this socially interactive world. It is the norm now to know a second or third language and it may be unusual to know only one, for language is at the centre of human life (Cook, 2016).

However, learning a foreign language is not a linear process and the difficulties to foreign language learning are multiple and varied, from learner-based factors to language-related difficulties and psychological pressures (Masri & Abu-Ayyash, 2020). This is further complicated when learners live in extreme conditions with unusual life experiences and trajectories such as is the case for refugees and asylum seekers (Cirocki & Farrelly, 2019). Carrying traumatic experiences is probably one of the most notable experiences impacting this group and learning a new language is surely not on the top list of priorities for refugees, at least at the beginning of their resettlement. Sinclair (2001) notes that trauma can be a major hindrance for refugees and can affect their learning abilities. In a review of literature on educational needs and barriers for refugee learners, McBrien (2005) points out that refugees have more obstacles to face in their education compared to their migrant peers. One pedagogical intervention that researchers have called for in recent years in order to create safe spaces especially in migrant English-as-a-foreign-language (EFL) settings is the adoption and inclusion of all communicative repertoires, including languages, that learners bring to the classroom.

As a result of this inclusion, EFL learners start to feel more comfortable with managing their negative emotions, reducing their traumatic symptoms, and subsequently making academic gains (Capstick & Ateek, 2021; Dovchin, 2021; Piller, 2016). However, little is known about how exploiting full linguistic repertoires helps in creating safe spaces for refugees and how interaction in different languages takes place in refugee EFL classrooms. Therefore, the aim of this article is twofold: to explore the challenges that face refugee learners when learning a foreign language, with a particular focus on trauma and learning in EFL settings, and to investigate teachers' and learners' translanguaging practices in the EFL classroom and examine how these practices facilitate or hinder the creation of safe spaces for language learning.

This article begins with a review of studies on how trauma negatively impacts foreign language learning. It then discusses monolingual ideologies that are prevalent in EFL settings and how academics and educators have challenged these ideologies in the last two decades, promoting multilingualism in the EFL classroom. The article concludes with a case study that is based on a previous research project to show how coaches and beneficiaries use translanguaging as a vehicle for psycho-social support.

2. TRAUMA AND FOREIGN LANGUAGE LEARNING IN REFUGEE SETTINGS

Some academics have grouped refugees with other immigrants (Clayton, 2015; Duran, 2017). While both groups may have similar motivations and characteristics, refugees are a particular group that are forced to leave their countries out of fear of persecution (McBrien, 2005). The UNHCR defines a refugee as an individual who:

> owing to a well-founded fear of being persecuted for reasons of race, religion, nationality membership of a particular social group or political opinion, is outside the country of nationality and is unable or, owing to such fear, is unwilling to avail himself of the protection of that country, or who, not having a nationality and being outside the country of his former habitual residence as a result of such events, is unable or, owing to such fear, unwilling to return to it (Convention and Protocol, 1951, n.p.).

The above definition demonstrates the adversity of the situation refugees must deal with. These life-threatening experiences invoke different levels of stress and trauma that many refugees live with even after being resettled into a new country. Research shows that trauma responses persist in the minds and behaviour of people for a long time after the traumatic experience has ended (Medley, 2012). Trauma is defined as "a response to a stressful experience in which a person's ability to cope is dramatically undermined" (Cole et al., 2005, p. 18). Many refugees might have gone through stressful experiences such as exposure to armed conflict, constant shelling, human trafficking, loss of close relationships and experiencing violence such as torture and rape. It is trauma that most notably differentiates refugees from the majority of EFL learners and trauma is more likely to lead to post-traumatic stress disorder (PTSD) than accidental stress (Charuvastra & Cloitre, 2008). PTSD and depression are highly prevalent in refugee populations and also among refugees resettled in high-income Western countries (Fazel et al., 2005; Tinghög et al., 2017; von Haumeder et al., 2019). Symptoms of PTSD might include difficulty beginning new tasks, blame, guilt, depression, disturbed sleep, eroded self-confidence, and an inability to concentrate (Kerka, 2002). Different studies have shown that trauma and PTSD can have negative effects on academic success in general and language acquisition in particular (Saigh et al., 1996; Sondergaard & Theorell, 2004). Steven's (2001) study of Cambodian refugees in Australia showed that 91 per cent of the participants to be experiencing at least one PTSD symptom, including trouble concentrating, memory loss and headaches.

Trauma and PTSD not only affect the mental wellbeing of refugees, but also negatively affect their language learning abilities. In a review of 43 articles from 1998 to 2015, Clayton (2015) investigated refugees' language learning and PTSD, and concluded that the articles "strongly support the hypothesis that PTSD has a direct effect on refugee language learning but that English-as-a-second-language (ESL) educators can implement procedures to minimize impediments to learning" (Clayton, 2015, p. 2). For example, in a longitudinal study of 49 Iraqi refugees in Sweden, Söndergaard and Theorell (2004) indicate that refugees who showed severe symptoms of PTSD learnt L2 at a slower speed. The authors also found that the speed of language acquisition is more highly correlated with the cumulative PTSD symptom load over time than the number of hours of language classes taken. In a more recent study, Masri and Abu-Ayyash (2020) explored the difficulties that face 45 Syrian refugees in nine countries while learning an L2. Being forced to flee their country and relocate to a new one is one of the stress factors refugee learners could face. One of the refugee participants in the study suffered from depression caused by the stressful kind of life he experienced in Sweden. "Such circumstances weakened the participants' self-confidence and made them feel shy to speak up in the new language in order not to make mistakes that the society may mock them for" (p. 380). Similarly, Ying (2001) reports a case study of a Vietnamese man who suffered from severe headaches and anxiety and was later referred for treatment because he had complained of poor concentration which made attending his ESL classes a difficult task.

The Canadian Centre for Victims of Torture (2002) explains the relationship between trauma and language, noting that the process of language learning requires noticing, control and meaning, and adults experiencing PTSD experience particular challenges to learning a new language as the effects of trauma interfere with many areas of cognitive processes, including all aspects of education and learning a new language.

Cognitive approaches to L2 learning placed much emphasis on the centrality of the processes of attention, noticing and memory (Ellis, 2015). These mental and cognitive processes are directly affected by trauma, as shown above. Specifically, traumatic experiences may alter neural pathways within the brain and impair working memory (Johnsen et al., 2008), which is critical for both processing and sorting new information such as grammar and vocabulary. One prominent hypothesis related to this discussion is the Noticing Hypothesis. Schmidt (2001) proposed that nothing is learnt unless it is noticed. In this regard, comprehensible input will not lead to successful language acquisition if the language learner is not aware of a particular language feature. Other approaches to language learning, such as the sociocultural perspective, assume that cognitive development, including language development, arises as a result of social interactions. Interaction facilitates giving access to language input that learners need to activate internal processes that play a major role in language learning (Vygotsky, 1986). However, refugees may struggle to take part in such social interactions. Studies such as Steel et al. (2002), who interviewed over 1,000 Vietnamese refugees in Australia, and Carlsson et al. (2006), working with 63 refugee survivors of torture, show that traumatic experiences and subsequent PTSD inhibit normal daily functioning and contact, reducing exposure to the L2 outside the classroom.

Finally, one more stressor that could trigger trauma and is of a central importance is linguistic discrimination that is led by monolingual ideologies. Language is one of the greatest assets that asylum seekers and refugees have and depriving them of this could result in emotional distress.

Although languages are viewed as practices, "they are practiced with socio-political norms and influences" (Duran, 2017, p. 24). Woolard (1998) notes that languages and their speakers are positioned in and through talk. In this sense, the dominant society (the host community in the case of refugees) views *nativism* as a preference, and deviation from monolingual practices could lead to exclusion and discrimination. Refugees' linguistic practices often work as markers of their ethno-cultural identities, which eventually leads to social comparisons, "in which the [language of] the in-group [dominant society] is perceived as better than that of the out-group [refugees/migrants]" (Bhatia, 2018, p. 423). This particular stressor is the main one to be discussed here. The argument, which is aligned with the research aims of this study, is that allowing teachers and learners to use all languages available at their disposal in the EFL classroom creates a seed for growing a safe space that is much needed for refugees' psycho-social support.

The next section will discuss monolingual bias and its effects on refugee language learning.

3. MONOLINGUAL IDEOLOGIES

Refugees are resourceful when it comes to languages. Their migration trajectory makes learning languages throughout their journey to the destination country a necessity. Most refugees had previous formal or informal education in another language (Duran, 2017). In addition, many of them are bilingual and can use two or more languages effectively. However, these linguistic resources are not recognised at schools in the host communities. The main reason for this non-recognition is the divergence of refugees' linguistic practices from those of the host communities, which brings the issues of socio-economic hierarchy, educational opportunity and social injustice that coexist with mass migration to the forefront (Blommaert, 2010).

Having arrived at their host communities, they are usually faced with monolingual bias and educational institutions that frown upon utilising their full linguistic repertoires and look at languages as separate, autonomous, and bounded entities. Recent research has advocated for translanguaging in L2 and FL contexts, where the language-of-instruction and the languages of the learners diverge (Al-Masaeed, 2020; Fallas Escobar, 2019; Li & Lin, 2019). These research projects provide rich examples of how multilingual practices enhance the learning process in the classroom, as they consider multilingualism to be the linguistic norm nowadays. These practices challenge and even resist monolingual ideologies that are prevalent in numerous L2/FL contexts. These same ideologies perceive switching between languages as a deficit and employing full linguistic repertoires as a dysfunction. This is evidenced in several studies that were published in a special issue edited by Li and Martin (2009). They show the conflicts and tensions between multilingual practices and language policies that prohibit using any language but that of the schools. Therefore, classrooms that celebrated multilingualism and allowed languages to breathe in classrooms were deemed to be unprofessional and accused of disrupting the pupils' learning.

One of the main drivers of these monolingual policies is the traditional understanding of bilingualism, where bilinguals were seen to have two separate language systems (Grosjean, 1989). This leads to defining bilinguals as L2 deficient learners, where employing a multitude of linguistic resources for communication is viewed as an error not a resource. Recently, Li and Lin (2019) argue that the "conflicts between everyday flexible multilingual practices of the individual, including teachers and pupils, and the societal-imposed policies of language-of-instruction in schools still remain in most parts of the world" (p. 209).

Although these conflicts may still exist, Larsen-Freeman (2018) notes that maximising the use of multiple linguistic resources will be on the rise in L2 classrooms because of the growing number of research studies that favour these practices. This means opposing the view that languages are separated following the philosophy of *separate bilingualism* (Creese & Blackledge, 2010), and emphasising that people's linguistic and semiotic resources can work as a whole, moving across and beyond languages for meaning-making and knowledge construction (Busch, 2012; Jonsson, 2019). In doing so, the monolingual bias (Block, 2003) is disrupted and the fluidity of languages, transcending boundaries, is highlighted.

4. TRANSLANGUAGING IN EDUCATIONAL SETTINGS

Viewing multilingualism as a resource draws on the flow of languages at larger community and international levels. This view has been developed because of living in *superdiverse* communities, which impose new dynamics on late modern society that require us to take account of mobility, fluidity, mixing and historical narratives (Creese & Blackledge, 2015). Meanwhile, a more popular language such as English has been widely used as a lingua franca among people from linguistically different backgrounds (Crystal, 2003).

Translanguaging is defined as "the deployment of a speaker's full linguistic repertoire without regard for watchful adherence to the socially and politically defined boundaries of named languages" (Otheguy, García, & Reid, 2015, p. 283). It is the flexible use of linguistic and non-linguistic resources by students to make sense of the world around them (García & Li, 2014). García and Li (2014) argue that translanguaging as a pedagogical practice could liberate the voices of minority students, whose languages are different from those of the local community. In educational contexts, Hornberger and Link (2012) propose that educators value the multiple communicative repertoires of the students and their families. Perhaps many still question the reasons for the distinction between code-switching and translanguaging. Lewis et al. (2012, p. 665) stress that such a distinction is ideological, where code-switching has associations with language separation. They note that especially in bilingual classrooms "translanguaging as a concept tries to move acceptable practice away from language separation, and thus has ideological, even political associations." Creese and Blackledge (2015) propose that translanguaging goes beyond code-switching, but it also encompasses it. A translanguaging lens focuses on the full deployment of linguistic resources and the discursive practices by individuals that cannot be assigned to one code or another, and that make up the full communicative repertoire (García & Li, 2014).

This new understanding of languaging in the classroom is derived from the transformative nature of translanguaging as it has the potential to challenge old understandings and generate new configurations of language practices in the classroom (Zhu, Jankowicz-Pytel, & Li, 2020).

According to García and Li (2014), the transformative nature of translanguaging is characterised by creativity and criticality. They argue that students, through translanguaging, construct and modify their identities as they respond to their historical and current conditions critically and creatively. Translanguaging focuses on the different ways in which students and teachers use their communicative repertoire across social contexts to negotiate their identities. Translanguaging brings together the different dimensions of the students' linguistic, cognitive, and social skills, and this in turn transforms their skills, values and beliefs, thus creating a new identity for these multilingual students (Li & Zhu, 2013). Palmer et al. (2014) investigated the practices of two bilingual teachers in a dual language programme in the USA. Drawing on the notions of identity positioning and investment, the teaching practices of the teachers suggested effective strategies to promote bilingual identities. These practices, translanguaging pedagogies, included modelling fluid language practices, positioning students as bilinguals, and celebrating language crossing. Language crossing "involves code alternation by people who are not accepted members of the group associated with the L2 that they are using (code switching into varieties that are not generally thought to belong to them)" (Rampton, 2010, p. 485). This is further illustrated by a research project by Langman (2014), who investigated how teachers organised their practices and how these practices compare with state expectation. She found that teachers initiate agentic actions (i.e., the socio-culturally mediated capacity to act) and engage with their learners in creative ways through translanguaging and transcultural connections. The current study (Section 6) draws on the notion of teacher agency in the second discourse topic and shows how agency is tightly linked with the theory of translanguaging (Li, 2018).

5. TRANSLANGUAGING SPACE AND TRAUMA

Li (2011) suggests that translanguaging creates a social space for the users by bringing in different dimensions of their personal experience and environment into one coordinated and meaningful performance. It is a space where different identities and ideologies not only coexist, but also combine to generate new identities. Thus, the boundaries of the translanguaging space are *ever shifting*, and the process of space construction is an ongoing and lifelong one, for the space exists in the mind of the individual who creates it.

Translanguaging space highlights the dynamic nature of multilingual practices, while showing the interconnectivity between multi-modal and multi-sensory resources that are deployed in communicative interactions. Translanguaging space is "a space where various semiotic resources and repertoires, from multilingual to multisensory and multimodal ones, interact and co-produce new meanings" (Zhu, Li, & Lyons, 2017, pp. 412–413). The transformative nature of translanguaging space can generate new configurations of language practice and new understanding and social structures. In this sense, these are spaces where different identities and ideologies (i.e., refugees and even language educators) not only coexist, but also combine to generate new identities in the sense that they are spaces where various semiotic resources and repertoires, from multilingual to multi-sensory and multi-modal ones, interact and co-produce new meanings. This means that the transformative power of translanguaging space would also

27

extend to challenge and transform old configurations and understanding of language practices. This is also true in educational contexts, in which classrooms and schools can be spaces, created for and by translanguaging practices, where both teachers and learners deploy a multitude of meaning-making semiotic resources and systems to incite new configurations of language and education practices.

One question that arises here is how these spaces could be used as safe spaces for refugees and asylum seekers. UNICEF (2016) suggest that safe spaces ensure positive identity and feelings through self-regulation as well as self-esteem and self-appraisal. They also suggest that safe spaces provide refugees with a voice and meaningful engagement and interaction with others. Safe spaces refer to physical or social spaces that allow vulnerable groups to meet and discuss challenging circumstances they experience (Harpalani, 2017). Safe spaces, in this sense, provide a platform to tackle difficulties in a supportive manner to alleviate anxiety, reduce isolation, and make connections with people who have similar experiences (Dryden, Tankosić, & Dovchin, 2021). In this context, safe spaces encourage their users to use their linguistic diversity fully and engage in greater linguistic and cultural practices. In this article, I apply the work on "translanguaging spaces to refugee settings where displaced learners' embodied repertoires can be called on to create a translanguaging space that is a safe space" (Capstick & Ateek, 2021, p. 4). This is because displaced learners often feel a disconnection from their linguistic and cultural heritage when they are displaced as their host schools and neighbourhoods may use different varieties to those of their countries of origin (Capstick & Delaney 2016). Symbolic violence (Bourdieu 1977) can result from this, compounding the trauma that many refugees seek to overcome in their psycho-social programmes. Outcomes of this trauma include poor memory, concentration and processing of information and increased anxiety, which interfere with language learning (Gordon, 2011) (see Section 2 for details). As mentioned above, displaced people may experience cultural and linguistic shock at the stage of pre-settlement as well as during the settlement process. To further complicate this, refugees are expected to use English only as it is the language of instruction in schools, university or work settings, not only in English-speaking countries, but in many EFL/ESL classrooms. Consequently, they are under constant pressure to think, write and communicate through standard English in both institutional and non-institutional settings in the host society (Piller, 2016). As a result, these stressful experiences can largely impact refugee EFL learners' emotional state and could cause foreign language anxiety, which interferes with learning and is one of the most accepted phenomena in psychology and education (Zheng, 2008). This means that language learning environments need to be safe rather than stressful. Gordon (2011, p. 2), for example, emphasises that "it is imperative for the ESL field to recognise and investigate trauma as a factor in language learning".

Dryden, Tankosić and Dovchin (2021) argue that the teacher's use of translanguaging may create emotional safe spaces to mitigate the negative reactions of foreign language anxiety. Such spaces permit them to manage and negotiate their emotions and feelings related to their lived linguistic and cultural experiences in a new country. The four participants in their study demonstrated calmer tones, emotional releases and semiotic actions that demonstrate relief, when they use translanguaging practices. In fact, translanguaging could travel beyond EFL/ESL classrooms to provide refugee EFL learners "with an emotionally and linguistically safe space where they feel comfortable in managing their negative emotions through employing multiple entangled layers of linguistic and paralinguistic resources" (Dovchin, 2021, p. 1). However, to what extent might translanguaging practices facilitate the creation of a safe space for reducing anxiety at times of increased trauma for refugee learners and asylum seekers? The next section will draw on one case study of an English language programme for refugee and host community students in a non-profit organisation (NGO) in the Kurdistan Region of Iraq (KRI) to answer this question.

6. RESEARCH METHODOLOGY (DESIGN, METHODS AND SETTINGS)

The case study presented here is based on a previous research project (Capstick & Ateek, 2021) that investigates the linguistic and non-linguistic resources used by refugees, internally displaced people (IDPs) and host coaches and beneficiaries (i.e., language learners) who teach and learn English in an international NGO that runs language programmes as part of its psycho-social support initiatives in the KRI. The EFL classes are made up of refugees from Syria, IDPs from Iraq and members of the host community from KRI, which constitutes a complex linguistic setting. The medium of instruction in schools in Kurdistan is Kurdish (Sorani dialect) and is therefore highly politicised as Kurdistan fights for independence from the Arabic-dominant central government in Baghdad (Shanks, 2016). Different languages compete for space in the education centres visited for this study.

The NGO's Advancing Adolescents Programme, which is designed to "strengthen the resilience of the host community and Syrian refugee young people through equitable access to psychosocial support, protection and informal learning opportunities" is made up of structured group-based activities (Mercy Corps, 2016, p. 2). These activities draw on the Profound Stress and Attunement framework in which a safe space is created, and prolonged stress is mediated in classroom activities (Macphail et al., 2017). Profound Stress and Attunement "provides a holistic platform for young people to develop empathy and resilience in response to their needs, and supports measurable psychosocial improvement" (Mercy Corps, 2016, p. 3). Elsewhere, it can be reported that this NGO demonstrated the need to create safe spaces that facilitate the conditions for post-stress attunement through English language lessons for the beneficiaries (Capstick & Ateek, 2021). Safe spaces in this context are of a significant importance to alleviate the anxiety that refugees and IDPs may face when trying to interact in English (Back et al., 2020), for their cognitive processes to still function so learning can take place. In the NGO centre where the study was carried out, English language lessons had been developed into a vehicle for *post stress attunement* programmes as English is a popular subject with adolescents in the region, though learners from low socio-economic groups (such as those in this study) will have had little or no access to English language teaching. The NGO claims that the implementation of these psycho-social support programmes through language lessons could increase the levels of diversity of social networks, trust and perceived confidence for learners.

The coaches who deliver the NGO's Advancing Adolescent Programme have been trained to understand the impact of trauma and stress on brain functions and how to respond to these issues to facilitate experiential learning. They had received two weeks of English language teacher training before starting their 8-week English language courses with the beneficiaries (learners). Six coaches, all under the age of 30 as a requirement for the programme, were observed twice and interviewed twice for the study: two from Syria (refugees), two from Kurdistan (host community) and two from the southern parts of Iraq (IDPs). While interviews provide rich data about the phenomenon under investigation and give the opportunity for the participants to provide their "story," a unique strength of classroom observations is that they yield more authentic data than mediated methods (Cohen et al., 2018). Furthermore, they serve as a reality check because people's actual behaviour may not correspond with what they say they do (Robson, 2002). In addition, detailed fieldnotes were recorded during the field visits. Having selected the six participants for this research (convenience sampling), the study was explained to them, and consent forms were obtained. The data analysed for this study consists of ten English language lessons which were video and audio recorded (a total of 8 h 3 m 36 s) with fieldnotes and copies of course materials – tailored and designed by the coaches. The number of students observed in each of these lessons ranged from 13 to 18 with an average of 15 students per lesson. Each lesson lasted approximately 45 minutes while post-lesson interviews with coaches lasted approximately 50 minutes. Semi-structured interviews with the coaches were conducted in English to explore their attitudes, opinions and thoughts about using language as a vehicle for psycho-social support and to investigate how their understanding of translanguaging practices compares with their actual use of these practices in the classroom. The principal reason for choosing this type of interview is that it provides information that is difficult to obtain by other means, and the social interaction during the interview provides in-depth discussion of the issue under investigation (Dörnyei, 2007).

6.1 DATA ANALYSIS

To analyse the data, thematic analysis was followed in both the interviews as well as the video-recordings (classroom observations) to identify discourse topics that the coaches orient to in their interviews and to explore the links between these discourses, the coaches' practices, and the beneficiaries' responses in the classroom. Thematic analysis is a common technique that is used mainly in qualitative research, and can be used to identify the important themes, derived from data, to answer the research questions (Gries, 2009). The main aims of the study, as mentioned in the introduction, are to investigate translanguaging practices in the EFL classroom by both coaches and beneficiaries and whether these practices create safe spaces for learners. To identify the discourse topics in the study, from interviews and classroom observations, coaches were all asked the same questions about language use in the classroom. Drawing on Krzyżanowski (2008), discourse topic is the basic analytic category and emerges through several sentences and appearances in discourse. In other words, a discourse topic is the salient theme that underlies a series of sentences in the interview data. Having established the themes from interview data (macro-level), a thorough analysis of the fieldnotes and observations of the classroom practices was conducted to make links between the macro and micro levels of discourse. Five discourse topics emerged from the data and all topics are related to home language use while learning the target language (i.e., English). These discourse topics are English first, translation, language and identity, coaches' agency through translanguaging and the last one is related to using movement and non-linguistic cues to support learning. Due to space limitations, I will present one extract from the interviews and another from classroom observations in relation to two discourse topics: *English first* and *coaches' agency through translanguaging* for their relevance to the research aims. These extracts and examples were selected to represent two discourse topics that appeared regularly in the larger dataset.

6.1.1 ENGLISH FIRST

This discourse topic about using the English language first in the EFL classroom was a common discourse topic in the interviews as well as the interactions between coaches and beneficiaries. In the interviews, the coaches describe the need to use English first before switching to a variety which is more familiar to the beneficiaries.

EXAMPLE FROM THE INTERVIEWS

> **Lanya:** Ok first I pronounce the word in English and then I translate into Kurdish then after pronouncing it in English I would tell them the meaning of that specific word in English and then in Kurdish.

The excerpt above is taken from an interview with one of the host community coaches (Lanya), who is from the KRI. Lanya usually teaches English with the presence of another Syrian Kurdish teacher assistant (Zakia) who also helps her to translate into Kurmanji (Syrian Kurdish dialect) and Arabic (so all students feel included in the learning process) when they feel that using English only is not enough. As shown in the above example, coaches lean into using English first before switching into either Arabic or Kurdish when there are communication breakdowns. This practice reflects the common preference among the NGO coaches to use the target language first. The monolingual ideology of using target-language only is dominant in EFL settings. Although using only one language at a time "may maximise exposure to the target language, it also leads to teacher-centred and textbook-focused pedagogies, due to limited, or even lack of, opportunity for students to engage in class interactions" (Zhang et al., 2020, p. 3). As a result, EFL learners, especially vulnerable groups such as refugees, might feel marginalised in the classrooms, which could lead to anxiety especially given that FL learning involves traumatic experience, thus leading to failure in creating safe spaces for learning, which the use of learners' L1 may have aided in setting up such spaces.

EXCERPT FROM THE CLASSROOMS

Bold= Modern Standard Arabic (MSA)

Italics/underlined: Syrian Arabic

Two underlines: Kurdish (Kurmanji)- Only in the second extract

Normal font= English

In between []: Translation

1. **Zakia:** The word tea. Nouns that are uncountable like tea, we cannot count tea. Can you count tea?

2. **Students:** (Nodding their heads but no response to the question).

3. **Zakia:** *ما فينا نعد الشاي لأن مو معدود. صح؟* [We cannot count tea because it's uncountable. Right?]

4. **Students: نعم لأنه** [Yes because] uncountable.

5. **Zakia:** We say a cup of tea for example. **يعني كلمة نضيفها قبل الشاي** Quantifier [means a word that we add before tea]. *منقول كاسة شاي مثلا* [We say a cup of tea for example].

6. **Student:** A cup of tea *كاسة شاي* [a cup of tea], two cups of tea *وهيك* [and so on].

This excerpt features translanguaging among Syrian Arabic, Modern-standard Arabic (MSA) and English. The dominant language at the beginning was English, in accordance with the NGO's policy. Zakia initiated her question in turn 1 in English, to which the students (beneficiaries) nodded their heads without any response, signalling some confusion and lack of comprehension. Zakia sensed this and that is why she resorted to using Syrian Arabic, in turn 3, to paraphrase the question she had initially asked in English. In doing so, the students showed more willingness to communicate and responded using Modern Standard Arabic, which is the official, high variety to mark the nature of content which is language grammar. Also, they used the last word (uncountable) in English to reference key content. The next turn (5) witnesses a complex use of multilingual repertoires. Zakia starts her turn by using English to adhere to the NGO's policy. Then, she employs MSA to explain the rule of using quantifiers before uncountable nouns, before using a shared variety (Syrian Arabic), as this could be a variety that both might feel most comfortable with. Zakia positions the student here as bilingual through transferability between resources of named languages. Zakia's effortless and successful use of translanguaging resulted in one student repeating Zakia's example (a cup of tea) and elaborating on another using English first and Arabic second, marking Zakia's use of translanguaging. All students started sharing examples of their own after that in the lesson.

The teacher's use and permission for the students to use Arabic in the EFL classroom could be seen as an act of resistance against the monolingual ideologies and an act of support to draw on their linguistic repertoires, build on their background knowledge and "engage in cross-linguistic transfer in order to improve their future learning" (Gynne, 2019, p. 359). Similar to Escobar's (2019) participants, what is noteworthy here is that students follow Zakia's practice of using English first and the initiation of translanguaging starts with the teacher, as shown in this example, which means that students do not have complete agency over using their full linguistic and semiotic repertoires. This shows the challenge that educators face to empower their learners to take more control of their learning (Gynne, 2019). Canagarajah (2011, p. 8) has criticised educational contexts in which "acts of translanguaging are not elicited by teachers through conscious pedagogical strategies."

This excerpt shows the integration and coordination among named languages for meaning-making, which happens in what Li (2011) calls the translanguaging space. Both the coach and the beneficiaries moved across different varieties and languages effortlessly when they felt a safe space was made available to do so. This space was not created randomly though; it is the teacher's translanguaging practice herself and her assurance to the student that made not only this student, but others as well engage in translanguaging. This translanguaging practice, as shown in the above excerpt, builds confidence and mutual trust between Zakia and her students, which could lead to reducing anxiety and traumatic symptoms. It is their personal histories and shared identities and experiences in displacement and refuge coming into contact with one another, which feed into Zakia's understanding of the vulnerability of this group and the impact of taking away parts of their linguistic repertoires on their self-concept and resilience. Blommaert (2015) points out that interactants employ their various and available resources to achieve their communication goals, and limiting these resources in the L2 context, guided by the influence of monolingual ideology, may limit the students' agency and the richness of interactions which are important for language learning (see Section 2 for details). The employment of the multilingual practices of MSA, Syrian Arabic and English for meaning-making and knowledge construction by Zakia and the students works as a tool of empowerment and an act of resistance to the English-only policy. In so doing, personal histories and shared identities not only come into contact with one another in this translanguaging space, but also develop together to create a safe space that could mitigate traumatic experience while learning.

6.1.2 COACHES' AGENCY THROUGH TRANSLANGUAGING

This discourse topic is about coaches' activation of their agency in the classroom through translanguaging practices. It relates to the psycho-social support that coaches provide to their students through pushing the boundaries of language use and resisting established ideologies that might hinder the creation of safe spaces.

EXAMPLE FROM THE INTERVIEWS

> **Mustafa:** If they [students] don't accept…in the English language we offer other languages. If not, we offer him music and if he didn't like music, we offer him football. We don't let him go.

The above example is taken from an interview with one of the coaches (Mustafa) – a Syrian Kurdish coach – who could speak in all the varieties existent in the EFL classroom (English, Sorani, Kurmanji and Arabic). Mustafa received training from the NGO and attended Skype sessions with UK-based language educators who acted as mentors for the coaches in the NGO. During the interview, Mustafa shows that he is willing to explore all options while teaching and change his techniques to build a good rapport with the beneficiaries to create a safe space for learning. This does not only include his *playful mix* of languages in the classroom, but also his use of body gestures and movement. His main reason behind such use is to *"show psycho-social support for everyone...and that I am here to support you"* (data from interview).

EXCERPT FROM THE CLASSROOM

1 **Mustafa:** if you cannot write it [word] you can draw it.

2 **Mustafa:** (sensing some confusion): اذا مابتعرفي الكلمة ارسميها [If you do not know the word, you can draw it] (while drawing a car on board).

3 **Student to another:** <u>Heger tu Peyvê nizanê bê, tu dikarê wê xêz bike</u> [if you don't know the word, you can draw it].

Image 1. Picture taken from Mustafa's lesson.

This excerpt is taken from an EFL lesson delivered by Mustafa about "picnics." Mustafa divided the 14 students in the classroom into four groups. The task is for each group to talk about a picnic that the group went on. They had to discuss food, games, conversations and other activities they engaged in on their last picnic. As with Zakia in the first example, Mustafa used English first to explain the rules of the task and what students are expected to write (turn 1). He wanted to maximise communication and involve all semiotic repertoires (linguistic and non-linguistic) in the task so students could be as much involved in the activity as possible. He managed to do this by employing not only English and Kurdish (Kurmanji), but also by drawing when he told students to draw any word they do not know (turn 2). This is also evidenced in Image 1 which shows the presence of various written languages and also Mustafa's drawing in the classroom. It is through translanguaging that Mustafa showed agency creatively and it is through his resistance to conform to classical understanding and activation of the English-only policy in the EFL classroom. This agentic action allowed the fluidity of languages in the classroom. It was mediated by the social, cultural and historic context in which it took place.

Tao and Gao (2021) note that teachers may display resistance against using a particular policy and this is a manifestation of agency. Relevant to this discussion on agency is translanguaging and how language teachers make agentic linguistic and non-linguistic choices and actions creatively and critically. This is manifested in the above extract through using translingual practices and drawing. Following Mustafa's use of different named languages, students were encouraged to follow his path and one of the students positioned herself as a more capable peer (turn 3). According to Vygotsky, instruction and learning should occur in the zone of proximal development (ZPD), which is defined as "the distance between the actual development level... and the level of potential development as determined through problem solving under adult guidance or in collaboration with more capable peers" (1987, p. 86). Learners construct meaning through social interaction, and experts play a facilitating role and assist the less capable learners in their learning and cognitive development. Therefore, ZPD is "a space for social interaction, which links learning with development" (Cirocki, 2016, p. 37).

7. CONCLUSION AND PEDAGOGICAL IMPLICATIONS

Based on this case study and other research studies, some pedagogical implications and recommendations are proposed for EFL/ESL practitioners about how to implement translanguaging while linking it to trauma and emotionality of refugee language learners. First, English language teachers should take refugee EFL learners' social-psychological state into account when they teach. They must be sensitive to the traumatic stress that these groups of learners have experienced and are still experiencing. Refugees who have experienced trauma take longer to acquire an L2 (e.g., Gordon, 2011). Traumatic experiences may also have an adverse impact on motivation to learn an additional language (Iversen et al., 2014). Therefore, proper teacher training programmes should be set in place for language teachers who work with students suffering from trauma. In this study, we have seen how coaches received training using the Profound Stress and Attunement framework and how such training raised their awareness of the impact of trauma on refugees and how to alleviate its effects. Teachers and educators need structured packages of training on the psychological and physiological effects of trauma. This could be provided through continuing professional development and in pre-qualification training. Such programmes could aim at reducing trauma symptoms that have a direct impact on learners' academic achievement and progress. Training should also include methods to organise and deliver teaching that is sensitive to the specific needs, strengths and difficulties of students who have experienced significant trauma. Training for teachers of refugees should include specific information about the context and experiences of the refugees with whom they work; this may include aspects of culture, politics, and displacement history.

Second, teachers should note that having to lose a culture and home is disempowering, and this can threaten to upset the balance of the relationship and trust with teachers who are not displaced. Being invited or allowed to exploit their full linguistic and non-linguistic resources to express their concerns could reset the power balance, so students feel that they have control over their agency. Self-expression is also very important to deal with the effects of trauma. Self-expression is not only manifested in linguistic means, but could also be shown through other communicative repertoires such as drawing, music, arts and other means, similar to what we have seen in Mustafa's classroom. This also brings the concept of teachers' agency to the fore and sheds light on the importance of these agentic actions to challenge established mandates and policies in EFL in general and in refugee settings in particular.

Having said that, it has been noted that foreign language teachers are reluctant to engage in translanguaging practices (Zhang et al., 2021). However, research shows that when students collaboratively draw on their linguistic repertoire and employ their L1 in L2/FL learning, more positive learning experiences take place (Capstick & Ateek, 2021). To put this into practice, Rowe (2018) suggested six practices which teachers could use to promote translanguaging: (1) discussing students' language backgrounds and potentially cultural backgrounds explicitly; (2) providing multilingual learning materials in students' various languages; (3) encouraging collaborative translation; (4) encouraging students to collaborate in order to create multilingual text; (5) providing opportunities for translanguaging through meaningful activities, such as encouraging discussion of curriculum content in relation to individual experience; and (6) designing projects that enable students to connect with multilingual audiences such as family members and the community. To add to this list, opportunities for students to disclose elements of their personal journey, using multiple languages, can be incorporated into lesson plans, but there will be variability in how ready individual students are to share that information. To this end, teachers need skills to provide non-directive support for students in distress and to signpost them to the available resources.

Finally, the L1 is an essential component of a learner's identity and a source of pride and cultural value. Therefore, making space for home languages in multicultural classrooms is important (Coelho, 2012). Different studies show that the L1 is a foundation for L2 learning and a tool for learning when there is a lack of L2 competence. Knowing more than one language may enhance cognitive abilities to learn an L2. Different activities could be designed to this end. As an icebreaking activity, coaches in this study asked students to do a pair activity where A's asked B's about their names, how they are pronounced and what they mean in their language. Students, then, tell the class about their peers' names. Another activity could be writing sentences or sayings in different languages on a board or screen. The teacher picks up a theme (e.g., study, sports, work, etc.) and asks students to provide sayings in their own languages. Students share these sayings/proverbs in their language with the class. There are many examples of such activities that teachers could find and use in different teachers' resources. Teachers are also encouraged to design their own activities based on their students' interests and language proficiency levels. Last, but not least, more research on the translanguaging practices of refugee language learners inside and outside the classroom is needed to check whether there is any transferability of these practices and whether they mirror each other.

REFERENCES

Al Masaeed, K. (2020). Translanguaging in L2 Arabic study abroad: Beyond monolingual practices in institutional talk. *The Modern Language Journal, 104*(1), 250–266.

Back, M., Han, M., & Weng, S. C. A. (2020). Emotional scaffolding for emergent multilingual learners through translanguaging: Case stories. *Language and Education, 34*(5), 387–406.

Bhatia, T. K. (2018). Accent, intelligibility, mental health, and trauma. *World Englishes, 37*, 421–431.

Block, D. (2003). *The social turn in second language acquisition*. Edinburgh: Edinburgh University Press.

Blommaert, J. (2010). *The sociolinguistics of globalization*. Cambridge: Cambridge University Press.

Blommaert, J. (2015). Meaning as a nonlinear effect: The birth of cool. *AILA Review, 28*(1), 7–27.

Bourdieu, P. (1977). *Outline of a theory of practice* (Vol. 16). Cambridge: Cambridge University Press.

Busch, B. (2012). The linguistic repertoire revisited. *Applied Linguistics, 33*, 503–523.

Canadian Centre for Victims of Torture. (2000). *Torture and second language acquisition*. Retrieved from http://ccvt.org/research-publication/publications/

Capstick, T. (2020). *Language and migration*. London: Routledge.

Capstick, T., & Ateek, M. (2021). Translanguaging spaces as safe space for psycho-social support in refugee settings in the Kurdistan region of Iraq. *Journal of Multilingual and Multicultural Development, 42*, 1–16.

Capstick, T., & Delaney, M. (2016). *Language for resilience: The role of language in enhancing the resilience of Syrian refugees and host communities*. London: British Council.

Carlsson, J., Mortensen, E., & Kastrup, M. (2006). Predictors of mental health and quality of life in male tortured refugees. *Nordic Journal of Psychiatry, 60*, 51–57.

Canagarajah, S. (2011). Translanguaging in the classroom: Emerging issues for research and pedagogy. *Applied Linguistics Review, 2*, 1–28.

Castles, S., De Haas, H., & Miller, M. J. (2013). *The age of migration: International population movements in the modern world*. London: Macmillan International Higher Education.

Charuvastra, A., & Cloitre, M. (2008) Social bonds and posttraumatic stress disorder. *Annual Review of Psychology, 59*, 301–328.

Cirocki, A., & Farrelly, R. (2019). Current perspectives on teaching English to refugee-background students [Special issue]. *The European Journal of Applied Linguistics and TEFL, 8*(1).

Clayton, M. (2015). The impact on refugee language learners. *Paper presented at CATESOL LA Regional Conference*, 4 March 2017, Mount San Antonio College, USA.

Cirocki, A., (2016). *Developing learner autonomy through tasks: Theory, research, practice*. Halifax: LinguaBooks.

Coelho, E. (2012). *Language and learning in multilingual classrooms: A practical approach* (No. 16). Bristol: Multilingual Matters.

Cohen, L., Manion, L., & Morrison, K. (2018). *Research methods in education*. London: Routledge.

Cole, S. F., O'Brien, J. G., Gadd, M. G., Ristuccia, J., Wallace, D. L., & Gregory, M. (2005). *Helping traumatized children learn: Supportive school environments for children traumatized by family violence*. Boston, MA: Massachusetts Advocates for Children.

Cook, V. (2016). *Second language learning and language teaching*. Abingdon: Routledge.

Creese, A., & Blackledge, A. (2010). Translanguaging in the bilingual classroom: A pedagogy for learning and teaching? *The Modern Language Journal, 94*(1), 103–115.

Creese, A., & Blackledge, A. (2015). Translanguaging and identity in educational settings. *Annual Review of Applied Linguistics, 35*, 20–35.

Crystal, D. (2003). *English as a global language*. Cambridge: Cambridge University Press.

Daubney, M., Dewaele, J-M., & Gkonou, C. (2017). Introduction. In C. Gkonou, M. Daubney, & J-M. Dewaele (Eds.), *New insights into language anxiety: Theory, research and educational implications*. Multilingual Matters.

Demirdjian, L. (2011). Introduction: Education, refugees and asylum seekers – A global overview. In L. Demirdjian (Ed.), *Education, refugees and asylum seekers: Education as a humanitarian response* (pp. 1–37). London: Continuum.

Dovchin, S. (2021). Translanguaging, emotionality, and English as a second language immigrants: Mongolian background women in Australia. *TESOL Quarterly*. Advance online publication. Retrieved from https://doi.org/10.1002/tesq.3015

Dörnyei, Z. (2007). *Research methods in applied linguistics: Quantitative, qualitative and mixed methodologies*. Oxford: Oxford University Press.

Dryden, S., Tankosić, A., & Dovchin, S. (2021). Foreign language anxiety and translanguaging as an emotional safe space: Migrant English as a foreign language learners in Australia. *System, 101*, 102593.

Duran, C. S. (2017). *Language and literacy in refugee families*. London: Springer.

Ellis, R. (2015). *Understanding second language acquisition*. Cambridge: Cambridge University Press.

Fallas Escobar, C. (2019). Translanguaging by design in EFL classrooms. *Classroom Discourse, 10*(3-4), 290–305.

Fazel, M., Wheeler, J., & Danesh, J. (2005). Prevalence of serious mental disorder in 7000 refugees resettled in western countries: A systematic review. *The Lancet, 365*(9467), 1309–1314.

García, O., & Li, W. (2014). *Translanguaging: Language, bilingualism and education*. London: Palgrave Macmillan.

Gordon, D. (2011). Trauma and second language learning among Laotian refugees. *Journal of Southeast Asian American Education and Advancement, 6*(1), 13.

Gries, S. (2009). *Quantitative corpus linguistics with R: A practical introduction*. London: Sage.

Gynne, A. (2019). 'English or Swedish please, no Dari!' – (trans)languaging and language policing in upper secondary school's language introduction programme in Sweden. *Classroom Discourse, 10*(3-4), 347–368.

Harpalani, V. (2017). "Safe spaces" and the educational benefits of diversity. *Duke Journal of Constitutional Law and Public Policy, 13*(1), 117–166.

Hornberger, N. H., & Link, H. (2012). Translanguaging and transnational literacies in multilingual classrooms: A bilingual lens. *International Journal of Bilingual Education and Bilingualism, 15*(3), 261–278.

Iversen, V., Sveaass, N., & Morken, G. (2014) The role of trauma and psychological distress on motivation for foreign language acquisition among refugees. *International Journal of Culture and Mental Health, 7*(1), 59–67.

Johnsen, G. E., Kanagaratnam, P., & Asbjørnsen, A. E. (2008) Memory impairments in posttraumatic stress disorder are related to depression. *Journal of Anxiety Disorders, 22*(3), 464–474.

Jonsson, C. (2019). 'What is it called in Spanish?': Parallel Monolingualisms and translingual classroom talk. *Classroom Discourse, 10*(3-4), 323–346.

Kerka, S. (2002). *Trauma and adult learning. Washington, DC: National Clearinghouse for ESL Literacy Education.* Retrieved from http://www.eric.ed.gov/PDFS/ED472601.pdf

Krzyżanowski, M. (2008). Analysing focus group discussions. In R. Wodak & M. Krzyżanowski (Eds.), *Qualitative discourse analysis in the social sciences* (pp. 162–181). Basingstoke: Palgrave Macmillan.

Langman, J. (2014). Translanguaging, identity, and learning: Science teachers as engaged language planners. *Language Policy, 13*(2), 183–200.

Lewis, G., Jones, B., & Baker, C. (2012). Translanguaging: Developing its conceptualisation and contextualisation. *Educational Research and Evaluation, 18*(7), 655–670.

Li, W. (2011). Moment analysis and translanguaging space: Discursive construction of identities by multilingual Chinese youth in Britain. *Journal of pragmatics, 43*(5), 1222–1235.

Li, W., & Lin, A. (2019). Translanguaging classroom discourse: Pushing limits, breaking boundaries. *Classroom Discourse, 10*(3-4), 209–215.

Li, W., & Martin, P. (2009). Conflicts and tensions in classroom codeswitching. A special thematic issue of the *International Journal of Bilingual Education and Bilingualism, 12*, 2.

Li, W., & Zhu, H. (2013). Translanguaging identities and ideologies: Creating transnational space through flexible multilingual practices amongst Chinese university students in the UK. *Applied Linguistics, 34*(5), 516–535.

Macphail, J., Niconchuk, M., & El-Wer, M. (2017). Conflict, the brain, and community: A neurobiology-informed approach to resilience and community development. In R. Phillips, S. Kenny & B. McGrath (Eds.), *The Routledge handbook of community development perspectives from around the globe* (pp. 340–357). London: Taylor & Francis.

Masri, H., & Abu-Ayyash, E. A. (2020). Second language acquisition from Syrian refugees' perspectives: Difficulties and solutions. *Open Linguistics, 6*(1), 372–385.

Mercy Corps. (2016). Advancing adolescents: Evidence on the impact of psychosocial support for Syrian refugees and Jordanian adolescents. Retrieved from https://www.mercycorps.org/research-resources/advancing-adolescence

McBrien, J. L. (2005). Educational needs and barriers for refugee students in the United States: A review of the literature. *Review of Educational Research, 75*(3), 329–364.

Medley, M. (2012). A role for English language teachers in trauma healing. *TESOL Journal, 3*(1), 110–125.

Otheguy, R., García, O., & Reid, W. (2015). Clarifying translanguaging and deconstructing named languages: A perspective from linguistics. *Applied Linguistics Review, 6*(3), 281–307.

Piller, I. (2016). *Linguistic diversity and social justice: An introduction to applied sociolinguistics.* Oxford: Oxford University Press.

Palmer, D. K., Martínez, R. A., Mateus, S. G., & Henderson, K. (2014). Reframing the debate on language separation: Toward a vision for translanguaging pedagogies in the dual language classroom. *The Modern Language Journal, 98*(3), 757–772.

Rampton, B. (2010). Linguistic ethnography, interactional sociolinguistics and the study of identities. In C. Coffin, T. Lillis, & K. O'Halloran (Eds.), *Applied linguistics methods: A reader* (pp. 234–250). London: Routledge.

Robson, C. (2002). *Real world research.* Oxford: Blackwell.

Rowe, L. (2018). Say it in your language: Supporting translanguaging in multilingual classes. *The Reading Teacher, 72*(1), 31–38.

Saigh, P. A., Mroueh, M., & Bremner, J. D. (1996). Scholastic impairments among traumatized adolescents. *Behaviour Research and Therapy, 35*(5), 429–436.

Schmidt, R. (2001). Attention. In P. Robinson (Ed.), *Cognition and second language instruction* (pp. 3–32). Cambridge: Cambridge University Press.

Shanks, K. (2016). The changing role of education in the Iraqi disputed territories: Assimilation, segregation and indoctrination. *Globalisation, Societies and Education, 14*(3), 422–433.

Sinclair, M. (2001). Education in emergencies. In J. Crisp, C. Talbot, & D. B. Cipollone (Eds.), *Learning for a future: Refugee education in developing countries* (pp. 1–84). Lausanne: United Nations Publications.

Söndergaard, H. P., & Theorell, T. (2004). Language acquisition in relation to cumulative posttraumatic stress disorder symptom load over time in a sample of resettled refugees. *Psychotherapy and Psychosomatics, 73*(5), 320–323.

Steel, Z., Silove, D., Phan, T., & Bauman, A. (2002) Long-term effect of psychological trauma on the mental health of Vietnamese refugees resettled in Australia: A population-based study. *Lancet 360*(9339), 1056–1062.

Stevens, C. A. (2001). Perspectives on the meanings of symptoms among Cambodian refugees. *Journal of Psychology, 37*(1), 81–98.

Tao, J., & Gao, X. (2021). *Language teacher agency.* Cambridge: Cambridge University Press.

Tinghög, P., Malm, A., Arwidson, C., Sigvardsdotter, E., Lundin, A., & Saboonchi, F. (2017). Prevalence of mental ill health, traumas and postmigration stress among refugees from Syria resettled in Sweden after 2011: A population-based survey. *BMJ Open, 7*(12), e018899.

UNHCR (United Nations High Commissioner for Refugees). (2021). *Refugee statistics*. Retrieved from https://www.unhcr.org/refugee-statistics/

UNICEF. (2016). *Language education and social cohesion (LESC) initiative*. Malaysia: UNICEF East Asia and Pacific Regional Office.

von Haumeder, A., Ghafoori, B., & Retailleau, J. (2019). Psychological adaptation and posttraumatic stress disorder among Syrian refugees in Germany: A mixed-methods study investigating environmental factors. *European Journal of Psychotraumatology, 10*(1), 1686801.

Vygotsky, L. (1986). *Thought and language*. Cambridge: The MIT Press.

Woolard, K. A. (1998). Introduction. In B. B. Schieffelin, K. A. Woolard, & P. V. Kroskrity (Eds.), *Language ideologies: Practice and theory* (pp. 3–47). New York and Oxford: Oxford University Press.

Ying, Y. (2001). Psychotherapy with traumatized Southeast Asian refugees. *Clinical Social Work Journal, 29*(1), 65–78.

Zhang, Q., Osborne, C., Shao, L., & Lin, M. (2020). A translanguaging perspective on medium of instruction in the CFL classroom. *Journal of Multilingual and Multicultural Development, 41*, 1–14.

Zheng, Y. (2008). Anxiety and second/foreign language learning revisited. *Canadian Journal for New Scholars in Education, 1*(1), 1–12.

Zhu, H., Li, W., & Jankowicz-Pytel, D. (2020). Whose karate? Language and cultural learning in a multilingual karate club in London. *Applied Linguistics, 41*(1), 52–83.

Zhu, H., Li, W., & Lyons, A. (2017). Polish shop(ping) as translanguaging space. *Social Semiotics, 27*(4), 411–433.

THE EUROPEAN JOURNAL OF APPLIED LINGUISTICS AND TEFL

3

HARVESTING DIGITAL SPACES FOR EMERGENT BILINGUALS: CULTURALLY-SUSTAINING MALL PEDAGOGIES FOR MIGRANT CHILDREN

Kathryn DePietro, Stevenson College, USA

Deniz Ortactepe Hart, University of Glasgow, UK

Xinxin Liu, Yu Ming Charter School, USA

ABSTRACT

In US schools, a particularly marginalised group of emergent learners are the children of migrant farm workers who move regularly to follow the crop seasons. This pedagogical article argues that mobile-assisted language learning (MALL) can provide affordances for language teachers to promote culturally sustaining pedagogies for migrant children. In this article, we will first discuss the importance of culturally sustaining pedagogies for the biliteracy development of migrant children. Next, we will introduce MALL and its affordances for culturally sustaining pedagogies in English language classrooms as well as in mainstream education. In the last section, we will discuss the principles for instructional design for culturally sustaining MALL pedagogies especially for novice teachers. While this article focuses on the migrant families located in Monterey, California to illustrate examples from their educational and life experiences, we hope that our suggestions are helpful for all educators working with any marginalised group of emergent bilinguals.

KEYWORDS

Mobile-assisted language learning, migrant learners, culturally sustaining pedagogies, emergent bilinguals.

1. INTRODUCTION

Migrant farm workers are groups of individuals who move to follow crop seasons in order to maintain financial income and improve economic mobility. Migrant families share characteristics similar to those of immigrants and refugees. These include, but are not limited to, fear of deportation, psychological stress from illegal entry, limited access to healthcare, parent's ineligibility for driver's licences and bank accounts, and lack of financial aid (Arzubiaga, Noguerón, & Sullivan, 2009; Free, Križ, & Konecnik, 2014). There are also a separate set of issues that make migrant children's educational experiences a bit more challenging. The instability of their family life, health concerns related to farm work (e.g., pesticide exposure), absence from or tardiness to school, interrupted schooling, and different conceptualisations of social worlds are some of the factors that threaten migrant students' educational and life trajectories (Green, 2003; Nevárez-La Torre, 2012). Teachers' lack of knowledge about and negative attitudes towards migrant students (Free et al., 2014) and lack of communication between migrant families and school administration (Purcell-Gates, 2013) are other factors that impair teachers' capacity to address migrant students' funds of knowledge and diverse cultural backgrounds in ways that enrich their classroom experience (González, Moll, & Amanti, 2005). Overall, the combination of poverty and mobility have "a lethal impact on the educational aspirations of migrant children" (Branz-Spall, Rosenthal, & Wright, 2013, p. 57).

In order to support the migrant populations in the United States, the Migrant Education Program (MEP) was authorised as an outcome of the civil rights movements in the 1960s, under the Elementary and Secondary Education Act of 1965. The federally-funded but state-administered programme aims to meet the particular educational and social needs of migrant children between the ages of 3 to 22 years old. The migrant education programmes coordinate direct student services to enhance migrant students' academic experience and access to a high-quality education, appropriate academic and social interventions, and physical and mental health well-being. Regional offices collaborate with school districts to recruit migrant-qualified students for the appropriate services and events. These services include academic instruction, remedial and compensatory instruction, bilingual and multicultural instruction, vocational instruction, career education services, counselling and testing services, health services, pre-school services and special guidance (Migrant Education Program, 2020). According to the 2015-2016 report of the Department of Labor in the United States, 68 per cent of the hired farmworkers were born in Mexico, 24 per cent born in the States, 6 per cent born in Central America and 1 per cent born in Puerto Rico (Hernandez & Gabbard, 2018). Eighty-three per cent of all the more than five thousand interviewed farm workers in this study were Hispanic (National Agricultural Workers Survey, 2015-2016). Therefore, bi/multicultural education is at the core of the migrant education programmes since most of the migrant students are emergent bilinguals.

Migrant farmworkers in the States are one of those vulnerable populations who have been disproportionately affected by the COVID-19 pandemic. In Monterey County, California, which provides a significant percentage of the food supplies in the United States, 51 per cent of the COVID-19 cases emerged in Salinas Valley where the majority of farm workers are located. Almost 22 per cent of the total number of COVID-19 cases in California emerged from the agriculture industry. Not only the migrant families who have to work in the farm collectively have been the primary targets of the pandemic, but also their children have been disproportionately impacted by the requirements and limitations of online education. While teachers all over the world have struggled to put their classes online due to the lack of instructional support and experience in online education, teachers who work largely with emergent bilinguals such as the migrant students have faced additional challenges to develop their biliteracy skills through online education. Therefore, this pedagogical article aims to argue that mobile-assisted language learning (MALL) can provide affordances for culturally sustaining pedagogies in English language classrooms and in mainstream education. In the next sections, we first discuss the importance of culturally sustaining pedagogies for the biliteracy development of migrant children. Subsequently, we introduce MALL and how it can be used in language classrooms to promote culturally sustaining pedagogies. In our last section, we will present principles for instructional design for culturally sustaining MALL pedagogies. Overall, this pedagogical article draws from both theoretical and practical aspects of culturally sustaining pedagogies and MALL to present readers both strategies and immediate take-aways to promote the biliteracy development of any marginalised group of emergent bilinguals.

2. CULTURALLY RELEVANT/SUSTAINING PEDAGOGIES

The widely held deficit ideology towards marginalised communities focuses on the differences and the observed weaknesses across learner groups and assumes that these groups are responsible for their low academic achievement, low level of English proficiency, suspension and expulsion rates (Bartolomé, 2004; Harven & Soodjinda, 2016). For instance, an educator who teaches migrant students within K-12 classrooms may perceive their interrupted education, their unconventional home life, poverty, time spent in the farms to assist their families, and the "nontraditional" forms of parental involvement as the reasons for the low achievement rates in English (and/or in a different subject matter). The previous literature which referred to these populations as English language learners (ELLs), English learners (ELs), and English as second language learners (ESL) only focused on their English language development within the dominant culture, and thus ignored that these populations are indeed emergent bilinguals who are in the process of developing language and literacy skills in their home and school languages simultaneously (Bauer, Presiado, & Colomer, 2017; Lopez, Turkan, & Guzman-Orth, 2017).

Migrant children are also emergent bi/multilinguals since they are in the process of acquiring both English and their home language(s). On the contrary to the deficit ideology that positions culturally and linguistically diverse students as "less intelligent, talented, qualified, and deserving" (Bartolomé, 2004, p. 99), migrant students have rich cultural and linguistic repertoires and bring their own cultural capital, norms and communicative practices of their communities into the language classroom. Many scholars have explored the effectiveness of pedagogies grounded in understanding, amplifying and sustaining linguistic and cultural practices of systematically marginalised students in order to support their academic success and biliteracy development (Bauer et al., 2017; Gay, 2010; Hammond, 2015; Ladson-Billings, 1995, 2012; Moll & Gonzalez, 1994; Paris, 2012; Paris & Alim, 2014). Some of these culturally and linguistically inclusive frameworks include *funds of knowledge* (Moll & Gonzalez, 1994), *culturally relevant pedagogy* (Ladson-Billings, 1995), *culturally responsive pedagogy* (Gay, 2010; Hammond, 2015) and *culturally sustaining pedagogies* (Paris & Alim, 2014).

According to Moll and Gonzalez (1994), *funds of knowledge* refers to "historically accumulated and culturally developed bodies of knowledge and skills essential for household or individual functioning and well-being" (p. 133). In other words, every student brings their own *funds of knowledge* to the language classroom in connection with their home, communities and social practices. Language teachers need to find ways to provide all learners with the space to integrate their *funds of knowledge* into the classroom activities and processes and relate instruction to their students' lived experiences which are rooted in their own historically community-based contexts (González et al., 2005). With this connection of home/cultural background and school/language classroom, migrant students can more actively engage in classroom discussions, knowing that their background is inseparable from and invaluable for their academic development even when they are newcomers to a particular school context. It is this process of promoting awareness of their *funds of knowledge* as well as its validation in educational contexts that enable language teachers to provide a culturally relevant pedagogy to migrant learners.

Ladson-Billings (1995, 2012) proposed the framework of *culturally relevant pedagogy* that is both relevant and responsive to the language, literacies, and cultural practices of marginalised students. Culturally relevant pedagogy emphasises three aspects of students' learning that are deemed essential for a multicultural and multilingual society: academic achievement, cultural competence and socio-political consciousness. The main principle behind this framework was the shift from deficit-based pedagogical frameworks towards holding high expectations for students from systematically disadvantaged backgrounds.

Taking Ladson-Billing's (1995) work as a foundation, Gay (2010) coined the term *culturally responsive pedagogy* which aims to empower students by underlining their cultural and ethnic identities as well as their linguistic and experiential backgrounds in the classrooms. Culturally responsive pedagogy maximises the affordances available to different cultural groups who are encouraged to draw from their own cultural resources to maintain their community and heritage while they are at the same time in the process of gaining access to the dominant culture. More recently, Hammond (2015) emphasised the connection between culturally responsive teaching and the brain. According to Hammond (2015), a *culturally responsive pedagogy* must be rigorous and stimulating to the brain, drawing not only on cultural frames of reference, but also on organised learning relationships and individualised learning goals.

However, given the power dynamics and the systemic inequality embedded in educational contexts, culturally "relevant" or "responsive" pedagogies may end up being potentially insufficient for maintaining migrant learners' cultural and linguistic heritage (Paris, 2012). According to Alim (2007), culturally responsive or relevant pedagogies refer to "classroom practices that use the language and culture of the students to teach them part of the 'acceptable' curricula cannon" (p. 27). To illustrate, in the White-dominated US society, the goal of education for many years has been to teach the youth of colour how to perform White middle-class norms rather than allowing them to explore, honor and extend their heritage and community practices (Flores & Rosa, 2015). Therefore, Paris (2012) proposed the term *culturally sustaining pedagogy* (CSP) that builds upon the previous frameworks while reframing and expanding them in a way to challenge already existing power dynamics that revolve around cultural pluralism and cultural equality. According to Paris (2012), educators embracing a CSP "meaningfully value and maintain the practices of the students in the process of extending their students' repertoire of practice" (p. 95). These practices are embodied in the home languages, cultural values and literacies that students bring to the classroom. Teachers become aware of their students' practices not only through discussions with the students outside of class time, but also through student-centred instructional materials, informal surveys and needs assessment.

CSP requires language teachers to reimagine schools as contested sites where diverse, heterogeneous practices are not only valued but *sustained* (Paris & Alim, 2014). In other words, a culturally sustaining pedagogy preserves and bolsters marginalised populations' cultural capital, funds of knowledge norms and values as well as their linguistic practices. CSP does not contain a particular set of practices teachers can take and apply to a particular context. Instead, it is a pedagogical framework that includes a set of beliefs and principles that can be adapted for classroom instruction depending on learners' subjectivities. Therefore, hereafter when we use the term culturally sustaining pedagogies (CSPs), we intentionally employ the plural form to underscore that there is no one particular CSP but CSPs that are tailored for the unique needs and interests of our learners.

CSPs are considered within social justice pedagogies due to their emphasis on equity, diversity and inclusion. CSPs challenge widely held but oppressive and assimilative beliefs and practices that are embedded in language instruction such as setting up middle-class White children as benchmarks for the working-class children of colour to speak and behave alike. Teachers who adopt CSPs understand that the goal of teaching is not assimilation through erasure of their students' languages, literacies, cultures and histories. On the contrary, educators embracing CSPs aim to more deeply understand and amplify the unique voices of their students and reflect on the question of whose culture is being sustained and for what purposes.

CSPs for the migrant students can take the form of teachers' individual actions such as including equitable instructional materials, validating and using students' home language(s) and culture(s), and creating classroom activities that sustain and strengthen their students' cultural knowledge and practices. CSPs can also extend to action-oriented institutional practices such as offering after-school classes to migrant families on economic self-improvement and health literacies. A comprehensive understanding of the migrant students' life circumstances and the social value systems is crucial for educators (Kozoll, Osborne, & García, 2003). Getting to know the migrant students beyond their academic performance and understanding their cultural and linguistic background is therefore key to their academic, social and cultural development. Overall, CSPs present all educators a new direction and ideology of transforming and decolonising the language classrooms as well as the mainstream education by legitimising and empowering all marginalised and disenfranchised learner groups. In that sense, MALL is highly potential for implementing CSPs in English language and mainstream classrooms, especially in today's pandemic-induced circumstances that demand online education.

3. MOBILE-ASSISTED LANGUAGE LEARNING

Mobile-assisted language learning (MALL) is "learning mediated via handheld devices" which are "potentially available anytime, anywhere" (Kukulska-Hulme & Shield, 2008, p. 273).

MALL differs from traditional computer-based learning in the sense that the former requires portability and accessibility from any device, not only a desktop or laptop computer. Pegrum (2014) described four different functions of MALL ranging from the least interactive to the most: content delivery, tutorial, creation and communication. MALL for *content delivery* entails the use of any online resource accessible from a mobile device for exposing language learners to the target language (e.g., the use of online newspaper applications (apps) or a podcast for listening practice). MALL as *tutorial* includes the use of apps that provide automated feedback on explicit grammar and vocabulary (e.g., language learning apps such as Duolingo or the use of Quizlet for vocabulary practice). The third function, MALL for *creation*, involves the use of social media or other interactive and mobile spaces to create and share discourses with an audience. Creation is tightly linked to the fourth use of MALL for *communication* where a mobile app's discourse is used to establish an interactive bridge between two or more people (e.g., messenger apps such as *Slack, WhatsApp* or *Google Chat*). Throughout this article, we draw upon all four intertwined uses of MALL when we discuss how MALL can help language teachers to provide culturally sustaining pedagogies for migrant students.

There are several affordances MALL provides for emergent bilinguals in general: providing a mobile platform for language and literacy development, lowering their anxiety and allowing them to take risks for communication, and fostering their learning agency and autonomy. As mentioned above, the aspect of "mobility" is what distinguishes MALL from computer-assisted language learning. This feature is incredibly important for migrant students as their migrant families move regularly to follow the crop season. While this move in California is more restricted within the borders of the state (from south to north, sometimes all the way up to Oregon and Washington states), a migrant family's journey might entail moving from Arizona or Texas to Midwestern states such as Minnesota and Michigan. Therefore, a combination of asynchronous and synchronous but "mobile" online environments provides students with the flexibility to attend school virtually and process classroom content from anywhere and in a self-paced manner (Chinnery, 2006; Merryfield, 2003).

Online environments also provide a learning context that reduces anxiety for all learners since they act "as a 'veil' to protect people as they reveal, question, and take risks" (Merryfield, 2003, p. 155). Therefore, MALL can be particularly helpful for migrant students, as having different first languages and distinctive conceptualisations of social worlds (Kozoll et al., 2003) may cause anxiety to some migrant students in the physical classroom environment. A plethora of empirical studies also observed a positive relationship between MALL, learner autonomy and learner agency (Demouy, Jones, Kan, Kukulska-Hulme, & Eardley, 2016; Kacetl & Klímová, 2019; Leis, Tohei, & Cooke, 2015; Zhang, 2016). Fostering learner autonomy and agency is fundamental if migrant educators are to move away from the deficit ideology and the *pobrecito syndrome* (Berzinz & Lopez, 2001) (i.e., setting up low expectations or simplifying tasks out of sympathy for the struggles in which a migrant student may face in their life beyond the classroom). In addition to these affordances of MALL for migrant populations and emergent bilinguals in general, we argue that MALL can assist teachers in providing culturally sustaining pedagogies that not only draw from migrant students' cultural capital and linguistic resources, but also cultivate these resources in a way to empower the migrant students.

4. AFFORDANCES OF MALL FOR CULTURALLY SUSTAINABLE PEDAGOGIES

Although scholars underlined the use of new technologies such as Web 2.0 tools, video blogs, podcasts and social network sites for empowering marginalised learner populations and for enabling exchange of knowledge and experiences (O'Hara, Pitta, & Pritchard, 2016), there are only a few studies that explored the intersection of MALL and culturally and linguistically inclusive frameworks to support English language learners (Burston, 2015; Chen, Carger, & Smith, 2017). Several studies have examined the relationship between technology and migrant student success (Carson, 1999; Levy, 2011; Meyertholen, Castro, & Salinas, 2004); however, there appears to be a gap in the literature with regards to the role of MALL for providing CSPs to migrant farm worker students in the United States.

Migrant farm worker families may or may not be a part of the larger population of immigrant populations who migrate from one country to another due to various social, economic and political reasons. However, as an exceptionally mobile population, migrant families recurrently move between Mexico and the United States and/or within the States to follow the crop season. Moving along with their families, migrant students often have their educational experiences interrupted and marked with changing communities, schools, teachers and friends. For these reasons, we believe the portability of MALL applications creates new digital learning spaces for educators to enact culturally sustaining pedagogies. In the following sections, we will discuss three overlapping affordances of culturally sustaining MALL pedagogies: building strategic learning networks and communities, constructing digital spaces for exploring intersectional identities, and sustaining and promoting native language skills.

4.1 BUILDING STRATEGIC LEARNING NETWORKS AND COMMUNITIES

The literature that focused on migrant children and on CSPs emphasise the importance of drawing upon community resources and knowledge to support learners' educational development. However, since migrant learners frequently uproot their lives to move to different communities, community resources and knowledge available for migrant students may often be limited to their family. Kozoll et al. (2003) noted the complexity of power dynamics within migrant familial relationships since the family unit is (re)conceptualised as a physical "home" for a migrant student. For instance, the decision to attend school by leaving the family and/or pursuing a life beyond the fields complicates the social dynamics within the migrant family. Thus, parental/familial involvement in migrant education is essential and has been a common call to action for educators of migrant students (Chavkin, 1996; Duarte & Rafanello, 2001; Green, 2003; Kozoll et al., 2003; López, Scribner, & Mahitivanichcha, 2001; Martinez & Velasquez, 2000).

Parental involvement, however, should go beyond the conventional understanding of the relationship between schools and families (López et al., 2001). Rather, schools should tactfully strategise social networks that provide migrant families with the kind of support that extends beyond the school doors. These activities include, but are not limited to, carrying out home visits, maintaining consistent interaction with families, fostering genuine school-family relations, offering educational/vocational programmes for parents to attend, and collaborating with health and professional agencies outside of the school. These activities should not simply be a list of systematic items to be checked off a list, rather, schools should consistently work to meet the social and economic needs of the migrant families on a daily basis to build learning networks and best support the migrant child (López et al., 2001). MALL can not only enable educators to meet migrant families wherever they are, but also provide students, caretakers, teachers and administrators with a flexible and mobile tool to build and maintain such educational and social networks.

Messaging apps that utilise grouping functions such as *Slack, WhatsApp* and *Google Chat* provide a practical way for administrators and teachers to more instantaneously contact migrant students and their families without revealing personal phone numbers. These apps also allow users to upload videos, voice recordings and PDF files in a quick and easy way. This function of multimodality allows for ease in communication of academic records, medical forms, school announcements, permission slips and other documents between families and schools as well as from one school to another. Most importantly, these applications help build community and are less formal than an email platform. Instead of using email, which is a more formal way of communication, educators can leverage messaging platforms to invite users to have interactions that extend beyond school-related matters and share publicly or privately about their lives, their languages, their cultures and the issues they care about in less formal ways. For example, a teacher or an administrator might give the messaging group a prompt such as "Share a picture of what you have been doing for self-care during the COVID-19 quarantine." Similar to the use of social media, these digital opportunities to connect and relate to one another could foster more meaningful connections between all stakeholders involved in a migrant student's life. Organising digital training seminars for migrant families and their children about applications that their school uses, in addition to tools such as a *mobile PDF Scanner*, is now more crucial than ever.

Beyond messaging apps, learning applications that emulate social media such as *FlipGrid* can be employed to foster a sense of community and ensure the continuity of after-school programmes that otherwise might have ceased to exist amidst the pandemic. For example, in December of 2020, the Monterey County's Migrant Education Program in Region XVI of California held its first ever virtual Speech Tournament. Migrant Speech and Debate competitions are treasured as an opportunity for students to build self-confidence, exercise their English or Spanish language skills, practise professional etiquette, and use both language and research to persuade an audience about their side of a controversial issue. Over 200 students participate only in this region's Speech Tournament yearly and students are allowed to choose between English and Spanish. In 2020's virtual Speech Tournament, 162 students enrolled and worked with volunteer speech coaches from the community. The topics students were able to select from were: (1) whether or not the government has the right to require people to wear facemasks, and (2) whether or not pesticides in agriculture do more harm than good. Eighty-two of the students made final submissions of their speech through *FlipGrid* and were evaluated asynchronously by 43 volunteer judges. The Speech competition was followed by a bilingual Spanish-English virtual award ceremony through *ZOOM* which hosted over 150 participants. During this virtual meeting, Simon Silva, an influential Mexican-American artist, poet, and writer who was also a migrant student, gave a keynote speech about the importance of creativity, persistence and community building.

This event made evident that a culturally sustaining pedagogy does not require a physical space to be executed successfully. Several salient features of this event helped sustain migrant students' language and culture: students' voluntary participation to present their viewpoint on a topic relevant and meaningful to them in the language of their choice; the English-Spanish bilingual communication; community building between students, coaches, administration, and the debate judges; and the contribution of Simon Silva not only as a keynote speaker, but also as a role model and a future reference for students as he continues to work with migrant students in after-school programmes in this particular region.

4.2 CREATING DIGITAL SPACES FOR EXPLORING INTERSECTIONAL IDENTITIES

Coined by Kimberly Crenshaw (1989) as a reaction to single-axis social movements that focused on only one social identity or one group membership (e.g., race, religion, ability, gender, sexuality, class) or one form of oppression (e.g., racism, sexism, ableism), intersectionality as a lens allows us to understand that identities are multiple, complex and act in accordance with one another. As Audre Lorde (2007) states, "we do not live single issue lives" (p. 138) but our consciousness and experiences are shaped by a constellation of identities that interact with each other. Intersectionality is an important element of culturally responsive pedagogies since educators must perceive the complexity of the identities of their learners as well as their families through this lens, rather than identifying them based on a single demographics or characteristics (Calafell, 2010), which is being a part of a farm worker family in the migrant students' case.

As mentioned above, the first-ever virtually held speech competition event organised by the Monterey County's Migrant Education Program in Region XVI through the use of *FlipGrid* and *ZOOM* enabled migrant students' opinions, narratives and voices to be amplified and heard despite the grave circumstances resulting from the pandemic. Since providing opportunities for learners to discuss how their race, ethnicity, gender and sexual identities interact with each other is essential for culturally sustaining pedagogies (Harven & Soodjinda, 2016), we argue that *FlipGrid* and other MALL tools can also be utilised in the everyday language classroom to allow all learners to discuss and draw from their own intersectional identities that have shaped their lived experiences and worldviews.

Effective pedagogical use of mobile social media platforms and other commonly used apps by both young teens and adults help educators to construct digital spaces for personal narratives, autobiographies and life stories to be conveyed. It is through these stories that educators can discuss how identities are shaped by the intersections of race, ethnicity, class, gender, sexuality and ability and how these intersectional identities influence the way we perceive and experience the world around us. These discussions will also help validate the intersectional identities of migrant students and their cultural capital, values and histories and decrease the stigmas around farm worker communities.

One particular context to explore intersectionality is through social media apps such as *Instagram*, *TikTok*, *Twitter* and *Reddit* that provide a familiar, realistic and fun complement to more mainstream language-learning apps and learning management systems. These social media apps provide migrant students with a voice, a platform, and perhaps even a means to find like-minded individuals who share similar experiences (Armfield, Armfield, & Franklin, 2016). There are an increasing number of individuals on *Instagram* and *TikTok* who use their platforms in a diary-like manner to discuss their experiences with issues of discrimination, immigration, migrant life and educational inequities in the United States. Some notable and migrant-relevant Instagram handles that can be referred to in language classrooms are: @wearemitu, @mira_immigrantrights, @fiercebymitu and @desertoranges.

It is noteworthy to mention that some of these social media apps may not be perfectly safe for especially younger learners to explore issues around intersectional identities. Opening social media accounts with pseudonyms or nicknames or establishing group pages with only class members having access can help overcome some of the privacy concerns. Since these apps are easily accessible and widely used among the youth beyond the school walls, teaching learners about digital citizenship and holding conversations about the privacy issues around these social media platforms and informing the students about the privacy settings of a particular app will also help them to take the necessary steps to protect their data both within and outside classroom use (Armfield et al., 2016). Additionally, these apps can very easily be emulated by language teachers who can take screenshots or download PDF versions of a webpage to create and provide students with a blank template. For applications that use video functions, such as *TikTok*, teachers can create a template in *GoogleSlides* and have the students embed a video created on their device into the presentation (Figure 1).

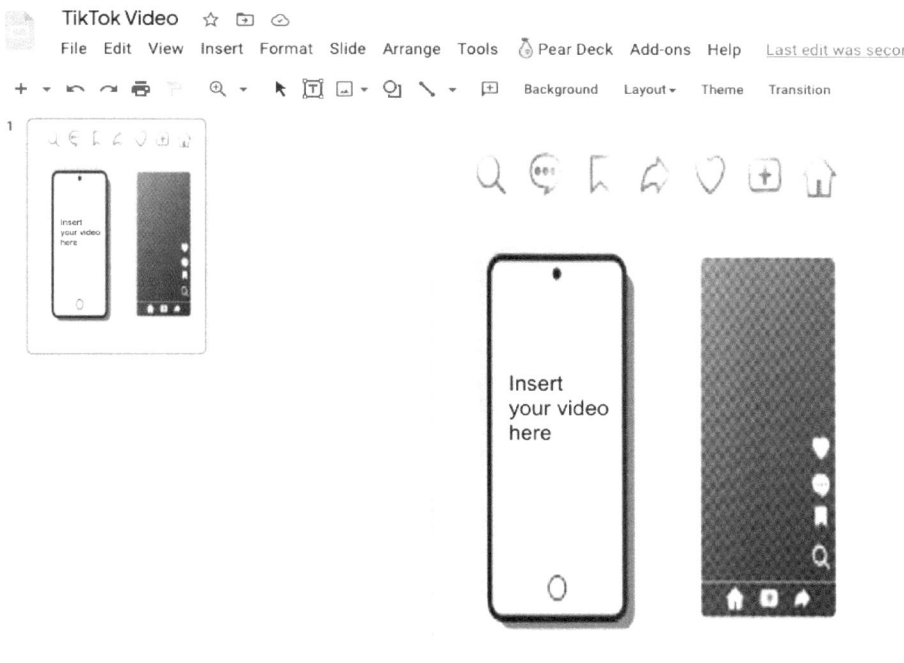

Figure 1. TikTok simulation through Google Slides.

4.3 PROMOTING BILITERACY SKILLS

As mentioned earlier, migrant children are emergent bi/multilinguals who are in the process of developing their literacy skills in two or sometimes more languages simultaneously. While there are several studies that presented the affordances of MALL for English language learners (ELLs) (Burston, 2015; Chen, Carger, & Smith, 2017), there is not much in the literature for how MALL can support the biliteracy development of migrant populations especially in relation to supporting their home languages. This article argues that culturally sustaining MALL practices can go beyond addressing the second language needs of migrant learners but also help them to preserve and develop their native language skills.

According to Paris and Alim (2014), sustaining one's language and cultural practices are two intertwined processes. According to Farquhar (2009), more than a quarter of Mexican migrant workers in the United States speak indigenous languages and this number seems to be growing larger. Mines, Nichols, and Runsten (2010) also observed that once a family settles in the United States, the familial encouragement for the child to speak their native indigenous language(s) decreases. Consequently, migrant students may face intra-family linguistic barriers, as many children of migrant families who are born in the United States learn English from a very early age. Often, Spanish becomes the lingua-franca of indigenous language-speaking households (Mines et al., 2010). While many schools offer services in Spanish, there are few schools that have abundant access to supporting indigenous languages such as Mexican Nahuatl, Mixteco, Triqui and the many other home languages of migrant students. MALL can provide a practical approach to implement CSPs in language classrooms where migrant students may not otherwise have access to speakers of their heritage languages and the teacher may not be competent in all the languages their students speak.

Language teachers can encourage migrant students to build upon their native languages by using applications that include indigenous languages such as *Vamos aprender Nahutl*, *Memrise* or *Master any Language*. In addition, the use of tandem resources such as conversation partners through video chat or weekend clubs and events can provide students with meaningful interactions in the students' first language that extend beyond the walls of their home or school (Ward, 2017). School administrators can seek out organisations of indigenous languages in their region, for example, *Indigenous Interpreters+*, to safely connect migrant students with other speakers of their native languages as possible volunteer virtual conversation partners. Teachers can also utilise mobile tools such as *Google Translate* or *iTranslate* to provide their students and their families with directions to tasks or class information in the student's mother tongue.

Strategic integration of mobile applications such as *Tandem* and *HelloTalk* into the educational curriculum can provide migrant students not only with native language practice and preservation, but also a digital social space to express themselves and perhaps form intercultural relationships that extend beyond their family members. *HelloTalk* in particular provides language partners the opportunity to offer feedback to each other, allowing them to refine their literacy skills in an interactive and authentic way.

However, we must be cautious that neither translation nor asking a student to use a mobile application equate to sustaining their language and culture. These tools should not be pushed onto migrant students as an additional task or "homework." Instead, online apps and/or language-learning specific apps must be applied in a meaningful and engaging way that promotes agency, autonomy and reflection. While language teachers during the early stages may prompt and assist migrant students to notice the linguistic differences between their home and school languages, the long-term goal for teachers should be facilitating the sustainability of these practices without scaffolding from teachers. This process might be challenging especially for novice teachers who are learning the ropes of the teaching profession. In the next section, we aim to provide principles for instructional design for successful integration of culturally sustaining MALL pedagogy.

5. INSTRUCTIONAL DESIGN FOR CULTURALLY SUSTAINABLE MALL PEDAGOGIES

Sound instructional design in a MALL-infused curriculum is synonymous with the process of *backwards design* which requires an educator to start with a learning goal, determine acceptable evidence of learning, and then plan instruction (Wiggins & Mctighe, 1998, 2005). To develop a culturally sustaining pedagogy that draws from MALL, an educator must first centre their language and culture, and possibly social justice goals, and only after doing so seek out the appropriate MALL application to assist students in reaching those goals. CSPs-centred learning goals should not only invite inquiry of cultural, academic and professional knowledge, but also inspire explorations of identity, intersectionality, positionality, real-world power dynamics and other social justice issues.

In order to determine which application to use in the classroom, a language teacher must analyse an app by asking themselves two fundamental questions: (1) What linguistic function(s) does this application target, and does it align with my learning goal? and (2) How can this application, rather than a pen and paper assignment, highlight and preserve the cultural and linguistic resources, perspectives and knowledge of my students? Table 1 below provides three sets of learning goals, lesson objectives and social media-based MALL apps that can be used for achieving such goals in any ESL and/or English Language Arts classroom with emergent bilinguals. Although Table 1 highlights English as the target language, to enact a culturally sustaining pedagogy, teachers should encourage students to produce an additional output/perform another task in their language of choice. These apps may be used both as crops of input for the language teacher to harvest authentic language use from and channels through which the students may produce such output.

Whether an educator personally embraces or rejects the use of social media or other MALL apps for personal use, they should not rob students of the opportunity of interacting with such interfaces as they reflect the current reality of the (digital) world outside the classroom. Lee (2017) highlighted that a culturally sustaining pedagogy "requires that we teach knowledge, skills, epistemologies, and dispositions that can serve as problem-solving resources for a wide array of problems within domains as well as across domains and tasks" (p. 270). The array of skills such as digital literacy and executive functioning that learners develop as they interact with MALL apps are certainly transferable not only within different academic subject areas, but also in their personal and professional lives. Educational apps, social media apps, messaging apps and even language learning apps have the potential to be useful and necessary to function in our present-day world that is inhibited by lockdowns, curfews and social distancing measures. Providing strategic and meaningful educational experiences to migrant students and their families through the use of MALL from an earlier age/level/grade may even help alleviate some of the systemic inequalities by providing more equitable opportunities that extend beyond the classroom walls.

Table 1

Mobile Apps for Culturally Sustaining Learning Objectives

Learning Goal	Sample Lesson/Unit Objective	Real-World Mobile Apps
Students will be able to (SWBAT) describe what constitutes a community and its values	SWBAT use the past simple tense to describe a moment in which they felt like a valued member of a community in English	TikTok Instagram Facebook Twitter Wordpress Blog
SWBAT argue and defend a viewpoint on a matter of personal meaning to them	SWBAT use the language of persuasion to articulate a viewpoint about the recent Green New Deal in English	Reddit Youtube Videos and Comments Section Instagram
SWBAT compare and contrast perspectives concerning nutrition, health and food access	SWBAT use imperatives to share a recipe that is important to them in English	Tasty Cookmate Food Network Kitchen TikTok
SWBAT compare and contrast cross-cultural perspectives of professionalism	SWBAT identify and use action verbs to discuss previous professional experiences in English	LinkedIn Indeed Jobcase

6. CONCLUSION

Before the era of COVID-19, the use of mobile apps such as *TikTok*, *Instagram* and *Tasty* during class time was perhaps considered a distraction or even shunned from the classroom. We hope that our article encourages all English language teachers and K-12 mainstream educators who work with emergent bilinguals to look at such applications through an entirely new perspective and leverage these applications for linguistic and culturally sustaining purposes. Social media apps and other blog/video-blog (VLOG) based platforms are authentic language use contexts to retrieve and teach about language-in-use as well as to provide students with a digital space to share and sustain their own linguistic and cultural practices. MALL also provides the affordance of a wider audience and a more permanent location for such personal narratives and educational projects to be preserved and passed along to communities that extend beyond the language classroom.

It is noteworthy to mention that MALL may come across as failing to take into account the needs of those students who may not have access to a mobile device, and therefore MALL itself may end up amplifying the class-based disparities in the classroom (Chen, Mayall, York, & Smith, 2019). As we mentioned earlier, each culturally sustaining pedagogy should take into account its own student population. In that sense, we perceive MALL as a means for CSPs rather than the end goal, a way to amplify curriculum rather than an attempt to completely replace it. It is only after educators establish the accessibility and usability of these online tools that decisions need to be made for learning objectives, activities and opportunities for assessment (Armfield et al., 2016). Moreover, integration of MALL activities alone is not sufficient in achieving CSPs. Educators adopting CSPs are required to constantly reflect upon their own perspectives, positionality, privileges and intersectional identities as well as the larger power dynamics embedded within educational contexts. MALL is but one piece towards achieving transformational social justice pedagogies in a largely white-dominated and systemically unbalanced educational system. There is still much work to be done by all of us who reject deficit ideologies and fight for all marginalised and oppressed learner groups.

REFERENCES

Armfield, S. W. J., Armfield, D. M., & Franklin, L. O. (2016). The shaming: Creating a curriculum that promotes socially responsible online engagement. In R. Papa, D. M. Eadens, & D. W. Eadens (Eds.), *Social justice instruction* (pp. 271–280). Cham: Springer.

Alim, H. S. (2007). "The Whig Party don't exist in my hood": Knowledge, reality, and education in the Hip Hop Nation. In H. S. Alim & J. Baugh (Eds.), *Talking black talk: Language, education, and social change* (pp. 15–29). New York, NY: Teachers College Press.

Arzubiaga, A. E., Noguerón, S. C., & Sullivan, A. L. (2009). The education of children in im/migrant families. *Review of Research in Education, 33*(1), 246–271.

Bartolomé, L. (2004). Critical pedagogy and teacher education: Radicalizing prospective teachers. *Teacher Education Quarterly, 31*(1), 97–122.

Bauer, E., Presiado, V., & Colomer, S. E. (2017). Writing through partnership: How emergent bilinguals foster translanguaging. *Journal of Literacy Research, 49*(1), 10–37.

Berzins, M. E., & López, A. E. (2001). Starting off right: Planting the seeds for biliteracy. In M. Reyes & J. Halcon (Eds.), *The best for our children: Critical perspectives in literacy for Latino students* (pp. 81–95). New York, NY: Teachers College Press.

Branz-Spall, A. M., Rosenthal, R., & Wright, A. (2003). Children of the road: Migrant students, our nation's most mobile population. *The Journal of Negro Education, 72*(1), 55–62.

Burston, J. (2015). Twenty years of MALL project implementation: A meta-analysis of learning outcomes. *ReCALL: The Journal of EUROCALL, 27*(1), 4–20.

Calafell, B. M. (2010). When will we all matter?: Exploring race, pedagogy, and sustained hope for the academy. In D. L. Fassett & J. T. Warren (Eds.), *The Sage handbook of communication and instruction* (pp. 343–359). Thousand Oaks, CA: Sage.

Carson, N. (1999). *Linking_learning: Migrant education technology projects*. Office of Elementary and Secondary Education, Washington, DC. Retrieved from https://files.eric.ed.gov/fulltext/ED425900.pdf

Chavkin, N. F. (1996). Involving migrant families in their children's education: Challenges and opportunities for schools. In J. L. Flores (Ed.), *Children of la frontera: Binational efforts to serve Mexican migrant and immigrant students* (pp. 325–339). Charleston, WV: ERIC Clearinghouse on Rural Education and Small Schools.

Chen, Y, Carger, C. L., & Smith, T. J. (2017). Mobile-assisted narrative writing practice for young English language learners from a funds of knowledge approach. *Language Learning & Technology, 21*(1), 28–41.

Chen, Y., Mayall, H. J., York, C. S., & Smith, T. J. (2019). Parental perception and English Learners' mobile-assisted language learning: An ethnographic case study from a technology-based Funds of Knowledge approach. *Learning, Culture and Social Interaction, 22*, 100325.

Chinnery, G. M. (2006). Going to the MALL: Mobile assisted language learning. *Language Learning & Technology, 10*(1), 9–16.

County of Monterey (2020, November 15). Summary Report. Retrieved from https://www.co.monterey.ca.us/government/departments-a-h/health/diseases/2019-novel-coronavirus-covid-19/2019-novel-coronavirus-2019-ncov-local-data-10219#sumaryreport.

Crenshaw, K. (1989). Demarginalizing the intersection of race and sex: A black feminist critique of antidiscrimination doctrine, feminist theory and antiracist politics. *University of Chicago Legal Forum, 1*(8), 139–167.

Demouy, V., Jones, A., Kan, Q., Kukulska-Hulme, A., & Eardley, A. (2016). Why and how do distance learners use mobile devices for language learning? *The EUROCALL Review, 24*(1), 10–24.

Duarte, G., & Rafanello, D. (2001). The migrant child: A special place in the field. *Young Children, 56*(2), 26–34.

Farm Bureau Monterey. (2020, November 15). *Facts, figures & FAQs*. Retrieved from http://montereycfb.com/index.php?page=facts-figures-faqs

Farquhar, S. A., Goff, N. M., Shadbeh, N., Samples, J., Ventura, S., Sanchez, V., Rao, P., & Davis. S. (2009). Occupational health and safety status of indigenous and Latino farmworkers in Oregon. *Journal of Agricultural Safety and Health, 15*(1), 89–102.

Flores, N., & Rosa, J. (2015). Undoing appropriateness: Raciolinguistic ideologies and language diversity in education. *Harvard Educational Review, 85*(2), 149–171.

Free, J. L., Križ, K., & Konecnik, J. (2014). Harvesting hardships: Educators' views on the challenges of migrant students and their consequences on education. *Children and Youth Services Review, 47*, 187–197.

Gay, G. (2010). *Culturally responsive teaching: Theory, research, and practice*. New York, NY: Teachers College Press.

González, N., Moll, L. C., & Amanti, C. (Eds.). (2005). *Funds of knowledge: Theorizing practices in households, communities, and classrooms.* Hillsdale, NJ: Lawrence Erlbaum Associates Publishers.

Groves, D. S. (2016). Excellence for all: How US schools can ensure student success. In R. Papa, D. M. Eadens, & D. W. Eadens (Eds.), *Social justice instruction* (pp. 43–56). Thousand Oaks, CA: Springer.

Green, P. E. (2003). The undocumented: Educating the children of migrant workers in America. *Bilingual Research Journal, 27*(1), 51–71.

Hammond, Z. (2015). *Culturally responsive teaching and the brain: Promoting authentic engagement and rigor among culturally and linguistically diverse students.* Thousand Oaks, CA: Corwin.

Harven A. M., & Soodjinda, D. (2016). Pedagogical strategies for challenging students' world views. In R. Papa, D. M. Eadens, & D. W. Eadens (Eds.), *Social justice instruction* (pp. 3–14). Cham: Springer.

Hernandez, T., & Gabbard, S. (2018). U.S. Department of Labor's National Agricultural Workers Survey (NAWS) (2015–2016). A demographic and employment profile of United States farmworkers. Research Report No. 13. Retrieved from https://www.dol.gov/sites/dolgov/files/ETA/naws/pdfs/NAWS_Research_Report_13.pdf

Kacetl, J., & Klímová, B. (2019). Use of smartphone applications in English language learning – A challenge for foreign language education. *Education Sciences, 9*(3), 1–9.

Kozoll, R., Osborne, M., & García, G. E. (2003). Migrant worker children: Conceptions of homelessness and implications for education. *International Journal of Qualitative Studies in Education, 16*(4), 567–585.

Kukulska-Hulme, A., & Shield, L. (2008). An overview of mobile assisted language learning: From content delivery to supported collaboration and interaction. *ReCALL, 20*(3), 271–289.

Ladson-Billings, G. (1995). Toward a theory of culturally relevant pedagogy. *American Educational Research Journal, 32*(3), 465–491.

Ladson-Billings, G. (2012). Through a glass darkly: The persistence of race in education research & scholarship. *Educational Researcher, 41*(4), 115–120.

Lee, C. (2017). What is culturally sustaining pedagogy and why does it matter? In D. Paris & H. S. Alim (Eds.), *Culturally sustaining pedagogies: Teaching and learning for justice in a changing world* (pp. 1–21). New York, NY: Teachers College Press.

Leis, A., Tohei, A., & Cooke, S. D. (2015). Smartphone assisted language learning and autonomy. *International Journal of Computer-Assisted Language Learning and Teaching (IJCALLT), 5*(3), 75–88.

Levy, M. S. (2011). Migrant laptops: Extending the academic day for the children of farm workers and their credit recovery via laptops. *Computers in the Schools, 28*(2), 140–157.

Lopez, A., Turkan, S., & Guzman-Orth, D. (2017). Conceptualizing the use of translanguaging in initial content assessments for newly arrived emergent bilingual students. *ETS Research Report 2017.* Princeton, NJ: Educational Testing Service.

López, G. R., Scribner, J. D., & Mahitivanichcha, K. (2001). Redefining parental involvement: Lessons from high-performing migrant-impacted schools. *American Educational Research Journal, 38*(2), 253–288.

Lorde, A. (2007). *Sister outsider: Essays & speeches*. Berkeley, CA: Crossing Press.

Martinez, Y. G., & Velazquez, J. A. (2000). *Involving migrant families in education.* Retrieved from https://files.eric.ed.gov/fulltext/ED448010.pdf

Merryfield, M. (2003). Like a veil: Cross-cultural experiential learning online. *Contemporary Issues in Technology and Teacher Education, 3*(2), 146–171.

Meyertholen, P., Castro, S., & Salinas, C. (2004). Project smart: Using technology to provide educational continuity for migrant children. In C. Salinas & M. E. Fránquiz (Eds.), *Scholars in the field: Challenges of migrant education* (pp. 181–196). ERIC Clearinghouse on Rural Education and Small Schools.

Migrant Education Program. (n.d.). Retrieved from https://results.ed.gov/about

Mines, R., Nichols, S., & Runsten, D. (2010, January). *California's indigenous farmworkers: Final report of the indigenous farmworker study (IFS)*. California Rural Legal Assistance. Retrieved from http://www.indigenousfarmworkers.org/IFS%20Full%20Report%20_Jan2010.pdf

Moll, L. C., Amanti, C., Neff, D., & Gonzalez, N. (1992). Funds of knowledge for teaching: Using a qualitative approach to connect homes and classrooms. *Theory into Practice, 3,* 132–141.

Moll, L. C., & Gonzales, N. (1994). Lessons from research with language minority children. *Journal of Reading Behavior, 26*(4), 439–456.

Nevárez-La Torre, A. A. (2012). Transiency in urban schools: Challenges and opportunities in educating ELLs with a migrant background. *Education and Urban Society, 44*(1), 3–34.

O'Hara, S. P., Pitta, D. A., & Pritchard, R. H. (2016). Implementing new technologies to support social justice pedagogy. In R. Papa, D. M. Eadens, & D. W. Eadens (Eds.), *Social justice instruction* (pp. 103–116). Cham: Springer.

Paris, D. (2012). Culturally sustaining pedagogy: A needed change in stance, terminology, and practice. *Educational Researcher, 41*(3), 93–97.

Paris, D., & Alim, H. S. (Eds.). (2014). Symposium: Culturally sustaining pedagogy. *Harvard Educational Review, 84*(1), 72–73.

Pegrum, M. (2014). *Mobile learning: Languages, literacies and cultures: New language learning and teaching environments*. Cham: Springer.

Purcell-Gates, V. (2013). Literacy worlds of children of migrant farmworker communities participating in a migrant head start program. *Research in the Teaching of English, 48*(1), 68–97.

Ward, M. (2017). The benefits of computer assisted language learning (CALL) for migrants and migrant families. In B. Covarrubias Venegas, M-T. Claes, & P. Namazie (Eds.), *21st Century waves of change: Cultural dexterity for turbulent times* (pp. 181–192). Dublin: IACCM.

Wiggins, G., & McTighe, J. (1998). *Understanding by design.* Alexandria, VA: Association for Supervision & Curriculum Development.

Wiggins, G., & McTighe, J. (2005). *Understanding by design* (2nd ed.). Alexandria, VA: Association for Supervision and Curriculum Development.

Zhang, S. (2016). Mobile English learning: An empirical study on an app, English fun dubbing. *International Journal of Emerging Technologies in Learning (iJET), 11*(12), 4–8.

4 "WE ARE ALL EQUAL?!" – GENDER, GENDER AWARENESS AND ATTITUDES TOWARDS GENDER IN FOREIGN LANGUAGE TEACHING AND LEARNING

Viviane Lohe, University of Erfurt, Germany

ABSTRACT

Gender is a topic that has only recently and slowly entered the spotlight of English as a Foreign Language (EFL) teaching and learning. Even though it is obvious that teachers should teach in a gender-aware and gender-inclusive way, it is shown in this article that there is still a need for systematic teacher training when it comes to gender in EFL classrooms. The article discusses the importance of EFL classrooms for dealing with gender and sexuality topics. A questionnaire study is presented that asked 79 students from one university in Germany, to shed light on their attitudes towards gender, gender awareness and teaching gender at schools in general and in EFL classrooms in particular. The results show that the vast majority have come across gender as a topic at universities, yet still, there is a need to develop gender awareness in many students, too, as they have traditional notions of gender or are not interested in the topic. In the last part of the article, the way that gender awareness can be raised with university students using critical incidents will be discussed. Critical incidents are a good way to foster gender awareness as they stimulate reflection processes and display alternative performative options that somehow deal with gender topics.

KEYWORDS

Gender, sexuality, university education, attitudes.

1. INTRODUCTION

Gender-related issues have found their way into universities and schools. This specifically applies to teaching pedagogy in general; however, when it comes to teaching foreign languages, the developments are comparably slow. And yet, FL teaching/learning contexts offer perfect conditions to raise gender awareness.

Starting with a theoretical introduction, the article shortly defines gender. Secondly, it will be unveiled why gender is a topic particularly suitable for foreign language classrooms. Teaching English as a Foreign Language (TEFL) classrooms inherently provide the opportunity for students to take on new perspectives and roles. They afford a safe space, as it can be easier to discuss sensitive topics in a foreign language, and they occasion the possibility to deal with authentic materials, as many texts about gender and gender studies in university education stem from Anglophone contexts. Thirdly, a research study with students from a German university will be presented. The study focuses on the German context only. However, the insights can be transferred to other EFL contexts, too. Lastly, it is concluded from the study's results that it is necessary to develop gender awareness among university students, university lecturers, (FL) teachers and students alike, and it will be shown how this can be done in any EFL context, not only the German one, using critical incidents.

2. GENDER IN THE EFL CLASSROOM

2.1 GENDER AS ONE CATEGORY OF HETEROGENEITY

First of all, I would like to note that I look at gender from a pedagogical perspective. Therefore, gender is, for me, a subcategory of heterogeneity. A heterogeneous class is often described as a class that has learners of different kinds in it as opposed to a class where learners are very similar in their learning preconditions (Ur, 1991). Heterogeneity in (EFL) classrooms may refer to different dimensions such as social, economic and cultural as well as linguistic backgrounds. Also, other categories like different levels of performance (students with learning difficulties or students who are highly talented) (Jaehner & Schick, 2013) come into play. Language skills, motivation, the pace of learning, learning styles and experience (of learning) can be incorporated under the umbrella term of heterogeneity. Likewise, physical and intellectual disabilities are covered by the term. Apart from these dimensions, and most importantly for this article, gender is another distinct part of heterogeneity (Walgenbach, 2014).

It is important that all individuals at school need to be enabled to unfold, develop and display their discrete varieties of heterogeneity, based on equal rights. Inclusion, which can be seen as an answer to heterogeneity in schools, demands that schools adapt to all students' learning requirements and needs and not the other way round, that students need to adapt to schools. In contrast to integration which refers to students adapting to the school system and not the other way round, inclusion entails actual participation in a group. In other words, all members of a group should be included into the group and the school system needs to adapt to the students' needs (Pompe, 2015), regardless of their heterogeneous prerequisites.

However, in this article, inclusion is not seen as creating a dichotomy between people who are tolerated and people who tolerate (Nelson, 1999). It is rather understood as a concept that does not entail minorities and majorities but views heterogeneity as the norm. Therefore, my perspective on inclusion is very similar to Nelson's, which incorporates queer theory rather than LGBT promotion, and thus takes a "universalizing view" (Nelson, 2002, p. 49). The aims of such a perspective are as follows:

- acknowledging that the domain of sexual identity may be important to a range of people for a range of reasons;
- examining not only subordinate sexual identities, but also the dominant one(s);
- looking at divergent ways of producing and 'reading' sexual identities in various cultural contexts and discourses;
- identifying prevailing, competing, and changing cultural norms that pertain to sexual identities;
- exploring problematic and positive aspects of this identity domain;

- considering sexual identity in relation to other acts of identity and vice versa.

(Nelson, 1999, p. 376)

Even though Nelson focuses mainly on sexuality, this can also be applied to gender in EFL classrooms as both topics are intertwined. The "sex-gender relationship entails differences or tendencies in what women and men do or say, stemming from the notion of gender as an idea about the importance of differentiation between women and men" (Sunderland, 2006, p. 29). Gender can be seen as a "correlate of sex" (Sunderland, 2006, p. 28), and therefore, both topics will be dealt with in this article.

2.2 GENDER – A SHORT DEFINITION

In contrast to the feminist movements of the 1970s, modern gender studies do not only focus on changing the social position of women (Pilcher & Whelehan, 2004). They also consider two other aspects: the socio-cultural constructedness of gender as well as the diversity of (sexual) identities, which go beyond simple binary structures like man and woman (Lohe & Viebrock, 2018). This means that gender issues concern questions like gender identity, heterogeneity, gender roles, gender differences, gender hierarchies, gender inequalities and gender stereotypes, gender subversion, gender equality, non-stereotypicality and how all these features are formed and constructed in societies (Frey Steffen, 2006). Therefore, the term "doing gender" is often used to highlight the social constructedness of gender (Lohe & Viebrock, 2018). It refers to aspects that define one's own and others' gender identities (Frey Steffen, 2006) and, conversely, to the ways in which gender shapes interactions. These processes and effects do embed not only social interactivity, but also discursive practices. Therefore, they are performative habits (Butler, 2004); not facts, but acts (Le Page & Tabouret-Keller, 1985). Regarding gender and TEFL a comprehensive definition that takes into account all important features discussed above has been provided by König et al. (2015, p. 3):

> [gender is] a social and discursive construct based on – but not limited to – the cultural opposition of femininity vs. masculinity (adjectives: e.g., feminine, gender-queer, masculine); often differentiated from 'sex' as the idea of an anatomical opposition of femaleness vs. maleness (corresponding adjectives: e.g. female, intersex, male).

2.3 GENDER IN THE EFL CLASSROOM

Established habits and constructs can and should be broken up, overcome and even deconstructed to provide an inclusive and healthy environment for everyone outside heteronormative structures. In schools, this can be done by raising gender awareness (Elsner & Lohe, 2016). Gender awareness can be developed in three steps that build on each other:

1. **identify** heteronormative stereotypes (e.g., finding out that you are "trapped" in a heteronormative assumption)

2. **reflect** on your own and on other people's stereotypes (e.g., thinking about the question where these stereotypes come from and what consequences they have)
3. **deconstruct** stereotypes (e.g., thinking about alternative options and ways of thinking to deal with gender sensitive situations) (Elsner & Lohe, 2016, p. 13).

The EFL classroom, as well as EFL teacher training in particular, offer a perfect place for fostering gender awareness, as they:

- are places for identity development and change of perspectives as core goals (König, 2018; Surkamp & Nünning, 2016),
- are safe spaces for explorative interaction and negotiation (Decke-Cornill, 2009; König, 2018)
- and provide authentic material on gender and inherent cultural openness (König, 2018, p. 39).

Regarding the first point, it can be argued that the EFL classroom offers perfect conditions for developing gender awareness, as it has identity formation as one of its core goals. It is the place where students are to learn how to change perspectives, be empathic, question their attitudes and stereotypes and deconstruct them (Kultusministerkonferenz, 2012). In other words, students can develop their identities in the EFL classroom.

The second point relates to the assumption that the foreign language, on the one hand, reduces complexity, as students do not yet master the language perfectly, and slows down processes of meaning negotiation, but, on the other hand, helps to talk more freely about sensitive topics such as gender (König et al., 2015). Through the foreign language, students can take on different roles than those they are used to. This may lead to a more open discussion of topics that might be emotional, taboo or somehow normatively loaded, as the foreign language is not as closely associated with cultural meaning as the first language (König et al., 2015).

The last point is connected to the fact that all material in the EFL classroom should be authentic material. This means that texts that deal with gender and gender studies can also be read in the EFL classroom (with older students), as most of the literature on the topic stems from Anglophone contexts. Besides, the EFL classroom fosters a general cultural openness (König, 2018), as inter- and transcultural competences are key elements of TEFL that need to be developed in class.

3. THE STUDY

The following section will outline one part of a larger research project on gender in EFL classrooms. The whole project aims to analyse various aspects of gender in class, focusing not only on university students, but also on teachers and learners. Therefore, I will first describe the bigger picture of the project (Section 3.1), and then discuss an individual study with university students about their attitudes and beliefs regarding gender and teaching about gender (sections 3.2-3.4).

3.1 NEED FOR RESEARCH

There is some research on the topic already. However, most of it is not connected to the EFL classroom but to general pedagogy or teacher training or deals with school students or teachers of English (e.g., Nelson, 2009). Nelson in her study with over 100 teachers and students combining observations and interviews discovered that there are various occasions in language classrooms where gender topics can and will be addressed by all social agents as well as classroom material. She concludes that five strategies need to be taken into account when raising gender awareness: "Recognizing that Sexual Literacy Is Part of Linguistic/Cultural Fluency," "Facilitating Queer Inquiry about the Workings of Language/Culture," "Unpacking Heteronormative Discourses for Learning Purposes," "Valuing Multisexual Student and Teacher Cohorts," and "Asking Queer Questions of Language-Teaching Resources and Research" (Nelson, 2009, pp. 206–218). She also describes how this should be done.

Other studies focus on didactic and methodological aspects of gender rather than on empirical research (e.g., Decke-Cornill & Gdaniec, 1992; Fliethmann, 2002; König, 2018). It is therefore of great importance to find out how teachers and students in teacher training programmes at universities position themselves towards gender aspects of EFL teaching and learning to find out what is needed in those programmes to raise gender awareness in students and students alike and, consequently, to foster real inclusion in German EFL classrooms. Therefore, the current article sheds light on university students' attitudes towards gender in EFL classrooms.

3.2 RESEARCH QUESTIONS

The overall aim of the study is to find out how the topic of gender is dealt with in learning and teaching environments, namely at universities and at (secondary) schools. It focuses on three phases of teacher training, namely students in university teacher training, future teachers in their traineeship and teachers who have accomplished their traineeship and work at schools, both less and more experienced. At the same time, students at schools will be observed.

The long-term objective of the study is to reveal how educational institutions (with both social agents and materials involved) deal with gender in foreign language learning contexts. The short-term objective of the study is to reveal university students' attitudes and needs in relation to gender. The results of the latter will be presented in this article.

The research questions for the whole study are as follows:

- How do universities and university students deal with gender and TEFL?
- How do schools and all social agents involved deal with gender and TEFL?

The research questions for the first part of the study include:

- What are university students' attitudes towards gender?
- What knowledge do they have about gender?
- What experiences with gender issues do they have?

3.3 METHODOLOGY

The following graph illustrates what is analysed:

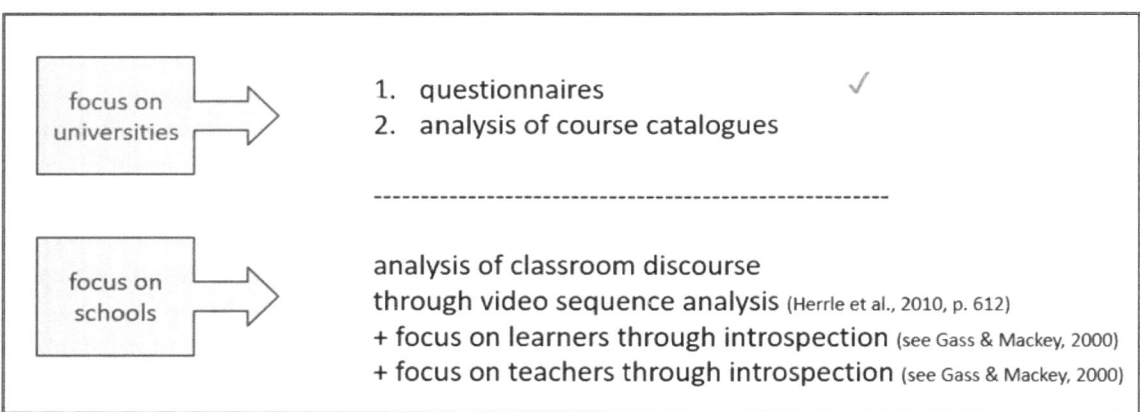

Figure 1. Methodology of the research study.

The study aims to be a multi-perspectival analysis of gender and TEFL (Jick, 1979; Lamnek, 1995). Both quantitative and qualitative methods will be combined in a triangulated way, so that it is a mixed-methods and between-methods approach (Denzin, 1970). Also, the triangulation happens in the shape of data-triangulation, as different sets of data (questionnaires, course catalogues, classroom discourse and introspective data) will be used and compared. To increase objectivity, different investigators will work with the data. They act as collectors, processors and analysers of data (Settinieri, 2014). The universal objective of the triangulation in the study at hand is to expand and deepen the multi-perspectival results (Aguado, 2014). It is not necessarily expected that the different data samples lead to the same or similar results, and therefore increase validity. Contrary results are possible.

The questionnaire study can be seen as a pilot study, as it is planned to collect a more extensive set of data in the future, also asking less advanced students to fill out the questionnaire. When developing the questionnaire, all relevant backgrounds were considered. All three dimensions that were determined according to the three fields identified in the figure above (Gender in general and at the university, Gender at school, Gender in English language classrooms) had at least two items to guarantee the reliability of the questionnaire. If the fields had only one item, the results would be too inaccurate. The questionnaire was analysed by experts on didactics and gender as well as pre-tested with seven university students. In the end, the questionnaire was adapted accordingly. It has 25 closed items and four open items in total (Appendix A).

In the study presented here, 79 advanced university students were asked about their knowledge, attitudes towards and experiences with gender in the winter and summer terms of 2019. All students studied TEFL in Germany. The data were collected in several seminars for TEFL. Most participants were students in their last two study semesters. The questionnaire was presented to the students in German, and all the answers were translated into English by the author. Due to the topic, it seemed important to ask the students about their gender: 71.6 per cent referred to themselves as female and 23.0 per cent as male, 0 per cent as diverse and 5.4 per cent made no indication.

3.4 RESULTS AND DISCUSSION

Not only for reasons of space, but also because the other items will be analysed within the wider scope of the study in future, not all results will be displayed here, just a selection for the dimensions "Gender in general and at the university" as well as for "Gender in English language classrooms." These dimensions are the focus of this article, as the field of "Gender at school" has been researched in other studies already. Besides, the items analysed here are supposed to provide the reader with first insights on university students' perspectives on gender, whereas some of the items go into detail too much. The items on gender-sensitive language (Appendix A), for example, were excluded as they rather focus on linguistic aspects and answer the research questions to a lesser extent. Some of the open answers will be analysed here as well. The open questions were selected to explain the closed items in more detail.

3.4.1 GENDER IN GENERAL AND AT UNIVERSITY

Question 1: I have often come across the topic of gender.
(1 not applicable at all; 6 totally applicable)

1	2	3	4	5	6
0%	0%	6.8%	5.5%	24.7%	63%

The vast majority of the test persons have already dealt with gender as a topic (93.2%) in general. The students seem to be well informed about the topic (see responses to open questions below, too). This means that there is already a starting point when talking about gender at universities.

Question 2: I am interested in the concept of gender.
(1 not applicable at all; 6 totally applicable)

1	2	3	4	5	6
2.6%	9.2%	15.7%	21.0%	30.3%	21.1%

When it comes to the question of interest in the topic, however, the results are different. Even though the majority of students are interested in the topic (72.4%), there is still more than a quarter (27.6%) that are not really interested. Yet again, the open questions will provide more insight into reasons for the students to be not too interested (for example, one student even seems to be annoyed by the topic; see below). However, for the majority, the topic is interesting, and they seem to be willing to deal with the topic as well.

Question 3: The role of gender in recent debates is too big.
(1 not applicable at all; 6 totally applicable)

1	2	3	4	5	6
9.3%	17.3%	13.3%	16.0%	24.0%	20.0%

This also applies to the question of whether the role of gender debates is too big. Sixty per cent of the students, a majority, say that this is true. Some students seem to be displeased with the role of gender in recent debates. For those students, it is still important to deal with gender topics. Teacher trainers should be aware of the fact that many students do not consider the topic sufficiently important. To help them to understand that the topic is important, teacher trainers should elaborate on the fact that many materials at school do not display various gender identities. It could, for example, be shown to future teachers that textbooks at schools often still depict traditional concepts of gender and sexuality to convince them to deconstruct these stereotypical notions.

Question 10: There are many seminars on gender at university.
(1 not applicable at all; 6 totally applicable)

1	2	3	4	5	6
6.8%	11.0%	23.3%	24.7%	27.4%	6.8%

Regarding seminars at the university, most of the students are aware that there are seminars on gender. This also applies to the non-representative observations I made when browsing the university's course catalogue (Summer Term 2019). There were many seminars on gender that students in their teacher training can attend, most of them on educational theory, many of them on literary and/or cultural studies, some on linguistics, none on EFL. In a wider scope of the study, it would also be interesting to see whether there has been a change in the university's offers of gender seminars.

Question 11: Gender does not play a significant role in teacher training.
(1 not applicable at all; 6 totally applicable)

1	2	3	4	5	6
45.9%	28.3%	17.6%	5.4%	2.7%	0%

In this vein, the majority of the participants (74.2%) also say that they disagree with the statement *"Gender does not play a significant role in teacher training."* They are familiar with gender in teacher training seminars. This can be seen positively, as it is the point of departure for avoiding a lack of confidence.

Question 12: Have you attended seminars on the topic of gender yet?

Yes	No	There were individual sessions on gender.	I don't know.
31.6%	40.5%	17.6%	5.4%

Many of the students have somehow dealt with gender in seminars, too. One third have attended whole seminars on gender, more than a quarter have attended seminars which had individual sessions on gender. However, even if there seems to be a wide variety of gender-related seminars at the university, 40.5 per cent have not dealt with gender at university yet. For the main study, it needs to be asked why they did or did not visit gender seminars. I hypothesise that students who are not interested in the topic avoid participating in gender seminars. If it transpires that this is the case, then it would be of utmost importance to support this group to further develop their willingness and confidence to deal with the topic. This could be done by telling them that gender is one subcategory of heterogeneity, and that inclusion is a teacher's main task in a well-managed classroom. Besides, gender is part of the German curricula. In Hesse, for example, it is a distinct part of higher secondary education in EFL classrooms ("gender issues;" "love, happiness, initiation, the troubled mind;" and "(in-)equality" (Hessisches Kultusministerium, 2014, p. 4)). Therefore, future teachers need to deal with the curricula as their binding guidelines to understand the importance of gender and sexual diversity for their EFL classroom.

3.4.2 GENDER IN ENGLISH LANGUAGE CLASSROOMS

Question 20: English language classrooms are particularly suitable for gender topics.
(1 not applicable at all; 6 totally applicable)

1	2	3	4	5	6
1.4%	17.8%	19.2%	35.6%	20.5%	5.5%

Most of the students (almost two thirds) think that the EFL classroom is particularly suitable for gender topics. They state several reasons for their answers (see below). Many of them are congruent with those that have been taken from the research literature (as discussed above), but the students also listed some more options.

Question 22: For girls, EFL is easier.
(1 not applicable at all; 6 totally applicable)

1	2	3	4	5	6
57.1%	22.9%	10.0%	8.5%	1.4%	0%

Fortunately, the students seem to reproduce a low amount of gender stereotypes, according to which girls are better language learners (Alexiou, 2016). Eighty per cent disagree with the statement. However, for almost 20 per cent, it is still important to raise awareness about heterogeneity in general and about gender in particular to avoid discrimination. Therefore, studies on gender and EFL learning need to be discussed in university education (e.g., Alexiou, 2016; Schmenk, 2009).

Question 19: For my future career, the topic of gender is of great importance.

(1 not applicable at all; 6 totally applicable)

1	2	3	4	5	6
2.5%	6.3%	6.3%	24.1%	35.4%	25.3%

Moreover, the students agree with the statement, *"For my future career, the topic of gender is of great importance"* (60.7%). The students seem to see the importance of being aware of gender topics. However, I hypothesise that social desirability could be a reason for these responses. Gender is a topic that is part of many public debates, not only academic ones. Students might know of the debates and might have known of my positioning towards gender in the EFL classroom, as I organised a lecture series on the topic beforehand. For this reason, they might have answered the way they thought I would want them to answer instead of reacting to the stimulus only (Stocké, 2004). For the future and main study, social desirability will be looked at more closely and it will be considered by employing a variety of investigators without identifying the main investigator and by using a wider variety of items. However, due to some of the answers that are fairly open and show negative attitudes towards gender, too, and due to the responses to the open questions in particular (see last part of the results), social desirability probably plays a minor role. In order to elaborate on the closed questions and to present a bigger picture, some answers to the open questions will be presented in the following section.

Responses to Open Questions on Gender and TEFL

> **Question 20 and 20a): The English language classroom is particularly suitable for the topic of gender. If so, why?**
>
> - **authenticity of texts (7)**
>   e.g., *"origin of the debate in the anglophone area (especially USA)"*
> - **cultural openness (11)**
>   e.g., *"stories, situations and topics that are the framework of teaching English as a foreign language provide good opportunities to deal with gender issues"*
> - **specific linguistic features (5)**
>   e.g., *"English is a gender-neutral language"*
> - **change of perspectives (3)**
>   e.g., *"literature and analysis of stories develops, and fosters change of perspective and contextualisation, also in the context of LGBTQI*- & feminist aspects"*
> - **gender is not subject-related (5)**
>   e.g., *"I think "gender" has to be dealt with interdisciplinarily; at the same time, it needs to be "de-dramatised"*

Responses to Open Questions on the Personal Meaning of Gender (Excerpts)

> **Question 27: What gender means to me personally...**
>
> The majority (58 students out of 79, 13 did not answer the question) of university students replied with sophisticated notions of gender such as:
>
> - e.g., *"to deal openly, tolerantly and without prejudice with others, irrespective of how they define their gender identity"*
> - e.g., *"social structures that might restrict me"*
> - e.g., *"the expression of identity"*
> - e.g., *"treating all students with the same form of respect and addressing individuals and their needs and dealing with their interests"*
> - e.g., *"becoming aware of how strongly socio-cultural circumstances shape my personality and my views/perception"*

Some students (8 students out of 79, 13 did not answer the question) seem to be not well informed and not interested (see last quote) in gender and gender debates. They think that there are more important topics than gender:

- *"natural differences between man & woman / weaknesses / strengths of man and woman"*
- *"I don't believe in gender-specific roles – it does not play a role – we are all equal – therefore, from my perspective, it should not be addressed permanently → creates 'artificial outrage'"*
- *"that people are doing too well when they are outraged about such topics. Everyone can be and live the way he wants to but should not bother me with it."*

From the research study, it can be concluded that:

1. There is a general interest and willingness to learn about gender topics at university, and there is also awareness about how important it is to deal with the topic in the EFL classroom.
2. Nevertheless, there are students who seem to have no interest in the topic and who have no gender awareness at all.

The results are very similar to the results that have been found in similar studies. Evripidou and Çavuşoğlu (2015), for example, have shown that most of the EFL teachers in their study have a positive attitude towards the integration of lesbian- and gay-related topics but with a number of hesitations as well. They conclude that if teachers are provided with suitable materials, they are willing to include gender topics, too. Both groups in the study at hand, meaning those university students who want to learn about gender topics at university as well as those university students who have no interest in the topic need further education about gender and gender awareness in EFL classrooms. The first group because they want to understand it and the second group because they do not want to discuss it. To avoid discrimination and homophobia, it is necessary though to deal with the topic at universities and at schools. As Sauntson (2018) found out, a lack of confidence on the teacher's side is a reason for not picking up gender and sexuality as concepts at schools. As Evripidou (2021) in his qualitative study in a Cypriot context found, some teachers questioned the weight of gender topics in EFL classrooms just because they have not dealt with them before. This also implies that it is still important to raise gender awareness in teacher training. In line with that, it was found in an Indian study that in-service teachers who have not dealt with gender before had a rather traditional view of gender roles (Agarwal & Shukla, 2017). Again, this shows how crucial it is to foster gender awareness. An older study from Israel (Tatar & Emmanuel, 2001) has shown that many teachers take gender equality as one subtopic of gender for granted, this is also confirmed by the quote above from my study (*"I don't believe in gender-specific roles – it does not play a role – we are all equal."*). Therefore, I believe that it is still necessary to educate this group about inequalities and gender topics. The first group in my study, however, has not necessarily completed its development of gender awareness either. For example, it could be the case that the first group dramatises gender in the EFL classroom, without knowing that this can lead to a reproduction of gender stereotyping (Faulstich-Wieland, 1996).

4. HOW CAN GENDER AWARENESS BE RAISED IN EFL TEACHER TRAINING?

A suitable tool to foster gender awareness in EFL classrooms has been developed by Cynthia Nelson. She lists questions that teachers might ask in EFL classrooms. However, following Nelson (1999, p. 378), they can also be used in university teacher training, for example, to start off a session or a seminar on the topic.

- In this country, what do people do or say (or not do or say) if they want to be seen as gay [lesbian] [straight]?
- How is this different in another country? How is it similar?
- Why do people sometimes want to be seen as straight [bisexual] [lesbian]? Why do they sometimes not want to?
- Why do people sometimes want to be able to identify others as straight [gay] [bisexual]? When is it important to know this about someone? When is it not important at all?
- Is it easy to identify someone as gay [straight] [lesbian]? Why or why not? Does it make a difference if the person is old or young, a man or a woman, someone you know or someone you only observe? What other things can make it easier or more difficult?
- Are there people who think their sexual identity is more [less] important than another part of their identity? Explain.
- In this country [in this city] [on this campus], which sexual identities seem natural or acceptable? Which do not? How can you tell?
- After people move to this country, do they change how they think about sexual identities? If so, how? If not, why not?

For further discussion and for more advanced students, critical incidents are an appropriate way to develop gender awareness. Critical incidents in EFL situations are defined as follows:

> Any unplanned event that occurs during class. In [sic] has been suggested that if trainee teachers formally reflect on these critical incidents, it may be possible for them to uncover new understandings of the teaching and learning process (Farrell, 2008, p. 3).

Critical incidents always entail reflective practice, which is defined as "the process of continually reflecting upon our interpretations of both our experience and the phenomena being studied so as to move beyond the partiality of our previous understandings and our investment in particular research outcomes" (Finlay, 2003, p. 108). It is very common practice in many (language) teacher education programmes as it helps university students "to think about what happened, why it happened, and what else could have been done to reach their goals" (Cruickshank & Applegate, 1981, p. 553). Critical incident practice is one way to enhance reflexivity in teacher training programmes. The aim of critical incident practice is to interrupt and/or reflect the taken for granted ways of thinking about teaching and learning (Brennan & Green, 1993). As Gumperz and Cook-Gumperz argued, gender is not a given parameter or boundary within which we develop our social identity. Rather, the parameters are "communicatively produced" and are thus discursive acts (Gumperz & Cook-Gumperz, 1982). An example of a gender-related critical incident has been discussed by Farrell (2008, p. 7):

> Another issue that was important for four teachers concerned the issue of student gender – in this case the realization that some students did not like working in groups with members of the opposite sex. Jasmine noticed that when she placed two boys and one girl together in a group, the girl was left out completely as the two boys only talked to each other. Jasmine also observed that this also occurred when the girls were in a majority – they also left the boy out of their discussion. Jasmine noted that: 'Arthur was left much out in the cold, not knowing what to do, while Weilin and Eunice just carried on without him'. When Jasmine reflected on these critical incidents, she said that she had not ever thought about gender issues in class before these incidents and now believes that 'cooperation among the genders can and should be cultivated, given the time and opportunity.'

The example deals with a situation very well known to experienced teachers but obviously not known to beginners of teaching. In primary schools as well as in secondary schools, some students tend to be not willing to work together with the opposite sex. With this example, university students can be induced to think about alternative ways to cultivate cooperation among boys and girls and any other gender. However, one must be careful with this example. It could reconstruct stereotypes about gender. Some students have no problem at all cooperating in mixed groups. Thus, it must be clarified that this situation is not necessarily the norm to de-dramatise the example. Moreover, to raise even more gender awareness, it could be pointed out that there are more genders than those presented in the example and how to deal with this issue. The problem that students are not willing to work in mixed-groups occurs in primary schools already. Therefore, working in mixed groups should be practised from the very beginning.

Interestingly, in his study, Farrell (2008, p. 4) points out that there are four out of 36 incidents from 18 teachers that were gender-related – a number that should not be neglected. Consequently, and also as a consequence of my observations in teacher training seminars, I believe that critical incidents about gender occur quite frequently, and they should be taken as opportunities for learning, reflecting and developing awareness about gender.

Another example of a critical incident regarding gender has occurred connected to a lecture series in 2015. The university student, who had already been working at a school, described the following (taken from Elsner & Lohe, 2016, p. 11):

> I remember that I once said to a boy in the classroom: "Stop sending messages to your girlfriend," as I assumed he is messaging to a girl. However, he replied: "Okay, but it is my boyfriend I am texting to."

> I was quite shocked and embarrassed that I did not think about using gender-neutral language, or why assuming [sic] that he is texting to his partner in the very first place. After this incident I always tried to be actively aware of what I am saying to my students. (Taken from an unpublished study log, anonymous author, 2015.)

This example is highly interesting for gender awareness in the EFL classroom as it does not only deal with the question of gender roles in language classrooms, but deals with sexual identities, too. The student very openly says that he has a boyfriend, and it can be assumed due to his very straightforward answer that he has fewer problems with his sexual identity than others who had remained quiet in the situation. Thus, the teacher trainee probably did not harm the student's identity, but still, she learnt from the situation and felt *"embarrassed."* Her gender awareness is quite sophisticated, as she identifies the incident, then reflects on it and, in the end, deconstructs it.

One more exemplification of a gender-related critical incident is the following situation (Élan Interculturel, 2012, p. 10) that happened to a "40-year-old, educated, middle-class woman, psychologist open to LGBT issues":

> A lesbian film club plays films about the life of lesbians and the problems they have. Afterwards the films are discussed by the audience with the involvement of subject-matter experts. Last time I was moderator of the discussion as a psychologist. In the audience there was a transgender woman (a man with a female identity) who actively contributed to the discussion. In one of my interactions, when I wanted to pass the floor to her, I said: "Now let's listen to a man's opinion."

The narrator then commented: "I had a cognitive dissonance: my slip of the tongue revealed that unconsciously I had a traditional gender conception." This situation occurred in an adult training scenario. It is very suitable to work with in university contexts, too, though. In EFL classrooms, teachers will encounter (knowingly or not knowingly) numerous gender identities. Not attributing the appropriate gender identity to a person can seriously harm the person's identity and self-esteem. Presenting this critical incident to trainee students at universities can lead to greater gender awareness – without putting them into the position to think about a critical incident themselves. Students can work individually or in groups through steps 2 to 4 on Farrell's list (see above). After they have thought about alternative and positive reactions (step 4), they hopefully develop gender awareness by deconstructing gender stereotypes, in this case, the stereotype that sex equals gender.

5. CONCLUSION

Gender is a topic that has only recently and slowly entered the spotlight of EFL teaching and learning:

> despite the increasing ex- and implicit mentioning of gender issues in the curriculum, teaching materials for the EFL classroom remain largely (identity and) gender-blind, which leads to a situation in which gender as a topic still continues to depend on the individual teacher or student (Eisenmann & Ludwig, 2018, pp. 17–18).

Even though it is obvious that teachers should teach in a gender-aware and gender-inclusive way, it has been shown in this article that there is still a need for systematic teacher training when it comes to gender in EFL classrooms. Even though the university students in my study had a general interest in gender topics at university and in the EFL classroom, there are also students who seem to have no interest in the topic and who have no gender awareness at all.

Therefore, analysing critical incidents is a powerful way to foster gender awareness in university seminars for teachers-to-be. They display situations that are both crucial and critical for teachers and learners. However, by thinking about alternative performative options, teachers positively gain new awareness and deconstruct their stereotypes. What is more, teachers can work in groups and not only – as stated in the quote above by Eisenmann and Ludwig – on their own.

REFERENCES

Agarwal, C., & Shukla, N. M. (2017). A study of in service teachers attitude towards gender discrimination. *Educational Quest: An International Journal of Education and Applied Sciences, 8/1*, 187–192.

Aguado, K. (2014). Triangulation. In J. Settinieri, S. Demirkaya, A. Feldmeier, N. Gültekin-Karakoç, & C. Riemer (Eds.), *Empirische Forschungsmethoden für Deutsch als Fremd- und Zweitsprache. Eine Einführung* [*Empirical research methods for German as a foreign and second language. An introduction*] (pp. 47–56). Paderborn: Ferdinand Schöningh.

Alexiou, T. (2016). Gender research in EFL classrooms or are girls better language learners? In D. Elsner & V. Lohe (Eds.), *Gender and language learning: Research and practice* (pp. 85–94). Tübingen: Narr.

Bortz, J., & Döring, N. (2016). *Forschungsmethoden und Evaluation für Human- und Sozialwissenschaftler* [*Research methods and evaluation for human and social scientists*]. Heidelberg: Springer.

Brennan, M., & Green, B. (1993). *Critical reflective writing*. Geelong: Deakin University.

Butler, J. (2004). *Undoing gender*. New York, NY: Routledge.

Cruickshank, D. R., & Applegate, J. H. (1981). Reflective teaching as a strategy for teacher growth. *Educational Leadership, 38/7*, 553–554.

Decke-Cornill, H., & Gdaniec, C. M. (1992). *Sprache – Literatur – Geschlecht. Theoretische Voraussetzungen für Gender Studies im fortgeschrittenen Englischunterricht* [*Language – literature – gender. Theoretical requirements for gender studies in advanced English teaching*]. Pfaffenweiler: Centaurus.

Decke-Cornill, H. (2009). Doing and undoing gender im klassenzimmer. Methodische Grundsätze und einige Anregungen [*Doing and undoing gender in the classroom. Methodological foundations and some recommendations*]. *Praxis Fremdsprachenunterricht, 6,* 14–19.

Denzin, N. K. (1970). *The research act*. Chicago, IL: Aldine.

Eisenmann, M., & Ludwig, C. (2018). Introduction. In M. Eisenmann, J. Hammer, & C. Ludwig (Eds.), *Queer beats: Gender and literature in the EFL classroom* (pp. 17–39). Frankfurt am Main: Peter Lang.

Élan Interculturel. (2012). *Compendium of critical incidents: Health, gender, sexuality, disability, body.* Retrieved from https://cesie.org/media/BODY-C.I.-Reader-EN.pdf

Elsner, D., & Lohe, V. (2016). Introduction to teaching gender in the EFL classroom. In D. Elsner & V. Lohe (Eds.), *Gender and language learning: Research and practice* (pp. 9–18). Tübingen: Narr.

Evipidrou, D., & Çavuşoğlu, Ç (2015). English language teachers' attitudes towards the incorporation of gay- and lesbian-related topics in the classroom: The case of Greek Cypriot EFL teachers. *Sexuality Research and Social Policy, 12/1*, 70–80.

Evipidrou, D. (2021). Deheteronormalising the EFL Classroom: Teachers' beliefs, doubts, and insecurities in exploring sexual identities in Cyprus. In D. L. Banegas, G. Beacon, & M. P. Berbaien (Eds.), *International perspectives on diversity in ELT* (pp. 113–129). London: Palgrave Macmillan.

Farrell, T. S. C. (2008). Critical incidents in ELT initial teacher training. *ELT Journal, 62/1*, 3–10.

Faulstich-Wieland, H. (1996). Abschied von der Koedukation? [*Farewell to coeducation?*] In E. Kleinau & C. Opitz (Eds.), *Geschichte der Mädchen- und Frauenbildung* [*History of girls' and women's education*] (pp. 386–400). Frankfurt/Main: Campus Verlag.

Finlay, L. (2003). Through the looking glass: Intersubjectivity and hermeneutic reflection. In L. Finlay & B. Gough (Eds.), *Reflexivity: A practical guide for researchers in health and social sciences* (pp. 105–119). Oxford: Blackwell.

Fliethmann, R. (2002). *Weibliche Bildungsromane. Genderbewusste Literaturdidaktik im Englischunterricht* [*Female educational novels. Gender-sensitive literature didactics in English language teaching*]. Tübingen: Narr.

Frey Steffen, T. (2006). *Gender. Grundwissen Philosophie* [*Gender. Basic knowledge of philosophy*]. Leipzig: Reclam.

Gumperz, J. J., & Cook-Gumperz, J. (1982). Introduction: Language and the communication of social identity. In J. J. Gumperz (Ed.), *Language and social identity* (pp. 1–21). Cambridge: Cambridge University Press.

Hessisches Kultusministerium. (2014). *Hinweise zur Vorbereitung auf die schriftlichen Abiturprüfungen im Landesabitur 2016 (Abiturerlass)* [*Notes on the preparation for the written examinations at upper secondary schools 2016*]. Retrieved from http://berufliche.bildung.hessen.de/bg/LA16-Hinweise_zur_Vorbereitung_auf_die_schriftlichen_Ab.pdf

Jaehner, C., & Schick, K. (2013). Wortschatzarbeit inklusiv [*Inclusive vocabulary work*] *Grundschulmagazin Englisch, 1/2013*, 10–13.

Jick, T. (1979). Mixing qualitative and quantitative methods: Triangulation in action. *Administrative Science Quarterly, 24/4*, 602–611.

König, L., Surkamp, C., & Decke-Cornill, H. (2015). Negotiating gender. Aushandlungs- und Reflexionsprozesse über Geschlechtervorstellungen im Fremdsprachenunterricht anstoßen [*Negotiating gender. Triggering negotiation and reflection processes about gender images in foreign language teaching*]. In L. König, C. Surkamp, & H. Decke-Cornill (Eds.), *Special issue: Negotiating gender. Der Fremdsprachliche Unterricht Englisch, 49/135*, 2–8.

König, L. (2018). *Gender-Reflexion mit Literatur im Englischunterricht. Fremdsprachendidaktische Theorie und Unterrichtsbeispiele* [*Gender reflection with literature in English language teaching. Foreign language theory and practical examples*]. Stuttgart: Metzler.

Kultusministerkonferenz. (2012). *Bildungsstandards für die fortgeführte Fremdsprache (Englisch/Französisch) für die Allgemeine Hochschulreife (Beschluss der Kultusministerkonferenz vom 18.10.2012)* [*Educational standards for the continued foreign language (English/French) for university admission*]. Retrieved from https://www.kmk.org/fileadmin/Dateien/veroeffentlichungen_beschluesse/2012/2012_10_18-Bildungsstandards-Fortgef-FS-Abi.pdf

Lamnek, S. (1995). *Qualitative Sozialforschung* [*Qualitative social research*]. Weinheim: Beltz.

Le Page, R., & Tabouret-Keller, A. (1985). *Acts of identity: Creole-based approaches to language and ethnicity*. Cambridge: Cambridge University Press.

Lohe, V., & Viebrock, B. (2018). Deconstructing gender stereotypes in EFL classrooms through contemporary movies. In M. Eisenmann, J. Hammer, & C. Ludwig (Eds.), *Queer beats: Gender and literature in the EFL classroom* (pp. 413–436). Frankfurt am Main: Peter Lang.

Nelson, C. (1999). Sexual identities in ESL: Queer theory and classroom inquiry. *ESOL Quarterly, 3/33, Critical Approaches to TESOL*, 371–391.

Nelson, C. (2002). Why queer theory is useful in teaching. A perspective from English as a second language teaching. *Journal of Gay & Lesbian Social Services, 14/2*, 43–53.

Nelson, C. (2009). *Sexual identities in English language education. Classroom conversations*. New York, NY: Routledge.

Pilcher, J., & Whelehan, I. (2004). *Fifty key concepts in Gender Studies*. London: Sage Publications.

Pompe, A. (2015). Inklusion [*Inclusion*]. In A. Pompe (Ed.), *Deutsch inklusiv. Gemeinsam lernen in der Grundschule* [*German inclusive. Learning together at primary level*] (pp. 1–14). Baltmannsweiler: Schneider.

Sauntson, H. (2018). *Language, sexuality and education.* Cambridge: Cambridge University Press.

Schmenk, B. (2009). *Geschlechtsspezifisches Fremdsprachenlernen? Zur Konstruktion geschlechtstypischer Lerner- und Lernbilder in der Fremdsprachenforschung* [*Gender-specific foreign language learning? On the construction of gender-typical learner and learning images in foreign language research*]. Tübingen: Stauffenburg.

Schößler, F. (2008). *Einführung in die Gender Studies* [*Introduction to gender studies*]. Akademie Verlag: Berlin.

Settinieri, J. (2014). Forschst Du noch, oder triangulierst Du schon? [*Do you still do research or do you triangulate yet?*] In D. Elsner & B. Viebrock (Eds.), *Triangulation in der Fremdsprachenforschung* [*Triangulation in foreign language research*] (pp. 17–35). Frankfurt: Peter Lang.

Stocké, V. (2004). Entstehungsbedingungen von Antwortverzerrungen durch soziale Erwünschtheit [*Conditions for the development of answer biases through social desirability*]. *Zeitschrift für Soziologie, 33/4,* 303–320.

Sunderland, J. (2006). *Language and gender. An advanced resource book.* London and New York: Routledge.

Surkamp, C., & Nünning, A. (2016). *Englische Literatur unterrichten. Grundlagen und Methoden* [*Teaching English literature. Foundations and methods*]. Seelze-Velber: Kallmeyer.

Tatar, M., & Emmanuel, G. (2001). Teachers perceptions' of their students' gender roles. *The Journal of Educational Research, 94/4,* 215–224.

Ur, P. (1991). *A course in language teaching: Practice and theory.* Cambridge: Cambridge University Press.

Walgenbach, K. (2014). Heterogenität als Grundlage pädagogischen Handelns [*Heterogeneity as a foundation of educational action*]. In S. Maschke, G. Schulz-Gade, & L. Stecher (Eds.), *Jahrbuch Ganztagsschule. Inklusion. Der pädagogische Umgang mit Heterogenität* [*Yearbook all-day school. The pedagogical approach to heterogeneity*] (pp. 22–32). Schwalbach/Taunus: Debus Pädagogik Verlag.

Questionnaire on Gender

Age
- □ 18-21
- □ 21-24
- □ 24-27
- □ 27-30
- □ 30-33
- □ 33-36
- □ older

Gender
- □ female
- □ male
- □ diverse

Semester (English)
- □ 1.-2.   □ 3.-4.
- □ 5.-6.   □ 7.-8.
- □ 9.-10.   □ 11.-12.
- □ higher

Teaching Degree
- □ L1 (primary)
- □ L2 (lower secondary)
- □ L3 (higher secondary)
- □ L5 (Special Educational Needs)

Subject Combination

GENDER IN GENERAL AND AT UNIVERSITY

I have often come across the topic of gender.
□ 1   □ 2   □ 3   □ 4   □ 5   □ 6
(1 not applicable at all; 6 totally applicable)

I am interested in the concept of gender.
□ 1   □ 2   □ 3   □ 4   □ 5   □ 6
(1 not applicable at all; 6 totally applicable)

The role of gender in recent debates is too big.
□ 1   □ 2   □ 3   □ 4   □ 5   □ 6
(1 not applicable at all; 6 totally applicable)

In my everyday life, I pay attention to gender-sensitive language.
□ 1   □ 2   □ 3   □ 4   □ 5   □ 6
(1 not applicable at all; 6 totally applicable)

At university, I pay attention to gender-sensitive language.
□ 1   □ 2   □ 3   □ 4   □ 5   □ 6
(1 not applicable at all; 6 totally applicable)

Gender as a topic should get more attention.
□ 1   □ 2   □ 3   □ 4   □ 5   □ 6
(1 not applicable at all; 6 totally applicable)

My lecturers pay attention to gender-sensitive language.
□ 1   □ 2   □ 3   □ 4   □ 5   □ 6
(1 not applicable at all; 6 totally applicable)

My fellow students pay attention to gender-sensitive language.
□ 1   □ 2   □ 3   □ 4   □ 5   □ 6
(1 not applicable at all; 6 totally applicable)

There are many seminars on gender at university.
□ 1   □ 2   □ 3   □ 4   □ 5   □ 6
(1 not applicable at all; 6 totally applicable)

Gender does not play a significant role in teacher training.
□ 1   □ 2   □ 3   □ 4   □ 5   □ 6
(1 not applicable at all; 6 totally applicable)

Have you attended seminars on the topic of gender yet?

□ yes

□ no

□ there were individual sessions on gender

□ I don't know

GENDER AT SCHOOL

Gender as a topic will overwhelm my students.

□ 1   □ 2   □ 3   □ 4   □ 5   □ 6

(1 not applicable at all; 6 totally applicable)

It is important to deal with gender issues in the classroom
(e.g. texts on homosexuality or the role of women).

□ 1   □ 2   □ 3   □ 4   □ 5   □ 6

(1 not applicable at all; 6 totally applicable)

It is important to use gender-neutral language at school.

□ 1   □ 2   □ 3   □ 4   □ 5   □ 6

(1 not applicable at all; 6 totally applicable)

In my experience, the boys tend to be a nuisance in class.

□ 1   □ 2   □ 3   □ 4   □ 5   □ 6

(1 not applicable at all; 6 totally applicable)

Girls are interested in other topics than boys.

□ 1   □ 2   □ 3   □ 4   □ 5   □ 6

(1 not applicable at all; 6 totally applicable)

In my classes, I will treat everyone equally, no matter if they are boys or girls.

□ 1   □ 2   □ 3   □ 4   □ 5   □ 6

(1 not applicable at all; 6 totally applicable)

For my future career, the topic of gender is of great importance.

□ 1   □ 2   □ 3   □ 4   □ 5   □ 6

(1 not applicable at all; 6 totally applicable)

GENDER IN ENGLISH LANGUAGE CLASSROOMS

English language classrooms are particularly suitable for gender topics.

□ 1   □ 2   □ 3   □ 4   □ 5   □ 6

(1 not applicable at all; 6 totally applicable)

If so, why?

In EFL classrooms, it is not so important to worry about gender-sensitive language.

□ 1   □ 2   □ 3   □ 4   □ 5   □ 6

(1 not applicable at all; 6 totally applicable)

For girls, EFL is easier.

□ 1   □ 2   □ 3   □ 4   □ 5   □ 6

(1 not applicable at all; 6 totally applicable)

For me, gender is a cross-cutting issue.

□ 1   □ 2   □ 3   □ 4   □ 5   □ 6

(1 not applicable at all; 6 totally applicable)

I will deal with gender in my English lessons
(e.g. in the form of texts that deal with gender identities).

□ 1   □ 2   □ 3   □ 4   □ 5   □ 6

(1 not applicable at all; 6 totally applicable)

I will deal with gender linguistically in English lessons
(e.g. discussing other forms of masculine and feminine).

□ 1   □ 2   □ 3   □ 4   □ 5   □ 6

(1 not applicable at all; 6 totally applicable)

I would translate gender in German as...

What gender means to me personally...

5

THINKING QUEERLY: IMPLICATIONS FOR TRANSFORMATIVE TEACHER PRACTICE IN THE ENGLISH LANGUAGE CLASSROOM

Benedict J. L. Rowlett, Hong Kong Baptist University, Hong Kong

ABSTRACT

Recent research conducted from a queer theoretical perspective in TESOL/TEFL demonstrates how issues of gender and sexuality can impact the language classroom in multiple ways. Featuring teachers' narrative reflections on their practices, many of these studies demonstrate the affordances that *thinking queerly* as a form of critical inquiry has brought to their understandings of diversity and inclusivity. In this article, by bringing together and discussing narrative reflections from previous research, I aim to explore more fully how thinking queerly is constructed as an affective process that can yield transformative actions and interventions in the English language classroom.

KEYWORDS

Classroom practices, queer theory, learner diversity, affect.

1. INTRODUCTION

The academic literature on teaching English to speakers of other/foreign languages (TESOL/TEFL) education has long been dominated by cognitive/psychological-based theoretical models that have generally treated language as a system of decontextualised forms and structures (Chun & Morgan, 2019) that can be acquired through instruction over time to achieve linguistic competence in the target language. However, in response to calls from scholars such as Pennycook (2001) and Benesch (2012), the past few decades have seen a growing number of studies dealing with critical sociocultural and political perspectives on English language learning/teaching practices. In other words, these perspectives look beyond traditional models of language acquisition to see language teaching and learning as practices impacted by both macro (society) and micro (the classroom) level forces (Douglas Fir Group, 2016; Peña-Pincheira & de Costa, 2020). In these approaches, the classroom, in particular, is conceptualised as a social space, or contact zone (Kaiser, 2017; Pratt, 1999), where students participate in and negotiate multiple societal discourses (and the power relations they (re)produce) that inform and shape their identities and positionalities, thus either enhancing or negatively affecting their (language) learning experiences. In this respect, a small, but growing, number of these studies have explored how issues of inclusivity and diversity vis-à-vis social categories and relations of gender and sexuality impact ESOL/EFL classrooms. Perhaps the most productive (yet challenging) examples of these gender/sexuality-focused inquiries have been those that have adopted queer theoretical frameworks to face up to the pervasiveness of regulatory heteronormative discourses in ESOL/EFL teaching and learning practices (Nelson, 2008a), that is, those discourses that privilege normative gender and sexual identities and performances. Studies from this theoretical perspective have therefore sought to remedy the erasure of a diversity of gender and sexual subjectivities from the language classroom and teaching profession; those which Vandrick (1997) calls *hidden identities*. In doing so, these studies have begun to address questions concerning the introduction of queer issues into language learning pedagogy, including the creation of gender/sexuality inclusive learning materials and raising awareness of these issues in teacher education programmes (Paiz, 2015, 2017).

Informing ongoing explorations of more practical questions concerning what a queer pedagogy might look like, a great deal of the TESOL literature that could be said to emanate from a queer perspective has focused on the learning experiences and motivations of lesbian and gay identified students. For example, Harrison (2011) reports on how the gay-identified Japanese learners of English he interviewed were, through their language learning, seeking alignments with Western concepts of positive sexual identities expressed by the LGBT+ community that would allow them the freedom to be themselves. Similar cases can also be found in King (2008), Moore (2013) and Nelson (2008a, 2010). Other studies, however, have looked at how the expression of non-normative sexual identities may be silenced in classroom discourse. Liddicoat (2009) presents the example of a student whose attempts to present a queer sexual identity in the context of a classroom discussion resulted in their efforts being constructed as *linguistic failure*. In tandem with these stories of learner experience, there have also been various research articles exploring classroom practices via the teachers' introduction of gender/sexual inclusivity and diversity issues into classroom discussion and learning materials, seen most notably in the work of Nelson (2008a) and also in Ó'Móchain (2006), Curran (2006), Paiz (2015), and Paiz and Zhu (2018). In addition, Nelson (2008b) touches on the experiences of lesbian and gay identified teachers in the ESOL profession. All of these studies have continued to offer us significant insight into how social categories of gender/sexuality, and the regimes of power in which they are involved, impact language learning classrooms and their teachers/learners in multiple ways.

In this article, I intend to draw on aspects of these previous insights, bringing them together into a discussion that focuses on queer approaches to TESOL/TEFL in terms of socio-critical action. More precisely, I wish to foreground instances from the literature, conceptualised here as instances of reflexive inquiry from ESOL/EFL classroom instructors, in which we can consider such actions through an analytical lens of what we might call *thinking queerly* (Fryer, 2010; Milani, 2014; Motschenbacher, 2011). Aligning with recent classroom-based research that has sought to account for the important role of affect (emotions) in language education (e.g., Benesch, 2012), I will demonstrate how these instances of queer thinking are constructed as affective and transformative processes that can yield positive actions and interventions in the classroom.

The article begins with a brief overview of the main principles and concerns of queer theory and how aspects of this theorising have been adopted in some of the TESOL literature thus far. The discussion is then extended towards an understanding of practitioners' actions in the literature on this theme as representative examples of queer thinking. From this discussion, I propose *thinking queerly* as a form of affective socio-critical action that can engage with and challenge the *normative effects* of entrenched, and often exclusionary, regimes of knowledge in language learning. A greater part of the article will then be taken up with a review of what thinking queerly may look like in practice, by focusing on a selection of narrative reflections by teachers that have been cited in previously published studies. The article ends with a discussion that brings together these reflections to consider ways in which we can (and should) harness forms of queer thinking in language education and classroom practice, but also to highlight what may still be missing from this discussion with respect to underrepresented ESOL/EFL teaching and learning contexts.

2. QUEERING TESOL/TEFL: A BRIEF OVERVIEW

As much of the literature on queer pedagogical approaches and practices in TESOL/TEFL has been comprehensively reviewed in previous publications (e.g., Paiz, 2017, 2019a) I do not intend to provide a detailed overview of this growing body of important work. However, in order to adequately contextualise the main focus of this article, i.e., thinking queerly as socio-critical action, I will briefly discuss how aspects of queer theory have informed research into language classroom practices. Queer theory emerged from Western feminist theorizing in the early 1990s to take as its critical focus of inquiry the hegemonic regimes of gender/sexual norms, or "heteronormativity", that regulate societies. Heteronormativity works ideologically to privilege certain essentialised, or "naturalised", forms of gender and sexuality; in other words, those which conform to versions of masculinity or femininity that are stereotypically associated with heterosexuality (Motschenbacher, 2011; Sauntson, 2018). Under this system, gender or sexual identity expressions that do not match those versions are rendered "unintelligible" to the majority and are thus effectively marginalised in (Western) society (Butler, 1990; Sauntson, 2018). It is in this respect that we can see heteronormativity as one of the many "norms" through which indicators of social difference are created (Hall, Levon, & Milani, 2019). Attending to how (hetero)norms or normativities are negotiated (taken up or contested) in discourse, and examining the material effects of these processes (e.g., sexism, homophobia, transphobia) is therefore key to queer theoretical approaches. In this way, taking a queer position, means taking a political stance that aims to deconstruct discursive regimes of heteronormativity, opening up a space for transformative critical inquiry that focuses on all expressions of gender and sexuality, including heterosexuality, as well as their intersections with other regulatory social categories (social class, race etc.).

Insights from queer theory caught the attention of educators from early on in its inception. These were in turn adopted by pioneering ESOL/EFL practitioner-researchers whose experiences in the classroom helped forge a critical interest in how heteronormativity pervades the lives and language learning experiences of their students (e.g., Nelson, 1993, 1999; Vandrick, 1997). In this way, the focus was on how regulatory discourses of (normative) gender and sexuality may have been inhibiting opportunities for successful language learning, as well as (mis)shaping the sociolinguistic competences needed for the successful navigation of the target culture (e.g., in ESOL classes for recent immigrants to the West) (Nelson, 2010). As outlined in the introduction, these early engagements have inspired ongoing research that has looked at aspects of queer pedagogy in TESOL/TEFL from multiple perspectives, for example, classrooms as dedicated spaces for LGBTQ+ learners (Moore, 2016) and inclusivity in curriculum and materials design (Paiz, 2015, 2017). One of the most influential of these pioneering teachers/researchers has been Cynthia Nelson, who has amassed a considerable body of queer work that investigates the intersection of gender/sexualities with the concerns and dynamics of ESOL/EFL classrooms and the students and teachers who inhabit these spaces. It is to her insights that I will now turn as I direct my attention to the conceptualisation of practitioner actions, presented in this review article as examples of queer thinking that can challenge and transform normative (and therefore often exclusionary) classroom practices.

3. THINKING QUEERLY

Nelson's early engagement with queer theory and her understanding of the pedagogic potential it offers language teachers is marked by the distinction she makes between a "pedagogy of inclusion" approach and a "pedagogy of inquiry" approach (1999, p. 373). While the former may seek to include the marginalised (e.g., lesbian and gay identities) into the language curriculum, it also raises a number of problematic questions regarding the premise on which this practice of inclusivity is based. In other words, simply "including" marginalised identities into the curriculum, in the spirit of "acceptance" (or at worst, "tolerance"), or as "a celebration of diversity" (Janks, 2010, p.102) may in fact only serve to re-emphasise and perpetuate the differences between the "normative" and "non-normative," thus reinforcing the minority status of the Other (Dumas, 2008; Nelson, 1999, 2008a; Wallace, 2002; Winans, 2006). In contrast, a pedagogy of inquiry approach is built on the (queer) premise that all identity categories are problematic as they tend to bring with them essentialising assumptions about the social and personal characteristics of those who identify as, for example, LGBTQ+, resulting in the forms of Othering addressed previously.

A pedagogy of inquiry therefore works to openly foreground and engage with the linguistic and cultural production of knowledges informing gender and sexual identities in everyday discursive practices (Nelson, 2005, 1999). For the ESOL/EFL classroom, which is of course a social space that aims to facilitate communication, participation and interaction, a pedagogy of queer inquiry seeks to incorporate and analyse those everyday discourses and their effects, in this way enabling learning, and equipping students with the socio-critical literacies and competences that can be deployed to challenge essentialising and limiting assumptions of fixed identities (Gray & Cooke, 2019; Nelson, 2016). It is thus within Nelson's body of work on this topic that we can begin to get a clear sense of what it might mean to think queerly and the implications this form of socio-critical practice has for re-imagining ESOL/EFL pedagogies. However, at this point, it is probably a good idea to offer a working definition of *thinking queerly* to lay the groundwork for the affective dimensions of this practice that the remainder of this article will focus on. To do so, I turn to the ethicist David Ross Fryer (2010, p. 6) who states:

> To think queerly is to think, *really to think* [italics in original], about gender, sex, sexuality, and indeed all forms of identity and expression as being open to various instantiations, and as having multiple – even infinite – modalities, as never being what we assume them to be from surface appearances or uninterrogated presuppositions...Queer thinking is critical through and through.

Fryer's position, as represented here, clearly emphasises the criticality of queer thinking. As such, it is offered as a challenge to normative thinking; in other words, a refusal to take for granted the world as it appears to be. Fryer's argument is expansive and thought provoking, and although it will not be the task of this article to examine what he proposes in detail, I would like to use his position as a working definition, or as a staging point, from which to hone in on what I identify as examples of queer thinking in narratives from the classroom. The call to think along non-normative lines is, in Fryer's view, a call for ethical practice. It is also, I suggest, a call that foregrounds the affective, or the emotional. After all, in order to think critically (queerly) about things that have long been taken for granted requires an affective shift – an emotionally-driven troubling of our assumptions and practices – shaking up in this way a reliance on comfortable ways of being/thinking (Luhmann, 1998). More specifically, in the case of this article's topic, this involves problematising orthodoxies in English language teaching from which socio-political issues of gender/sexuality are often sidelined or erased entirely.

Following this line of inquiry, the examples of queer thinking in these narratives from the ESOL/EFL classroom are approached as forms of transformative practice, where affective shifts in experience allow teachers to *feel*, and therefore *think* differently (Åhäll, 2018) about their teaching. By deploying the notion of affect in this article I therefore follow Ahmed (2004) by focusing on what emotions do rather than what emotions are. In other words, the focus is not on the inner workings of affect from the perspective of individual speaking subjects but rather on how affects are manifested socially in discourse (Weatherell, 2014) to inform and enable (transformative) social action. A consideration of affect has until recently, and like queer issues, only occupied a marginal place in research on teaching and learning practices in ESOL/EFL. However, scholars such as Sarah Benesch (2012) have made it clear that affect is not tangential to English language teaching and learning but, on the contrary, is integral to the critical work teachers and learners carry out in their classroom. Most importantly, affect can be seen as a tool for understanding how pedagogical decisions can result in small shifts in perception that cumulatively may result in positive and transformative socio-critical action (even beyond the walls of the classroom) (Benesch, 2012). The examples from the TESOL/TEFL literature I will now present and discuss are, in this way, often highly affective, and thus demonstrate the affordances that thinking queerly can offer by way of fresh insights and understandings into a critical pedagogy of inquiry in English language teaching. However, to begin with, it is important to address the pervasiveness of (hetero)normative thinking in the TESOL/TEFL profession, to provide a baseline from which to examine those affective shifts in perception in context.

4. NORMATIVE AFFECTS

Surveys and interviews conducted by Macdonald and colleagues (2014) for a British Council project titled *Exploring LGBT Lives and Issues in Adult ESOL* highlight teachers' various positions with respect to the role of gender and sexuality in language learning and teaching. While a number of respondents expressed a willingness to engage more with these issues, it is also clear that those interviewed had, until that point, never really considered the relevance of gender/sexual diversity to their teaching, and, in a few cases, were openly hostile to doing so (Gray & Cooke, 2019). Citing reasons such as a lack of confidence in introducing sexuality issues to their classes, not wanting to offend students' sensibilities, and worries over how to address and contest homophobic remarks in class, the responses of these teachers clearly illustrate the *normative affects* of entrenched (institutional) orthodoxies in the ESOL profession. In line with the topic of this article, I use the term *affects* here to underscore that, in this research, these teachers' responses are mostly expressed in emotional terms. I add *normative* to *affects* to create a collocation that emphasises that norms, as markers of social difference (of what may be acceptable, or not), are regulatory. In terms of affects, this means that not only do they generate and sustain ignorance or even antipathy towards the non-normative, but also that any broach of these norms is likely to cause discomfort with relation to the risk of sanction.

On the one hand, those teachers from the survey who expressed ambivalence (or even hostility) towards sexuality issues in their teaching provide fitting examples of what Felman (1987, see also Winans, 2006) calls the "desire to ignore." Rather than simply seeing these kinds of positionalities as ignorance, Felman makes clear that ignorance is "less cognitive than performative" (p. 79). In other words, taking such a position on these issues indicates a refusal to engage with anything that may unsettle, but even more importantly, a refusal, "to acknowledge one's own implication" (p. 79) in that disengagement. On the other hand, for those teachers who do acknowledge the importance of these issues, and even if they identify as queer themselves, their responses often emphasise the potentially disruptive affects of any further engagement, especially with respect to institutional demands and expectations. For example, one respondent in Macdonald et. al.'s (2014) study expressed a vulnerability towards acts of self-disclosure and addressing sexual diversity in class, where, in this teacher's words, "putting your neck on the line" would result in "a change or even breakdown in your relationship to students and possible further ramifications for you within your organization" (Gray & Cooke, 2019, p. 201).

A similar example to the above can be found in Nelson (2008b) where Tony, a self-identified gay male teacher from the United States, seeks to explain the reasons why he is not "out" to his students. In his brief narrative, he explains that he wishes to present himself as straight, so that he maintains a good relationship with his students – "I wanna gain their trust…show them…that we have a lot of things in common" (p. 30). For Tony, this position relies on the essentialising, and normative, assumption that his (mostly) Asian students will not understand what it means to be gay so he does not want to add to the many experiences of *culture shock* they will have on arrival to the US.

In this way, Tony's desire to present himself to his students as "the normal American guy" (p. 30), and the positions represented in Macdonald and Gray and Cooke (see also many of those in Nelson, 2008a), succinctly capture the normative affects that continue to infuse the ESOL profession and classroom. Expressed in terms such as "vulnerability," "maintaining good relationships," and "anxiety not to cause offence," it seems that those teachers who may wish to bring issues of gender/sexual diversity and inclusion into their classrooms are compelled to navigate a complex path where addressing these issues represents potential disruptions to their (established) teaching practices, and thus contains elements of risk. It is at this juncture where Winans's (2006) conceptualisation of processes of normalisation as the "places where thinking stops" (p. 113) makes a lot of sense, as the risk to selves, to careers, to interpersonal relationships for example may be, for some teachers, too great. However, it is precisely that element of risk that drives queer pedagogy (Luhmann, 1998) and the forms of queer thinking it entails, where the central pedagogic focus is on confronting and interrogating discourses of heteronormativity that construct and regulate selves and others. In the following, examples of reflexive practice will therefore be presented that detail how a queer pedagogical approach acknowledges this risk but moves beyond that position to find spaces for transformation and further inquiry.

5. CRITICAL SHIFTS IN THINKING:
EXAMPLES OF AFFECTIVE PRACTICE AND RELATIONALITY FROM TEACHERS

In a personal narrative from the classroom related by Christy Rhodes (2019), she draws attention to the homophobic attitudes displayed by one of her students, George, who frequently justified his comments as being "manifestations of his culture" (p. 162). This had the effect of silencing any challenges to his position as he maintained that his fellow students did not understand his country's values. Rhodes's initial reaction to these uncomfortable episodes was to "self-consciously stop the discussion and return to the "comfort" of comprehension and grammar questions" (p. 162), thereby demonstrating how heteronormativities, co-constructed in classroom interaction, result in the regulation of teaching practices. Her reflections on these episodes clearly reveal the affects of the normative TESOL classroom, expressed in her "disappointment" and "unease." She was, like many of those teachers surveyed in Macdonald et al. (2014) and Nelson (2008a, 2008b), unable at that time to form an effective response to the "risk" of stepping "on anyone's cultural toes" (p. 162). However, her narrative goes on to relate how these experiences represented a pivotal point in her practice, affording her the opportunity to think (queerly) about the affects her actions may have had on her students – "I cringe to think of the lesson my LGBQ students internalized about who had a voice in my classroom" (p. 163). She concludes her brief story with reflections on how she could have dealt with George, following the queer discourse inquiry approach advocated by Nelson (1999). As such, she voices an understanding of new strategies via discussion questions that are directed towards reframing and deconstructing heteronormative (or homophobic) positions expressed in class, for example, "What makes us believe that being straight or gay is natural? What do we think we base that on?" (p. 163). Rhodes's affective response to the uncomfortable experiences she faced in her classroom is therefore seen to afford her the shift in perception to open up a space for thinking queerly, facilitating a practice that fosters the critical sociolinguistic skills needed for both her and her students to question their (stereotypical) assumptions about gender and sexual identities.

Likewise, transcending the risk inherent in challenging and reframing heteronormative classroom practices is a featured concern of Joshua Paiz's short narrative from his EFL classroom in China (Paiz & Zhu, 2018). Although Paiz makes clear that his institution had actively encouraged diversity and inclusion initiatives, he also refers to the normative affects of institutional practice that result in stances taken by some students and faculty who see the presentation of queer issues in the classroom as an unwanted politicising of the curriculum. With this risk in mind, and despite stating his commitment to a queer teaching philosophy, Paiz explains that the decision to queer his own practices in this context was accompanied by strong feelings of anxiety. These feelings were both related to how presenting himself as an openly queer teacher would be received and his concern about how to accomplish this critical work in a way that would be culturally responsive, given that he had only just begun to teach in the Chinese context. His decision to confront the risk and take action, however, was vindicated by the excited response he received from his students, with many of them choosing to focus on sexuality issues in their final research papers (Paiz & Zhu, 2018). In this way, Paiz's embrace of queer thinking reveals how affective shifts in experience – thinking differently – can drive practitioner actions towards facing heteronormativities head-on and, in the process, generating transformative classroom practices.

A distinguishing feature of the narratives from both Rhodes and Paiz is the affective relationality (Wetherell, 2014) that emerges between teachers and their students when exploring together the forms of knowledge (discourses) that produce and regulate identity categories. I use the term affective relationality in this way to refer to how people forge relationships in particular encounters or spaces (e.g., the classroom) and how these relations are co-constructed in discourse, that is, in their classroom interactions and in their reflective narratives that are purposed towards making sense of these encounters. As we have seen from the survey and interview data from Macdonald et al. (2014) and the teacher narratives from Nelson (2008b), affective relationships between teachers and students are of central concern, especially when contemplating the potential breakdown in those relationships when queer issues are broached by either side. However, discussion from Rhodes and Paiz indicates that students are both sensitive and receptive to the actions taken by their teachers to queer their practices (or not). Paiz chooses to complement his own narrative with that of one of his students, Junhan Zhu, who responds to Paiz's use of queer learning materials in their course (Paiz & Zhu, 2018). Zhu's narrative is framed via his curiosity to explore queer issues, and his reception to the course materials is expressed in terms such as "excitement" and a growing sense of "comfort" in being able to express an understanding of these topics, resulting in his becoming a "more respectfully and critically involved student" (p. 4). The affective relationality afforded through these classroom encounters therefore sees both teacher (Paiz) and student (Zhu) experience together a shift in thinking that opens up a space for an examination of selves through acts of queering. Returning to Rhodes's (2019) narrative, we see an example of emergent affective relationality that prompts Rhodes to critically evaluate her reliance on tried and tested classroom activities. In this instance, one of Rhodes's queer students, Susan, complains to her that the icebreaker activities in which students were encouraged to relate aspects of their lives and social activities as conversation practice were causing her many difficulties – "…I hated those questions…I had to pretend and sometimes make up lies about who I went to the movies with. That was the only way I could keep who I was hidden" (p. 164). This admission resulted in Rhodes re-examining her assumptions about what she believed would be effective pedagogical activities in building community amongst her students. The affective incitement to think queerly, for example by replacing "monosexual assumptions about learners' identities with a multi-sexual approach" (p. 164; Nelson, 2008a), afforded Rhodes the capacity to create a learning environment that would not only be inclusive, but one in which the heteronormativity of the classroom would be brought to the fore and be open to critical inquiry.

To round off this section on constructions of affective practice (and relationalities) with respect to queer inquiry in the language classroom, I focus on two reflective and complementary articles from a special (and seminal) issue of the Journal of Language, Identity and Education (2006), *Queer Inquiry in Language Education,* edited by Cynthia Nelson. The first by Greg Curran (2006), and informed by his developing understanding of queer theory, relates how the author re-evaluates his teaching practices about gender and sexuality and the miscommunications these may have caused in his EFL classroom lessons. The second, by Constance Elwood (2006), is a highly affective reflection on teacher (researcher) and student subjectivities and affective relationalities that link to the co-construction and exploration of heteronormative discourse. The queer thinking that emerges from Curran's article comes in response to explanations he provided about queer sexualities to his students, building on the course materials he introduced on the topic of Sydney Mardi Gras. In his narrative, Curran expresses his frustration at not only what he perceived to be the inadequacy of his explanations, but also by recognising how he had fallen into the "comfortable 'teller' role" (Curran, 2006, p. 90), where the teacher imparts knowledge, and the students listen. As he explains, his best-laid intentions to trouble the heterosexual/homosexual binary through emphasising a non-essentialist understanding of sexual identities, as espoused in queer theory, conversely resulted in confusing his students. Despite positioning himself as the *expert*, he explains that their curiosity and questions about queer identities and concepts was frustrated by his lack of direct answers. As such, he realises that this top-down approach had not given room for his students' perspectives to emerge through discussion and debate, thus probably leaving, "the heteronormative knowledge they brought to the learning situation…intact and undisturbed" (p. 94).

Curran's narrative therefore draws attention to two aspects of critical practice that I wish to foreground in this article. The first relates (again) to how queer thinking is constructed as deeply affective, fostering the shifts in perception that allow us to think and feel differently about our classroom practices. The second follows this trajectory as it relates to the processual, where thinking does not stop (Winans, 2006), but often uncomfortable experiences and dissonances provide the impetus to re-examine and re-conceptualise – that is, queer thinking as ongoing socio-critical action, in contrast with, for instance, a resubmission to pedagogical orthodoxies because they are likely to be more comfortable. Curran's reflections and explorations in his article thus provide representative, and particularly useful, examples of the processes of queer thinking in practice. Moreover, the suggestions he provides as to how to pursue a pedagogy of queer inquiry in the language classroom underscore the very real benefits this approach can bring to students' learning. Drawing on Nelson (1999), he advocates strategies of reframing and deconstructing (Rhodes, 2019). Therefore, heteronormative and essentialising questions from students such as, "Are gays born that way," can be reframed to pay attention to the norms that inform and shape sexualities in different cultural contexts, for example, "What leads people to think that they're straight, gay, lesbian or bisexual" (p. 92). The strategy of deconstruction, similarly, can be directed towards questioning the values and assumptions embedded in discourse, and in doing so, maximise the language learning opportunities such discussions present (Curran, 2006).

Finally, and in a move away from actual classroom practices in this case, Elwood's (2006) compelling narrative study recounts the emotional trajectory she underwent when reflecting on and analysing an interview she conducted with a second language learner, as part of a study on cultural identities in English language learning. The focal point of her narrative hinges on how their navigation of (Western) heteronormative discourses during the interview, for example, "the confessional," and the "drive to self- knowledge," resulted in this learner's "coming out." This act of coming out is considered in this study to be an unavoidable product of these discourses, where self-representations and identifications encourage self-disclosure – "in answering my questions about 'who they were', the students were 'obliged' to produce themselves in terms of discourses in which I could recognise them" (p. 69) (see also Moore, 2016).

While Elwood's narrative reflection and analysis not only provides an extremely illuminating account of how regulatory discourses of heteronormativity shape interaction and actions at the micro level (a research interview on language learning experiences in this case), I have included a brief outline of her reflections here to once more draw attention to how an engagement with the affective results in forms of queer thinking. Characterising her experience as an emotional process of *coming undone* as she deals with the affects of the interview and her responsibilities to this student, she also makes clear that this process allowed her rethink both her practices and the formation of her own subjectivities through a troubling of heteronormative discourse. In doing so, she stresses (and resonating in Fryer, 2010) the "ethical reflexivity" (p. 82) that is required when addressing the complex issues of sexuality and sexual difference that are brought to bear on the language classroom and the experiences of learners. In this sense, and to re-emphasise a point made earlier, it is not enough to simply celebrate the diversity of learners by encouraging them to feel comfortable in coming out in the classroom, but to recognise the tensions that are created by such processes of (hetero)normalisation and the identities they may enforce, and how this may result in acts of misrecognition or othering that lead to further marginalisation and disengagement (see also Paiz & Zhu, 2018).

6. THINKING QUEERLY: IMPLICATIONS AND FUTURE DIRECTIONS

The above teacher (and student) narratives have been brought together and discussed with the intention of shedding light on what it may mean to think queerly. That is, a reflective process of interrogating the discursive regimes of (hetero)normativity that often shape language teaching and learning practices in TESOL/TEFL. As we have seen, what binds these selected narratives together is a consideration of affect as fundamental to the decisions made by teachers to critically evaluate and rethink their pedagogical approaches in the language classroom, together with their responsibilities to their students. In this way, their engagement with queer theory and pedagogy has provided them with the socio-critical tools to seize upon different ways of feeling and thinking, and to transcend the risk that challenging the normative affects of the ESOL profession and its institutions may entail. More importantly, and as presented in Paiz and Zhu (2018), teachers' affective responses may have direct benefits to learners, motivating them to become more "critically involved" (p. 4) in the world that the language learning classroom opens up to them.

It therefore remains, in the concluding sections of this article, to consider the ongoing and future implications that thinking queerly may have on the practicalities of pursuing a queer pedagogy of inquiry (or discourse inquiry) approach (Nelson, 1999) in our classrooms and institutions. In order to do so, I briefly return to Paiz (2006) who's own (affective) experiences of thinking queerly have resulted in a number of articles (2015, 2017, 2019a, 2019b) in which he lays out strategies for queering the language classroom. These strategies reiterate those advocated by Nelson (1999) and Curran (2006), in terms of a discourse inquiry approach, but further highlight the need for teacher trainers to add space in their programmes for readings and discussion of the queer ESOL literature, and the need for an ongoing critical examination and reworking of (largely heteronormative) commercially produced teaching materials (Paiz 2017, 2019). It is not my intention to rehearse Paiz's very useful directives and suggestions here. However, two areas that emerge from his recommendations deserve further discussion, as they relate most directly to the themes of this article.

The first concerns the necessity for more examples (published and widely disseminated) of how processes of queer thinking are co-constructed in practice (Paiz, 2017). As such, it would be good to see many more reflective accounts of how teachers and students may work together to co-construct affects in their negotiation of heteronormativities, and how such affects may positively impact both students' language learning and teacher practices in various or unexpected ways. In fact, in going about the task of selecting teacher experiences for discussion in this article I was struck by how few of these reflections are actually represented in the literature on queer approaches in TESOL/TEFL, despite the growing number of research articles on this topic. Of course, the (normative) research paper genre demands adherence to a structure that favours a rather impartial presentation of methods, data and results. As a result, these demands can often mask important and, I would stress affective, processes of thinking that have led to research interventions inspired by queer thinking – what Slembrouck (2001, p. 45) would call the "shadow conversations" that are integral to the research project but are often omitted as the research is packaged as journal articles and book chapters.

What is clear from the reflections I have discussed in this article, however, is that forms of narrative may offer a means by which to make these shadow conversations visible, enabling the affective to take centre stage and revealing the (often) messy processes through which teachers have sought to think queerly in the re-thinking of their practices. Indeed, as Nelson (2005), with reference to Bruner (1996), explains, narratives, as forms of inquiry or knowledge creation, can "violate canonicity" in the sense that they can "tell something unexpected", clarifying in this way "the expected" and thus serve, "to differentiate what is normative from what is not" (p. 111). Nelson also makes clear that narratives can be directed towards engaging others in processes of knowledge production. As we read, reflect on and question what is related in these stories from the classroom, narratives make effective pedagogic materials for both teachers (pre- or in-service) and students to interrogate discursive constructions of heteronormativity in the ESOL/EFL classroom and respond to the forms of queer thinking that aim at challenging them (Paiz, 2017). In short, what we need more of is what Zembylas (2005) identifies as "genealogies of emotions," specified in this way as "accounts of the strategies and tactics that have taken place in various emotional practices at different moments in relation to one's teaching" (p. 936). Assembling *genealogies* of affective queer thinking across diverse times and spaces (contexts) and using them in teacher training programmes and in our curricula may serve to both unsettle (a good thing as I have explained previously) and inspire. This position extends also to our exploring different forms of (academic) writing, in contrast to the generic research paper, where affect is foregrounded rather than side-stepped, resulting in fresh insights and the opening up of spaces for potential transformation (see Thurlow, 2016, for an excellent example of how he sets about accomplishing this challenge to conventional genres in his writing).

The second area for discussion that arises from Paiz's recommendations (2019), and one that I have previously addressed on the topic of gender and sexuality in language education (Rowlett & King, 2016), is the Western-centric position the work in queering TESOL/TEFL generally adopts. Queer theory and the forms of thinking it generates is very much a construct of the Western academy, and as such, may (and should) be interrogated in its relevance to areas and cultures that lie outside these centres of knowledge production. That said, much of the literature in ESOL from this perspective actually focuses on non-Western contexts (for example Moore, 2016, in Japan, and Paiz, 2018, in China). Moreover, it is evident from the above that queer issues, gender and sexual identities, and the (now global) discourses through which they are constructed, hold much significance and appeal for learners around the world who are engaging in their own explorations and constructions of (queer) selves through the learning and use of English (Dovchin, 2019; King, 2008; Rowlett, 2020). The question that remains, in this sense, is therefore of how to get around the binary of "the West and the Rest" in the challenge of queering TESOL/TEFL (Appleby, 2009; Rowlett & King, 2016).

A response to this challenge is, in tandem with the above, a call for not only more classroom-based research, but also many more (narrative) reflections of research and teaching practice to add to our *genealogies* of queer thinking. These should be from teachers who encounter and deal with the very real effects/affects of gender and sexuality in their English language classes in diverse contexts around the world, namely with respect to local constructions of heteronormativity and their intersections with other forms of social regulation, for example, race and class (Appleby, 2009). Such reflections, I hope, would therefore also be forthcoming from researcher-practitioners working in sites that sit outside of the typical private language school, a space often occupied by the privileged (i.e., those who can afford the fees) to encompass sites of compulsory schooling (primary and secondary) and perhaps more informal sites of learning (e.g., community centres/ NGOs – areas in which I am personally invested in my ongoing research). It is via these future narratives that we can expect to learn how forms of affective and queer thinking vis-à-vis teachers' (and their students') troubling of heteronormative classroom practices might be constructed in ex-centric (hence underrepresented) sites of investigation. Additionally, we might expect to learn more about alternative (Southern) theoretical perspectives, or ways of thinking, that can be purposed towards the deconstruction/decolonization of (hetero)normative or (neo)colonial pedagogies (Makoni & Pennycook, 2019). Most importantly, the emphasis should continue to be on how such stories from the ex-centric English language classroom (like those from Western contexts) might be deployed to inform strategies of redressing gender and sexuality-based inequalities in language education; inequalities that continue to impact access to linguistic (and material) resources, and therefore life opportunities in multiple sites of language contact and in multiple ways.

7. CONCLUSION

In wrapping up this contribution, I am very much aware that what I have *not* provided is a set of guidelines or activities on *thinking queerly* that can be selected and applied in any given English language classroom (a decision that may be seen as somewhat remiss in a paper submitted to a teaching journal!). For teaching and learning activities that adopt a queer inquiry approach, I urge the reader to explore in greater depth the inspiring articles I have discussed above (Curran, 2006; Paiz, 2017, 2019a, 2019b; Rhodes, 2019) as well as Ó'Móchain (2006) and Moore (2016). Instead, my purpose in this article has been to draw attention to important processes of knowledge production and socio-critical action in ESOL/EFL, by focusing on what it might mean to think queerly with respect to how we approach our professional practices as teachers/researchers. It must therefore be stressed that thinking queerly is not a method – like queer theory, it cannot be tied down to a notion of best practices or rules of pedagogic engagement (Winans, 2006). On the contrary, queer thinking represents those moments of *coming undone* (Elwood, 2006), when the unexpected happens or when questions or issues arise that cannot be simply dealt with by taking solace in the tried and tested. Those affective moments can, as I hope I have demonstrated in this article, afford us the opportunity *really to think* (Fryer, 2010) about how we can create a better and more critically inclusive learning environment for our students in all their diversity, despite our being in a world that often stifles or seeks to erase that diversity. I therefore hope that our actions, forged through processes of feeling and thinking with difference (and publications resulting from those actions), will continue inspiring future generations of teachers and students to capitalise on what they learn in the English language classroom, and the interactions they have there, to actually make that difference.

REFERENCES

Åhäll, L. (2018). Affect as methodology: Feminism and the politics of emotion. *International Political Sociology, 12*, 36–52.

Ahmed, S. (2004). *The cultural politics of emotion* (2nd ed.). Edinburgh: Edinburgh University Press.

Appleby, R. (2009). The spatial politics of gender in EAP classroom practice. *Journal of English for Academic Purposes*, *8*(2), 100–110.

Benesch, S. (2012). *Considering emotions in critical English language teaching: Theories and praxis.* New York, NY: Routledge.

Bruner, J. (1996). *The culture of education.* Cambridge, MA: Harvard University Press.

Butler, J. (1990). *Gender trouble: Feminism and the subversion of identity.* New York, NY: Routledge.

Chun, C. W., & Morgan, B. (2019). Critical research in English language teaching. In X. Gao (Ed.), *Second handbook of English language teaching* (pp. 1–19). New York, NY: Springer.

Curran, G. (2006). Responding to students' normative questions about gays: Putting queer theory into practice in an Australian ESL classroom [The Forum]. *Journal of Language, Identity, and Education*, *5*, 85–96.

Douglas Fir Group. (2016). A transdisciplinary framework for SLA in a multilingual world. *The Modern Language Journal*, *100*, 19–47.

Dovchin, S. (2019). Translingual English, Facebook, and gay identities. *World Englishes, 39*, 54–66.

Dumas, J. (2008). The ESL classroom and the queerly shifting sands of learner identity. *TESOL Canada Journal, 26*(1), 1–10.

Elwood, C. (2006). On coming out and coming undone: Sexualities and reflexivities in language education research. *Journal of Language, Identity, and Education*, *5*, 67–84.

Felman, S. (1987). *Jacques Lacan and the adventure of insight: Psychoanalysis in contemporary culture.* Cambridge, MA: Harvard University Press.

Fryer, D. R. (2010). *Thinking queerly: Race, sex, gender, and the ethics of identity.* Boulder, CO: Paradigm.

Gray, J., & Cooke, M. (2019). Queering ESOL: Sexual citizenship in ESOL classrooms. In M. Cooke & R. Peutrell (Eds), *Brokering Britain, educating citizens: Exploring ESOL and citizenship* (pp. 195–211). Clevedon: Multilingual Matters.

Hall, K., Levon, E, & Milani, T. M. (2019). Navigating normativities: Gender and sexuality in text and talk. *Language in Society, 48*, 481–489.

Harrison, M. (2011). *Discovering voices, discovering selves: Auto-ethnographic examinations of the relationships between Japanese queer sexualities and English as language and culture* (Doctoral dissertation). Indiana University of Pennsylvania, Indiana, PA.

Janks, H. (2010). *Literacy and power.* New York, NY: Routledge

Kaiser, E. (2017). LGBTQ+ voices from the classroom: Insights for ESOL teachers. *The CATESOL Journal, 29*(1), 1–21.

King, B. W. (2008). "Being gay guy, that is the advantage": Queer Korean language learning and identity construction. *Journal of Language, Identity and Education, 7*(3/4), 230–252.

Liddicoat, A. J. (2009). Sexual identity as linguistic failure: Trajectories of interaction in the heteronormative language classroom. *Journal of Language, Identity, and Education, 8*, 191–202.

Luhmann, S. (1998). Queering/Querying pedagogy? Or, pedagogy is a pretty queer thing. In W. F. Pinar (Ed). *Queer theory in education* (pp. 141–55). Mahwah, NJ: Lawrence Erlbaum.

Macdonald, S., El Metoui, L., Baynham, M., & Gray, J. (2014) *Exploring LGBT lives and issues in adult ESOL*. London: British Council.

Makoni, S., & Pennycook, A. (2019). *Innovations and challenges in applied linguistics from the global south.* London: Routledge.

Milani, T. M. (2014). Sexed signs–queering the scenery. *International Journal of the Sociology of Language, 228*, 201–205.

Moore, A. R. (2013). The ideal sexual self: The motivational investments of Japanese gay male learners of English. In P. Benson & L. Cooker (Eds), *The applied linguistic individual: Sociocultural approaches to identity, agency and autonomy* (pp. 135–151). Sheffield: Equinox.

Moore, A. R. (2016). Inclusion and exclusion: A case study of an English class for LGBT learners. *TESOL Quarterly, 50*, 86–108.

Motschenbacher, H. (2011). Taking queer linguistics further: Sociolinguistics and critical heteronormativity research. *International Journal of the Sociology of Language, 212*, 149–179.

Nelson, C. D. (1993). Heterosexism in ESL: Examining our attitudes. *TESOL Quarterly, 27*(1), 143–150.

Nelson, C. D. (1999). Sexual identities in ESL: Queer theory and classroom inquiry. *TESOL Quarterly, 33*(3), 371–391.

Nelson, C. D. (2005). Transnational/Queer: Narratives from the contact zone. *Journal of Curriculum Theorizing, 21*(2), 108–117.

Nelson, C. D. (2008a). *Sexual identities in English language education: Classroom conversations.* New York, NY: Routledge.

Nelson, C. D. (2008b). A queer chaos of meanings: Coming out conundrums in globalised classrooms. *Journal of Gay and Lesbian Issues in Education, 2*(1), 27–46.

Nelson, C. D. (2010). A gay immigrant student's perspective: Unspeakable acts in the language class. *TESOL Quarterly, 44*(3), 441–464.

Nelson, C. D. (2016). The significance of sexual identity to language learning and teaching. In S. Preece (Ed.) *The Routledge handbook of language and identity* (pp. 351–365). New York, NY: Routledge.

Ó'Móchain, R. (2006). Discussing gender and sexuality in a context-appropriate way: Queer narratives in an EFL college classroom in Japan. *Journal of Language, Identity and Education, 5*(1), 51–66.

Paiz, J. M. (2015). Over the monochrome rainbow: Heteronormativity in ESL reading texts and textbooks. *Journal of Language and Sexuality*, *4*(1), 77–101.

Paiz, J. M. (2017). Queering ESL teaching: Pedagogical and materials creation issues. *TESOL Journal*, *9*(2), 348–367.

Paiz, J. M. (2019a). Queering practice: LGBTQ+ diversity and inclusion in English language teaching. *Journal of Language, Identity and Education*, *18*(4), 266–275.

Paiz, J. M. (2019b). Queer ELT classroom practices: Suggestions for educators. *WATESOL newsletter, Winter 2019*, 5–7.

Paiz, J. M., & Zhu, J. (2018). Queering the classroom: A teacher's action and a student's response. *TESOL Journal, e371*, 1–4.

Peña-Pincheira, R. S., & de Costa, P. (2020). Language teacher agency for educational justice-oriented work: An ecological model. *TESOL Journal*, 1–13. Retrieved from https://onlinelibrary.wiley.com/doi/10.1002/tesj.561

Pennycook, A. (2001). *Critical applied linguistics: A (critical) introduction.* New York, NY: Routledge.

Pratt, M. L. (1999). Arts of the contact zone. In D. Bartholomae & A. Petrosky (Eds.), *Ways of reading: An anthology for writers* (pp. 581–596). Bedford: St. Martins.

Rhodes, C. M. (2019). A practical guide to queering the adult English language classroom. *Adult Learning, 30*(4), 160–166.

Rowlett, B. J. L. (2020). Second language socialization in the margins: Queering the paradigm. *Multilingua, 39*(6), 631–662.

Rowlett, B. J. L., & King, B. W. (2017). Language education, gender and sexuality. In S. May & T. McCarty (Eds.), *Encyclopedia of language and education*, (pp. 85–97). New York, NY: Springer.

Sauntson, H. (2018). *Language, sexuality and education.* Cambridge: Cambridge University Press.

Slembrouck, S. (2001). Explanation, interpretation, and critique in the analysis of discourse. *Critique of Anthropology, 21*(1), 33–57.

Thurlow, C. (2016). Queering critical discourse studies or/and performing 'post class' ideologies. *Critical Discourse Studies, 13*(5), 485–514.

Vandrick, S. (1997). The role of hidden identities in the postsecondary ESL classroom. *TESOL Quarterly, 31*(1), 153–157.

Wallace, D. L. (2002). Out in the academy: Heterosexism, invisibility, and double consciousness. *College English, 65*, 53–66.

Wetherell, M. (2014). *Affect and emotion: A new social science understanding.* London: Sage

Winans, A. E. (2006). Queering pedagogy in the English classroom: Engaging with the places where thinking stops. *Pedagogy: Critical approaches to teaching literature, language, composition, and culture, 6*(1), 103–122.

Zembylas, M. (2002). Structures of feeling in curriculum and teaching: Theorizing the emotional rules. *Educational Theory, 52,* 187–208.

6 DISRUPTING ENGLISH HEGEMONY AND PROMOTING CRITICAL LANGUAGE PEDAGOGY IN PHILIPPINE ELT

Jayson Parba, University of Hawai'i at Mānoa, USA

Irish Fernandez-Dalona, Mindanao State University-Iligan Institute of Technology, Philippines

ABSTRACT

Critical language pedagogy (CLP) has gained more attention in recent years although research that draws from this perspective remains wanting in applied linguistics, specifically in ESL and EFL contexts outside the US. Drawing on the Freirean principle of *praxis*, which allows the authors to reflect on their teaching experiences and legitimise their teacher-as-intellectual identities, this article explores various entry points through which to engage in critical language teaching. The discussion first situates Philippine ELT in its socio-cultural, historical, and political contexts, in which the English language enjoys a hegemonic privilege in education and in many other aspects of the society. It then proceeds to highlight the various entry points of engaging in critical ELT by encouraging teachers to disrupt English language hegemony. These entry points encourage Filipino ESL teachers to orient themselves towards a non-essentialist view of language and language learning, to leverage students' multilingualism through translanguaging, and to unpack the English for economic success myth. Moreover, the discussion underscores the value of incorporating critical teaching materials to create a space for underrepresented voices in the curriculum and to foster critical awareness among students. Lastly, the article highlights CLP's practical contributions in the field of English language teaching in the Philippine context.

KEYWORDS

Critical language pedagogy, Philippine ELT, critical materials, critical teachers, praxis.

1. INTRODUCTION

In recent decades, the field of applied linguistics experienced a critical turn as inspired by the works of Pennycook (1999, 2001), Canagarajah (1993; 1996) and other leading scholars in the field (Crookes, 2010, 2013, 2021; Kubota; 1998; Kubota & Lin, 2006). This critical orientation in terms of philosophy, research and pedagogy has encouraged and challenged a generation of applied linguists and language teachers to look at language learning and teaching as socially, culturally and politically situated (Crookes, 2021). In the field of English language education, for instance, an increasing number of works explore various ways of rethinking English language philosophy, curricula and pedagogy from a critical language pedagogy (CLP) perspective. Crookes (2013, p. 9) describes CLP as:

> teaching for social justice, in ways that support the development of active, engaged citizens who will, as circumstances permit, critically inquire into why the lives of so many human beings, perhaps including their own, are materially, psychologically, socially, and spiritually inadequate.

The same scholar also states that the main goal of a critically oriented curriculum is to prepare students to become citizens who will find solutions and take concrete steps to solve problems they identify and experience in their lived realities in a society that is often bereft with inequalities and status quo discourses that sustain power structures. It is important to note that CLP underscores the notion of agency, or a certain level of freedom, expected of and given to students to engage in what matters to them. Students in a CLP classroom are expected to ask relevant questions and to challenge various forms of inequalities in education and in the bigger social and historical contexts in which their lives are embedded. Additionally, the learners become critical co-investigators in continuous dialogue with the teacher. This means that students are empowered to "obtain and question knowledge as well as learn about themselves, their opinions on issues, and the influence of a dominant culture on these factors" (Kincheloe, 2008, pp. 163–164; see also Giroux, 2020) through engaging in purposeful discussions with their peers, their teachers and other experts, and learning from a variety of critical materials. In his work, which explores critical theories of learning, Brookfield (2005) maintains that students need to work on seven learning tasks, which include: challenging ideology, contesting hegemony, unmasking power, overcoming alienation, learning liberation, reclaiming reason and practising democracy.

While admittedly still marginal within the field of applied linguistics, it is encouraging to see several ways in which critically-oriented practitioners have engaged in transformative and reflexive educational practices, exploring various dimensions of critical language pedagogy. To be more specific, some of these scholars have explored the topics of race, racism and racialisation (Hammond, 2006; Kubota & Lin, 2006), social class (Menard-Warwick, 2008; Vandrick, 1995), war and politics (Morgan, 1992) and gender through a dialogic approach (Benesch, 1999; Valdez, 2012). In the Asian context, critical language teaching also became the focus of the work of Shin and Crookes (2005) and a growing number of scholars (e.g., Izadina & Abednia, 2010; Konoeda & Watanabe, 2008; Lin, 2004; Takayama, 2009) who share the same interest.

One way of engaging in CLP is by introducing critical materials in the hope of fostering sympathy for marginalised and minority groups and by engaging students in critical dialogues to foster critical awareness. Teaching at a Japanese university in the EFL context, Stillar (2013) enacted CLP through having his students write journal entries from the perspective of people who are seen as *others*. He carved a space for his students to form a new set of perspectives on controversial topics such as the life of a North Korean living in Pyongyang, the challenges of having a fiancée/fiancé from a Buraku caste, and the controversial whaling operations in Japan. In a somewhat similar vein, Shin and Crookes (2005) introduced critical dialogue to students in a Korean EFL context despite common essentialist perceptions that position South Korean students as passive and uncritical. The two scholars maintained that given the right classroom environment and critical stance by the teacher, students are able to engage in the dialogic process involving critical issues found in the society. What these studies suggest is that given the right theoretical background and mindset, teachers are able to successfully incorporate CLP in their own teaching practices despite common institutional constraints (e.g., standardised curriculum and assessment standards) (see also West, 2019).

Despite this growing interest in CLP among teachers and scholars in language education, however, research that explores the specific entry points of doing critical language teaching in various contexts remains wanting (Crookes, 2013). Many ESL teachers in the Philippines have limited familiarity with CLP, as teaching philosophies and approaches in the country have continued to reflect mainstream pedagogical approaches and frameworks like Communicative Language Teaching (CLT), Task-based Language Teaching (TBLT) and English for Specific Purposes (ESP) (Martin, 2014). With language teachers as the primary audience, this article hopes to address this scholarly lacuna to make the conversations on critical language teaching more accessible and practical to classroom teachers. More specifically, this article explores the following questions: *How might Filipino ESL teachers engage in critical pedagogical perspectives? What are some of the specific entry points for incorporating critical language pedagogy in their classroom practices?* In answering these questions, we reflect on our own experiences of teaching English in the Philippines while drawing and building on the extant literature in the field of applied linguistics. The exploration of these questions and the discussions that follow are therefore both theoretical and practical in nature. While this article is not empirical, the vignettes presented in the discussions that follow are conceived as *praxis*, which allows us to reflect on our pedagogical and curricular decisions to inform both teaching philosophy and practices (Freire, 1970), specifically in social-justice and action-oriented language classrooms (see Section 4 below). As such, the discussion intends to open more spaces for conversations, especially for teachers who are interested in learning more about critical language pedagogy and its possible manifestations in different contexts.

2. CONTEXTUALISING ENGLISH LANGUAGE TEACHING IN THE PHILIPPINES

2.1 ENGLISH AS A COLONIAL AND NEOCOLONIAL LANGUAGE

As a country that experienced brutal oppression through colonialism, English language teaching in the Philippines can be traced back to the American occupation of the archipelago in the early 20th century. The introduction of the American educational system, initially viewed as one of the various ways that paved for the attainment of democracy, for Filipinos to govern themselves, and for ultimate independence, rationalised the American settlement in the Philippines. The Americans' regard for education, seen from their establishment of the first public school system, left an indelible mark in the culture and values of the Filipinos as well as in the entire Philippine educational system. In fact, the institutionalisation of the public school system and the imposition of English as one of the official languages in the country produced enduring colonial structures and ideologies, and at the same time sustained the grip of English in the archipelago (Lorente, 2013).

Teaching English to Filipinos during the American period was practical since there were no teachers and teaching materials in Philippine languages (Bernardo, 2008) and was perceived to bring together Filipinos from different regions who spoke different languages. This move was also strategic compared to the previous Spanish colonisers, who depicted "hard power," owing to narratives of force and coercion. The Americans constructed themselves as liberators – a label which ironically designates to them the role of "liberating," instead of "colonizing" the entire archipelago. The Americans demonstrated "soft-power", a term coined by Nye (2017, p. 2), to mean "the ability to influence the behavior of others to get the outcome one wants, and the ability to get what you want with attraction rather than coercion and payments."

The American colonial government successfully encouraged more and more Filipinos to learn English by giving them incentives such as job opportunities, career in politics and access to government services. In the early 20th century, for instance, civil service jobs created by the US government in the Philippines required applicants to pass the English language exam. Passers of the said exam had more chances of getting hired than those who passed the Spanish language exam (Kramer, 2006). In other words, English became the official language not only in education, but also in the civil service sector; it had become a prerequisite qualification for Filipinos to participate in nation-building. In addition, "the positive attitude of Filipinos towards Americans; and the incentives given to Filipinos to learn English in terms of career opportunities, government service, and politics" provided a social climate receptive to the rule of Americans (Gonzalez, 1980, pp. 27–28). Additionally, the discourse associating enlightenment, democracy and self-governance with the acquisition of English was proliferated under the US occupation. The American colonial government assumed that through English as a common language, "Philippine society would…evolve…from the tribal chaos…to the emergence of – far in the future – of a nation characterised by 'homogeneity'" (Kramer, 2006, p. 201). English was, in other words, turned into "the wedge that separated Filipinos from their past and…was to separate Filipinos from the masses of their countrymen" (Constantino, 1970, p. 5). In the Philippines, to be able to think and speak in English became a condition for colonial subjects to meet.

The grip of English has persisted decades after the Philippines attained its independence from the US in 1946. In fact, the English language has secured a permanent position in Philippine society with the help of locals since day one. Often, viewed as the key to the Western societies, or a thoroughfare for upward social mobility, English has become deeply embedded in the everyday lives of Filipinos. A few studies revealed how Filipinos view the language, to wit: as a tool for "unification and social integration" (Ocampo, 2006, as cited in Koo, 2008, p. 22), along with economic advancement, greater academic pursuits (Racca & Lassaten, 2016) and globalisation (Lorente, 2012; Tupas & Salonga, 2016).

2.2 CONTEMPORARY SOCIO-ECONOMIC AND POLITICAL CONTEXT

It is important to point out that Philippine ELT exists against the backdrop of pervasive social inequality and human rights violations in the Philippines as can be seen in the persistence of income inequality and cases of poverty (Balisacan, 2003; Steele, Miller, & Britain, 2014) and the increasing number of cases of state-sponsored violence towards legitimate and peaceful dissent under Rodrigo Duterte (Coronel, 2017; Human Rights Watch, 2021). In terms of poverty reduction, for instance, Balisacan (2003) observes that the Philippines has been rather slow, and a high incidence of economic inequality and absolute poverty remain persistent in the country. This social context is worth mentioning because social and economic inequality often results in unequal Englishes (Tupas, 2015a), whereby certain groups of Filipinos, especially the middle class and the elites are privileged in terms of acquiring "good" English and the value associated with the variety of English they have in their communicative repertoire. As a case in point, Tupas (2019) argued that there is only a small portion of Filipino Overseas Workers (OFWs) who may be considered elite migrants, and they are often "products of elite Philippine universities, most of whom come from well-to-do and highly educated families" (p. 8). In the BPO (Business Processing Outsourcing) industry in the Philippines, Salonga (2010, 2015) states that only three to four of 100 applicants get hired, and these "exceptional applicants" often come from privileged backgrounds. The others who do not make it are often perceived to lack the proficiency in English or have possessed the "undesirable" variety of English. Salonga (2015) asserts, "only particular kinds of people, usually those who are privileged...can take part in what the industry has to offer" (p. 139).

More importantly, the concerning situation of the Philippines with regard to human rights is an important context worth mentioning, as this current environment makes it even more difficult to challenge the status quo and inequality through a CLP perspective and curriculum. In recent years, particularly during Rodrigo Duterte's presidency, both local and international observers have noted that the human rights situation in the Philippines has deteriorated. The international organisation Human Rights Watch (2021) has observed and reported an increase of killings, threat, harassment and attacks against activists, journalists, lawyers, community leaders and news media outlets (see also Coronel, 2017). They also stated that under Duterte, "[t]he military, national security agencies, and the police have actively used social media to convey threats that have resulted in tens of red-tagged people being killed in the past year" (Human Rights Watch, 2021, n.p.). Even more worrying is the most recently enacted Anti-Terrorism Law in July of 2021. Critics of the law claim that it has provisions that are vague and far-reaching that embolden the government to unfairly target critics and dissenters. As a case in point, the law creates an Anti-Terrorism Council, members of which are appointed by the government, "that can designate a person or a group as a terrorist, making them immediately liable to be arrested without warrant or charges and be detained for up to 24 hours" (Human Rights Watch, 2021, n.p.).

Another important context worth underscoring is globalisation as a force that shapes Philippine ELT. Globalisation is not only limited to economic expansion, as it also includes the instantaneous sharing of communication resources, knowledge or perspectives and cultures

(Quijano, 2012). With English-speaking nations at the helm of discourses related to trade, other global economic players are forced to strengthen and secure the position of English in their country to participate. For instance, Tullao (2003, pp. 227–228) states:

> Among the requisites of a global economy is for people to acquire a more profound level of proficiency in foreign languages, specifically English, which is why the demand for learning, acquiring, and using the language has increased. The need for English in the preparation for national and international licensure examinations, believed to lead the individual to a 'greener pasture', provides another impetus to learning and acquiring the language. Moreover, communication skills, competence, and confidence in the use of English contributes positively to skill-based professions (i.e., providing health care services, etc.).

While it is often perceived that proficiency in English helps the individual to reach their professional goals and even helps the country in its struggle for self-sufficiency, policies that favour the sole use of English violate the principle of equality (Kumaravadivelu, 2008). As pointed out by some scholars (Smokotin, Alekseyenko, & Petrova, 2014), the dominance of English language and culture has continued to be a threat to minority languages and cultures all over the world and could eventually lead to the suppression, degradation and even extinction of other languages (Chureson, 2013). In Cabigon's (2015) work, it is clear that the motivation for the acquisition of an acceptable level of fluency in the English language is primarily economic. The Philippines has capitalised on its English-speaking citizens making the country one of the top business process outsourcing (BPO) destinations in the world; furthermore, the relatively affordable English language schools that mushroomed all over the archipelago have paved for the influx of foreign learners of English (Haisa, 2016, 2017; Parba & Morikawa, 2022), which, on the one hand, helps the country's economic development, but, on the other hand, serves the neoliberal agenda of big corporations and service-oriented industries.

3. RESEARCHER POSITIONALITY

We are both language teachers and researchers. Jayson, the first author, was trained in the areas of English language teaching and applied linguistics. He taught English language and literature courses for eight years in the Philippines both at high school and university levels. Although no longer based in the Philippines, he continues to engage with Filipino teachers and scholars through his research and by engaging in conversations which examine the teaching of English in the country. Moreover, Jayson's research has mainly focused on exploring the potentials of critical language pedagogy and in critically unpacking multilingualism in the Philippines and in Hawai'i. The second author, Irish, is a professor in the area of English Language Studies and teaches both undergraduate and graduate students in one of the leading State Universities in Mindanao. Her work and engagements have allowed her to gain perspectives about issues that continue to plague the education system. She has observed the lack of thorough understanding amongst her students and teacher colleagues of the value of critical pedagogy and how this understanding would have made a difference in instigating changes within the Philippine academic landscape.

4. *PRAXIS* AS THE GUIDING PRINCIPLE

This article draws on the Freirean principle of *praxis* as a guiding principle to inform the discussion that follows. Thus, the suggestions we offer spring from our reflections and yearning for concrete actions (Freire, 1970; see also Crawford-Lange, 1981). In the field of language education, scholars like Osborn (2000, 2006) and Shor (1992) have likewise called for praxis. This may take in various forms such as *reflection-for-practice, reflection-on-practice,* and *reflection-in practice*. Reagan and Osborn (2002) define *reflection-for-practice* as "the reflective planning and preparation that necessarily precedes the classroom teaching event" (p. 22). This involves "the teacher's analysis of likely pedagogical, learning, and management problems that might emerge in a particular class dealing with specific subject matter" (Reagan & Osborn, 2002, p. 22). In contrast, the reflections that often happen outside the classroom after the lesson is finished are called *reflection-on-practice*. The process involves reflecting retrospectively on what happened inside the classroom and on how students received and engaged with the learning materials. Lastly, *reflection-in-practice* is the utilisation of "tacit knowledge in the classroom setting" and "involves the teacher's ability to utilise unarticulated knowledge about content, pedagogy, and learners in the classroom contexts" (Reagan & Osborn, 2002, p. 23). Moreover, praxis allows us to call out the disempowerment that has been happening to teachers, who have long been excluded from the conversations of educational reforms. Praxis brings back the power to the teachers, encouraging them to take on more active roles such as doing research and publication to gain better perspectives of curriculum and policies (Cirocki & Farrell, 2017a). Through this Freirean principle, we are able to conceive schools and schooling as "spheres that embody and express struggle over what forms of authority, regulations, and versions of the past and present should be legitimated and conveyed to students" (Giroux, 2020, pp. 44–45; see Cirocki & Farrell, 2017b, and Cirocki & Widodo, 2019, for practical applications of reflective practice in teacher development contexts).

5. ENTRY POINTS FOR CLP IN PHILIPPINE ELT

From a critical perspective, schooling and educational institutions reproduce inequality, but they are also a fertile ground for disrupting various forms of oppression and injustice. Educators are therefore invited to take a more active role in dismantling social inequalities in education and in society (Freire & Macedo, 1995; Kincheloe, 2008). Critically oriented teachers need to identify and challenge everyday beliefs, ideologies, practices, and discourses that lead to the marginalisation and oppression of certain individuals (Auerbach, 1995; Canagarajah, 1996). As previous studies have indicated, there are many ideologies and practices that continue to proliferate in and shape the Philippine educational system, especially in regard to language teaching (Parba, 2018; Tupas, 2015b). We are also aware of the existence of relevant literature that offers comprehensive and practical discussions of CLP (see for instance Akbari, 2008; Crookes, 2010, 2013). However, as noted earlier, the discussions in this article are specifically situated in the Philippine ELT context. Because of space constraints, we specifically engage in the discussion of the most pressing issues that need to be addressed. Thus, in the sections that follow, we identify these pressing issues as 1) the hegemony of English and 2) a limited engagement with critical teaching materials. Our discussion then provides some ways through which Filipino English teachers may adopt a critical praxis to address each of them.

5.1 DISRUPTING ENGLISH HEGEMONY

In an interview with young school children, parents and teachers in an elementary school in Bukidnon in the Philippines, Parba (2018) found that English continues to enjoy its hegemonic privilege in spite of the implementation of the Mother Tongue-Based Multilingual Education Policy (MLE) since 2012 (see also Dawe, 2014). In one of the interviews the author conducted with grade school children, even at a young age, they often invoked the discourse of English as the language of economic opportunity and upward mobility: *"Kinahanglan gyod ang English sir kay para makakita og trabaho"* (English is very important so we can find jobs). In fact, English is so dominant in the Philippines that many schools continue to implement the English-only-policy on school grounds and enforce a punitive stance when students are caught speaking their mother tongue. As a case in point, three students in the Ilocos region in the Northern Philippines were expelled from their school after being caught speaking Ilokano within school grounds (Dawe, 2014; Tupas, 2015b). What is worrying about this policy and action is the fact that the school treated speaking the vernacular as a form of delinquent behaviour or misconduct together with smoking and drinking liquor (Dawe, 2014). Such school policy and action are rooted in language ideologies that position English above all Philippine languages and underscore the enduring structures of colonialism that continue to denigrate local languages and cultures.

Not only is English privileged in the Philippines, but also its native speakers and the notion of "standard English," which has been unpacked and criticised by various scholars (e.g., Holliday, 2006; 2008; Kubota, 2019; Phillipson, 1992). As an example, many learning materials emphasised and idealised the American and British English as the standards, as if the language were monolithic and unchanging (Martin, 2018), and that Filipino students should emulate in order for them to find good paying jobs. Both authors for instance are aware of the USAID sponsored Job Enabling English Proficiency (JEEP) programme that has been implemented in Mindanao. Jayson taught in the programme for three years. While well-intentioned and often viewed as helping students to develop their proficiency in English, the learning materials and assessment mechanism of JEEP typically centred on standard British English, marginalising and illegitimising Philippine English (Tupas & Tabiola, 2017). For instance, in some sections of the online materials, students need to listen and repeat a sentence or phrase. The students are instructed to enunciate or mimic the way "native speakers" speak. When students speak with a

Filipino accent, they have a bigger chance of being told, *"Sorry, I don't understand you. Please say it again."* by the computer, which is programmed to listen to and recognise British English only. Even if students speak clearly while using the programme, they still sometimes get assessed negatively, and this assessment adversely impacts their academic achievements. What is more, students develop a sense of linguistic insecurity, which is a pervasive experience among multilingual learners (Ortega, 2019). Very often, many multilinguals, including Filipino multilingual learners of English, tend to evaluate their English negatively. Because they see themselves as inadequate, many multilinguals "criticise their [own] mastery of language skills, others strive their hardest to reach monolingual norms, others still hide their knowledge of their 'weaker' language, and most simply do not perceive themselves as being bilingual" (Grosjean, 2008, p. 224).

Another case in point is Irish's observation of how Philippine academic institutions perpetuate the hegemony of English through a strong emphasis on American English. Reflecting on her experiences as an instructor at a university and collaborator with other academics in research endeavours, Irish has observed that a strong emphasis is placed on standard grammar in writing and standard American pronunciation (Arcilla, Soriano, & Bayeta, 2017; Estioco & Eroa, 2015; Pangket, 2019) in speaking, ruling out as errors or disfluencies when Filipinos fail to "properly enunciate." Additionally, audio-video materials, including songs and films, provided in classrooms mostly present the voice of the American culture, or textbooks fail to present culturally relevant perspectives (Mangila, 2018), and learners' academic performances, either in writing or speaking, are evaluated using rubrics and frameworks forwarded by authors whose contexts are either British or American (Jugo, 2020). Many local universities also prefer either (mostly white) native English speakers, or individuals who at least received education abroad, as resource speakers in teacher-training programmes. Through these instances, Irish believes that the hegemony of English is produced, spread and sustained in the academic setting. This ideology is deeply entrenched among Filipino academics and students so that it has remained unquestioned and dominant.

How then can language teachers disrupt the hegemony of English and the standard English myth? As teacher-researchers, we draw on the scholarship of applied linguistics, bilingual education, sociolinguistics and educational linguistics in order to inform and offer the following suggestions. As a reminder, the following discussions are not in any way canonical, as depending on school milieu teachers may find other ways through which to critically engage in this conversation.

5.1.1 A NON-ESSENTIALIST VIEW OF LANGUAGE AND LANGUAGE LEARNING

Multilinguals are not monolinguals, and yet, many of our students are expected to use their language resources like monolinguals. Very often, in many language programmes around the world, including in the Philippines, languages are seen as bounded entities so that in bilingual settings, for instance, these languages are seen as "two solitudes" (or three or four solitudes depending on how many languages co-exist) (Cummins, 2007). Because of this ideology languages are often taught separately, and the monolingual norm is often set as the yardstick to assess students' language proficiency. In the Philippine context, many schools, including universities, enforce an English-only policy and penalise students (and yes, even teachers) when they deviate from the monolingual norm through translanguaging (Garcia & Wei, 2014) or "the flexible use of linguistic resources by bilinguals in order to make sense of their worlds (Garcia, 2009, p. 33; see Cenoz & Gorter, 2017; Creese & Blackledge, 2010; Wei, 2018). These instances are a common experience in the Philippines because teachers continue to consider the target language only policy as the best approach "in spite of extensive research that supports the superiority of bilingual [or translingual] techniques" (Valdes, 2020, p. 127).

An essentialist view of language learning is also prevalent in Philippine settings. From this perspective, language learning is seen as a linear process that has a finish line or like a ladder that one climbs to reach the top (Ortega, 2019). This often results in linguistic insecurity among multilinguals that also impacts identity development. As educators working in multilingual settings, Filipino ESL teachers need to orient themselves to a heteroglossic view of language to legitimise their own dynamic language practices and those of their students. As a practical example, we have observed in many ESL classrooms in the Philippines in which students would raise their hand to ask a question. However, students' curiosity is often stifled because they are told *"to speak only in English"* as they try to form their questions. This practice needs to be abolished, as this not only delegitimises students' multilingual identities and language practices, but also deprives their right to learn. In some instances, we have also observed that when a high frequency and low frequency (subject related) lexical item (or sometimes a concept) appears in readings or discussions in the classrooms, some teachers tend to spend so much time trying to unlock the meaning of the word only in English even if the said word or concept is already familiar with the students in their first language (L1). While this may be good to some extent, as it challenges students to think more, in some cases, teachers are wasting their time as these words may be explained in the vernacular so that the students' understanding is optimised, and class time is spent on more productive undertakings.

5.1.2 GIVE TRANSLANGUAGING A CHANCE

In relation to the discussion above, we echo the call to give translanguaging a chance in language learning and teaching (Ortega, 2019). In order to do this, Filipino ESL teachers need to engage in the growing literature on translanguaging as pedagogy (Creese & Blackledge, 2010) and theory of language (Wei, 2018). This call is especially relevant because, as mentioned earlier, the monolingual approach or English-only attitude remains pervasive in Philippine ELT (Martin, 2014). In one presentation that Jayson gave to Filipino language teachers, for instance, one teacher suggested that translanguaging is the "bastardization" of the language. We have also observed that code mixing and other dynamic language use are frowned upon by teachers and school administrators (Häusler, et al, 2018), as these are often viewed from a language deficit perspective. Metila's (2009) study, for instance, has shown that most high school students in a private college are apathetic towards code-switching or think that it is a manifestation of poor language performance in either English or Filipino. This is of course not surprising because most people, including multilinguals, have been immersed in the ideology of language separation and are conditioned to embrace normative ways of language practices (Garcia & Tupas, 2019). And yet, it is axiomatic that many of our students are multilinguals and their everyday language practices involve the dynamic assemblage and deployment of multimodal resources and linguistic signs (e.g., De Los Reyes, 2019; Parba, 2018; Perfecto, 2020). In other words, multilingual speakers routinely reassess, break or adjust assumed boundaries between languages and the link between nation-states and languages (Wei, 2018; Pennycook & Otsuji, 2016) in their daily lives, including in the classrooms.

For the reasons discussed above, teachers and administrators involved in Philippine ELT are encouraged to consider carefully creating a "translanguaging space" (Wei, 2011, p. 1222) in order to respond to the complex (and messy) realities on the ground. For starters, although the context is a little different, there are useful translanguaging guides created and put together by professors and educators at the City University of New York. The project is spearheaded by leading scholars in the field of Bilingual Education and offers "dozens of strategies and approaches for teachers working with emergent bilingual students at all grade levels and in all programs" (Otheguy, Garcia, & Menken, n.d.). Simply put, language teachers are encouraged to leverage students' multilingualism rather than consider it as a problem in their acquisition of English. This means allowing the use of the students' L1 (Akbari, 2008) and other linguistic and semiotic resources to participate in meaning-making activities.

One example of this is demonstrated by Irish's colleague teaching Philosophy courses, who encourages his students to reason in class (either oral or written) in a way that is most linguistically comfortable for them. There was hesitation at the onset, because of the linguistic purism movement, in the guise of the aim for communicative competence, that is widespread in Philippine universities. But for him, communicative competence does not at all refer to competence in the use of the English language alone, but in any language that allows learners to engage with others comfortably and effectively. For years of doing this, he has observed how students have become more participative, more articulate in their arguments. This proves that translanguaging facilitates creativity from students to pull from their wide range of linguistic repertoire they bring with them to school (Garcia & Wei, 2014; Oliver, Wigglesworth, Angelo et al., 2021) such that it will serve them well in becoming more engaged in class, rather than stressing over grammar and mechanics. Also, when given a chance to thrive in class, translanguaging motivates students into thinking that their native language is valid and worthy of academic recognition which in turn empowers both learners and teachers (Miller, 2020).

Teachers need to take advantage of students' holistic linguistic repertoire (Garcia & Tupas, 2019) "in various different ways and following numerous carefully-thought-out strategies" (Valdes, 2020, p. 129), especially those supported by empirical research. Teachers can also learn from Irish's interactions with some indigenous communities in the Philippines. Prior to one of her teacher-training projects, she noticed a mismatch in the teaching materials provided by the founder with the context of teachers and their learners. While materials are highly American-based and the strategies effectively improve motivation and interaction in the classroom, there is a need to modify teachers' output into allowing them to use concepts that are endemic to the indigenous communities. This allowed the teachers to understand the strategies and materials more, at the same time, advance their and their students' cultural identities. Meanwhile, from a recent webinar organised by a learning institute for indigenous students, Irish learnt how teachers and volunteers, and the indigenous people (IP) effectively coped with the challenges of the pandemic. Aside from providing IP students and their families COVID-prevention materials that are written in their local languages, they have benefitted much from the community-based activities, such as: regular community cleaning for all households, creation of coin banks for the younger population, backyard vegetable gardening, tree planting and the creation of bins from recycled materials for the younger generation and for men. Learning, after all, is facilitated not only through lectures but through application of various skills in the respective activities. Furthermore, teacher-volunteers (they call para-teachers) have been very active in doing home-based reading tutorials using culture-sensitive texts (i.e., lores, songs, etc.). In the case of IP schools, therefore, translanguaging activities have inspired students to overcome any negative feelings attached to their minoritised language/s and cultures and have given them a sense of belonging, which is another major strategic goal in education for social justice. The activities have also preserved the entire community's social and emotional health because they feel that the school has validated and valued their identities and aspirations (Ryoo, 2017), whilst these have taught them skills to sustain their needs during this time.

Adopting a translingual view allows teachers to challenge the hegemonic position of English, as it becomes one language within a full linguistic repertoire that students draw on to communicate meaningfully and effectively. As a manifestation of critical praxis, it changes the way teachers think about language and language learning. By orienting towards a translingual view of language teaching and learning, Filipino ESL teachers can also become agents of countering our "internalised, but certainly colonially induced, hatred towards the mother tongues even if we (sometimes) profess explicit support for them in school" (Tupas, 2015b, p. 120). It is important for teachers to recognise that the acquisition of English and maintenance of other Philippine languages are not mutually exclusive. In other words, both can co-exist and expand students' communicative repertoire, or students' mother tongues are not a threat to the development of English proficiency.

5.1.3 UNPACK THE ENGLISH FOR ECONOMIC BENEFIT DISCOURSE

Disrupting the hegemony of English also involves unpacking the myth of English for economic benefit (Watts, 2011). Kubota (2011) and Park (2011) argue that this myth is often used to justify the promotion of English in many parts of the world, where it enjoys a hegemonic status in education. This myth is so pervasive that even in the age of MLE in the Philippines and elsewhere, teachers and parents often assume that learning English would "guarantee better and financially more lucrative job opportunities" (Watts, 2011, p. 286). In the case of the Philippines, many Filipinos believe that proficiency in English automatically brings economic benefits and success. Unsurprisingly, when news about the consistent decline of Filipinos' English proficiency circulated, the Department of Education and the Commission on Higher Education immediately laid out plans and aggressive educational policy and curricular reforms, one of which was to remove Filipino and Panitikan (literature) courses from the curriculum (Baclig, 2020; Jimenez, 2018; Valderama, 2019). However, the myth that English guarantees economic success ignores the fact that, more than English proficiency, other factors (e.g., one's technical and social skills, gender, social capital, socio-economic background, race, etc.) may have stronger impacts in determining economic success. Additionally, English language ability and access to language education in the Philippines is often class-based (Salonga, 2015; Tupas, 2019; Tupas & Salonga, 2016) so that it becomes another way through which those who have the financial resources gain more, while those who do not are locked out. Moreover, Kubota (2019), in her work that criticises ten common beliefs about language teaching, cited the work of Terasawa (2015) that explored the correlation between English language skills and income. Teresawa's work showed that there is no significant relationship between the two variables, especially when considering the actual necessity of English use for work. Therefore, it is very important for teachers to realise that the economic value people associate with a certain language varies depending on geographical locations and types of work.

One of the ways to unpack the economic benefit myth that comes with English is to engage students in ideological conversations. This can be explored on a topic that on the surface may reflect the necessity of English to participate in the market for personal and economic gains but, when examined closely, may not be necessarily true (all the time). To illustrate this point, the topic on Overseas Filipino Workers (OFW) can be used as a springboard in discussing and problematising this belief. Students can be assigned to survey friends and/or family members who work abroad to share their experiences of applying for a job. Students can also be asked to survey Filipino employers about the factors that make an employee competitive. After their survey, students can then share the important factors that employers look for and value in job applicants or employees. For sure, English skills may be mentioned during the discussion but teachers can use this opportunity to underscore the other skills deemed important by employers. Teachers can also discuss that some jobs may not require very technical skills of English and that the English language may not be necessarily used among workers in the workplace for efficiency. Moreover, teachers can then discuss with students why economic benefits that may come with English are not equally distributed or attainable (Lorente, 2012).

To be clear, this is not to say that English is not important, and that teachers and students should not aim to develop their English language skills. The truth is, not gaining mastery in a dominant language such as English has real and material consequences on students. In fact, it may even further the marginalisation of certain groups of people if they are not able to avail themselves of the opportunities that may be present in the job market that requires English proficiency. However, teachers, students and parents must realise that various factors come into play when we look at economic success and opportunities, so much so that reducing it to English language skills alone becomes problematic and worth questioning (Kubota, 2019).

5.2 INCORPORATING CRITICAL MATERIALS

Critical materials that draw and build on social issues are key components of critical language teaching. These materials play a vital role in generating critical dialogues and fostering critical awareness about pressing issues happening in the outside world (Shor, 1996). However, in many English classrooms, learning materials are often "anesthetized to make them politically and socially harmless" (Akbari, 2008, p. 281) and materials developers and textbook writers are also advised to refrain from incorporating controversial topics in their textbooks. As a result, the voices of marginalised individuals and oppressed groups are not represented in coursebooks, as they are sometimes viewed as conflicting to the beliefs and ideologies of the dominant group of the society. This often results not only in the further marginalisation of the minorities, but also in the denial of certain rights and opportunities (Akbari, 2008).

While critical dialogues on social issues do happen in some English classrooms in the Philippines, only a limited number of studies (Fajardo, 2016; Paterno, 2009; Valdez, 2012) reported the process and described the experiences of Filipino ESL students and teachers. Thus, drawing on the works of other teacher-practitioners (Akbari, 2008; Benesch, 1999; Hammond, 2006; Shin & Crookes, 2005; Stillar, 2013;), it is recommended that Filipino ESL teachers find ways to incorporate critical teaching materials into their curriculum. For instance, in the Philippine context, it is common knowledge that social and economic inequality remains an everyday experience of a large portion of the students and their families (Balisacan, 2003). And yet, poverty is sometimes discussed as a neutral topic or as something that naturally exists in the society. This perspective glosses the fact that power mechanisms are involved in the unequal distribution of wealth in the Philippines, which drives millions of people into hopelessness and sometimes even despair. Another relevant topic that is often missing in the English classrooms in the Philippines is the discussion of human rights issues even though the country has observed an increase in human rights violations in recent years (Human Rights Watch, 2021). A language lesson built around the topic of human rights will engage students in critically thinking about its inherent value, but also in possibly building sympathy and alliances (Stillar, 2013) with certain individuals and groups (e.g., Lumad or Indigenous Peoples, LGBTQ people, victims of extrajudicial killings; community leaders and organisers, Martial Law victims) whose basic human rights are violated and denied.

Besides the ones already mentioned, the following topics are worthy of consideration in a critically-oriented English language curriculum: illegal logging, pollution and other environmental issues; corruption in Philippine government; linguistic and cultural discrimination targeting minoritised groups; violence against women and children; sexism; racism; sending/exporting Filipinos abroad; deprivation of basic services; (in)accessibility of healthcare services; plight of senior citizens and persons with disabilities; wage and unemployment issues; workers' rights to unionise; misinformation on and responsible use of social media; teenage pregnancy; suicide; language discrimination; and bullying among others. These topics are in no way an exhaustive list, and teachers who wish to explore other relevant topics are encouraged to engage their students in dialogues and tasks in which the latter can express their real-life concerns

(Shor, 1996). In addition, as mentioned above, these critical contents may be absent from English textbooks, and teachers are encouraged to look for these in other sources. For example, in Jayson's own context, he uses editorials or news articles that deal with the aforementioned issues as supplementary materials for students to read, respond to and critically reflect on during critical discussions in class. This implies that teachers will need a certain degree of familiarity with current events and history, including ongoing social, political, cultural, economic and gender-related conversations happening outside the classroom.

By creating language lessons around the aforementioned critical topics, teachers are able to bring to the fore and centre the lived realities of students. When learners see themselves reflected in resources (Martens, Andersen, & Rinnert, 2018), the more they are encouraged to take on active roles in the learning process. Consistent with a Freirean view of education, engaging students in dialogues with critical materials is a step towards fostering critical consciousness, which involves identifying, challenging and rethinking status quo discourses that can be acted upon in progressive and creative ways to open opportunities for action (Jennings, et al, 2010). Additionally, when students' real-life concerns form part of the curriculum, the classroom is transformed into a shared learning space where the teachers themselves become aware of students' real-life struggles, hopes and aspirations. Consequently, both the teachers and students become fellow enquirers of the subjects to be known (Young, 1992).

6. FUTURE OF CLP IN PHILIPPINE ELT

Reflecting from a recent webinar hosted by the second author's university and drawing from the participants' feedback, we are both optimistic that there is room for espousing CLP in Philippine ELT. We have had conversations with teachers who are genuinely curious and interested in a critically oriented practice, and we hope that these entry points are useful to them and their context. As an example, Irish's colleague who teaches a humanities class integrated socio-political issues in an art-installation project that his students worked on. Although this project was eventually censored by the school administration for being "disconcerting," this gives us hope about the future of CLP in the Philippine ELT context, as there are critically minded teachers who are willing to incorporate socio-political issues in their curriculum and engage students in democratic conversations on these topics. As Freire (2021, p. 110) highlighted in the *Pedagogy of Hope*, it is through democratic dialogue that individuals are "opening up to the thinking of others," a start towards transforming oppressive conditions.

The incident mentioned earlier is also a concrete example of the challenges facing critically oriented teachers. There are teachers in Philippine ELT who are favourable of translanguaging and the judicious and strategic use of students' L1 in the classroom in order to empower their students (De Los Reyes, 2019; Parba, 2018) despite institutional English-only policy enforced by school administrators. Additionally, there are critically oriented academics in Philippine academia who continue to challenge the structures of power that marginalise and suppress dissent. These are instances of hope in which teachers challenge normative and status quo discourses and practices. These teachers have our support, and we would like to encourage them

117

to share their stories of critical engagement within the Philippine educational landscape through research and publication, attending talk-stories and reaching out to like-minded teachers.

7. CONCLUSION

Considering the historical, social and economic conditions of the Philippines within which ELT is situated, teachers involved in English language education need to take a more active role in making the language-learning experiences of their students more meaningful and transformative. This article highlighted various entry points through which teachers may find a space for exploring critical language pedagogy in their classrooms. The use of "entry points" in this work is intentional in order to draw attention to various institutional conditions, state mechanisms and other external forces that might constrain teachers from incorporating critical perspectives into their teaching. These entry points also show a terrain of possibilities, but careful consideration of the contextual contours must be taken as teachers try to explore them. While the CLP framework gives us some possibilities of hope (Freire, 2021) in transforming our educational practices and institutions, it is important to underscore that this invitation may not apply to some contexts. This means that teachers do not have to radically change the curriculum, as the prospect of harm is tangible in being perceived as "leftist," "activists" or "radical" in many contexts where democracy and democratic institutions are fragile and unstable, including in the Philippines.

REFERENCES

Akbari, R. (2008). Transforming lives: Introducing critical pedagogy into ELT classrooms. *ELT Journal*, *62*(3), 276–283.

Arcilla Jr, F. E., Soriano, E. A., & Bayeta, P. B. (2017). First Language influence on second language phonology among Visayan speakers. *IAMURE International Journal of Multidisciplinary Research, 16(1),* 18–34.

Auerbach, E. (1995). The politics of ESL classroom: Issues of power in pedagogical choices. In J. Tollefson (Ed.), *Power and inequality in language education* (pp. 9–33). Cambridge: Cambridge University Press.

Baclig, C. E. (2020, November 20). Philippines drops further in global English proficiency rankings. Retrieved from https://newsinfo.inquirer.net/1362951/philippines-drops-further-in-global-english-proficiency-rankings

Balisacan, A. M. (2003). Poverty and Inequality. In A. M. Balisacan & H. Hill (Eds.), *The Philippine economy: Development, policies, and challenges* (pp. 311–341). Quezon City: Ateneo de Manila University Press.

Benesch, S. (1999). Thinking critically, thinking dialogically. *TESOL Quarterly, 33*(3), 573–580.

Bernardo, A. B. (2008). English in Philippine education: Solution or problem? In M. L. Bautista & K. Bolton (Eds.), *Philippine English: Linguistic and literary perspectives* (pp. 28–48). Hong Kong: Hong Kong University Press.

Brookfield, S. (2005). *The power of critical theory: Liberating adult learning and teaching*. San Francisco, CA: Jossey-Bass.

Cabigon, M. (2015). State of English in the Philippines: Should we be concerned? *British Council Philippines*. Retrieved from https://www.britishcouncil.ph/teach/state-english-philippines-should-we-be-concerned-2

Canagarajah, S. (1993). Critical ethnography of a Sri Lankan classroom: Ambiguities in student opposition to reproduction through TESOL. *TESOL Quarterly, 27*(4), 601–626.

Canagarajah, S. (1996). From critical research practice to critical research reporting. *TESOL Quarterly, 30*(2), 321–330.

Cenoz, J., & Gorter, D. (2017). Minority languages and sustainable translanguaging: Threat or opportunity? *Journal of Multilingual and Multicultural Development, 38*(10), 901–912.

Chureson, O. (2013). The impact of English as a global language on Filipino language practices. *International Forum Journal, 16*(2), 22–36.

Cirocki, A., & Farrell, T. S. C. (Eds.). (2017a). Reflective practice for professional development of ELT practitioners. *The European Journal of Applied Linguistics and TEFL, 6*(2), 5–22.

Cirocki, A., & Farrell, T. S. C. (Eds.). (2017b). Reflective practice in the ELT classroom [Special Issue]. *The European Journal of Applied Linguistics and TEFL, 6*(2).

Cirocki, A., & Widodo, H. P. (2019). Reflective practice in English language teaching in Indonesia: Shared practices from two teacher educators. *Iranian Journal of Language Teaching Research, 7*(3), 15–35.

Constantino, R. (1970). The miseducation of the Filipino. *Journal of Contemporary Asia, 1*(1), 20–36.

Coronel, S. (2017). Murder as enterprise: Police profiteering in Duterte's war on drugs. In N. Curato (Ed.), *A Duterte reader: Critical essays on Rodrigo Duterte's early presidency* (pp. 167–198). Quezon City: Ateneo de Manila Press.

Crawford-Lange, L. M. (1981). Redirecting second language curricula: Paulo Freire's contribution. *Foreign Language Annals, 14*(4), 257–268.

Creese, A., & Blackledge, A. (2010). Translanguaging in the bilingual classroom: A pedagogy for learning and teaching? *The Modern Language Journal, 94*(1), 103–115.

Crookes, G. V. (2010). The practicality and relevance of second language critical pedagogy. *Language Teaching, 43*(3), 333–348.

Crookes, G. V. (2013). *Critical ELT in action: Foundations, promises, and praxis*. New York, NY: Routledge.

Crookes, G. V. (2021). Critical language pedagogy. *Language Teaching*, 1–18.

Cummins, J. (2007). Rethinking monolingual instructional strategies in multilingual classrooms. *Canadian Journal of Applied Linguistics, 10*(2), 221–240.

Dawe, C. J. (2014). Language governmentality in Philippine education policy. *Working Papers in Educational Linguistics (WPEL), 29*(1), 61–77.

De Los Reyes, R. A. (2019). Translanguaging in multilingual third grade ESL classrooms in Mindanao, Philippines. *International Journal of Multilingualism, 16*(3), 302–316.

Estioco, J. C., & Eroa, M. G. (2015). The use of multimedia drills in college students' English pronunciation training. *Asia Pacific Journal of Multidisciplinary Research, 3*(4), 1–8.

Fajardo, M. F. (2016). *Teaching critical literacy using multimodal texts to college students in the Philippines* [Unpublished doctoral thesis]. University of Wollongong, Australia.

Freire, P. (1970). *Pedagogy of the oppressed* (M. B. Ramos Trans.). New York, NY: Continuum Books.

Freire, P. (2021). *Pedagogy of hope: Reliving pedagogy of the oppressed* (R. Barr, Trans.). London & New York: Bloomsbury Publishing.

Freire, P., & Macedo, D. (1995). A dialogue: Culture, language, and race. *Harvard Educational Review, 65*(3), 377–403.

García, O. (2009). Education, multilingualism and translanguaging in the 21st century. In T. Skutnabb-Kangas, R. Phillipson, A. K. Mohanty, & M. Panda (Eds.), *Social justice through multilingual education* (pp. 140–158). Bristol: Multilingual Matters.

García, O., & Tupas, R. (2019). Doing and undoing bilingualism in education. In A. De Houwer & L. Ortega (Eds.), *The Cambridge handbook of bilingualism* (pp. 390–407). Cambridge: Cambridge University Press.

García, O., & Wei, L. (2014). *Translanguaging: Language, bilingualism, and education*. Basingstoke: Palgrave Macmillan.

Giroux, H. A. (2020). *On critical pedagogy*. New York, NY: Bloomsbury Publishing.

Gonzalez, A. B. (1980). *Language and nationalism: The Philippine experience thus far*. Quezon City: Ateneo de Manila University Press.

Grosjean, F. (2008). *Studying bilinguals*. Oxford: Oxford University Press.

Haisa, A. (2016). The influence of studying English in the Philippines on Japanese learners' language attitudes. *Sagami Women's University Kiyo, 80*, 11–24.

Haisa, A. (2017). Analysis of Filipino teachers' English as an instructional language for Japanese learners. *Sagami Women's University Bunka Kenkyu, 35*, 37–52.

Hammond, K. (2006). More than a game: A critical discourse analysis of a racial inequality exercise in Japan. *TESOL Quarterly, 40*(3), 545–571.

Häusler, A. H., Leal, P., Parba, J., West, G. B., & Crookes, G. V. (2018). "How did you become political?": Narratives of junior researcher-practitioners in applied linguistics. *Critical Inquiry in Language Studies*, *15*(4), 282–301.

Holliday, A. (2006). Native-speakerism. *ELT Journal, 60*(4), 385–387.

Holliday, A. (2008). Standards of English and politics of inclusion. *Language Teaching, 41*(1), 119–130.

Human Rights Watch. (2001). Philippines: Events of 2020. Retrieved from https://www.hrw.org/world-report/2021/country-chapters/philippines

Izadina, M., & Abednia, A. (2010). Dynamics of an EFL reading course with a critical literacy orientation. *Journal of Language and Literacy Education, 6*(2), 51–67.

Jennings, L. B., Messias, D. K. H., & Hardee, S. (2010). Addressing oppressive discourses and images of youth: Sites of possibility. In L. B. Jennings, J. Jewett, T. Laman, M. Souto-

Manning., & J. Wilson (Eds.), *Sites of possibility: Critical dialogue across educational settings* (pp. 36–67). Cresskill, NJ: Hampton.

Jimenez, R. (2018, August 14). The decline of English proficiency in the Philippines from Punto! Retrieved from https://punto.com.ph/the-decline-of-english-proficiency-in-the-philippines

Jugo, R. R. (2020). Language anxiety in focus: The case of Filipino undergraduate teacher education learners. *Education Research International,* 1–8.

Kincheloe, J. L. (2008). *Knowledge and critical pedagogy*. New York, NY: Springer.

Konoeda, K., & Watanabe, Y. (2008). Task-based critical pedagogy in Japanese EFL classrooms. In M. Montero, P. C. Miller, & J. L. Watzke (Eds.), *Readings in language studies* (vol. 1, pp. 45–61). St. Louis, MO: International Society for Language Studies.

Koo, G. S. (2008). English language in Philippine education: Themes and variations in policy, practice, pedagogy and research. *Asia-Pacific Journal of Research in Early Childhood Education, 2*(1), 19–33.

Kramer, P. (2006). *The blood of government: Race, empire, the United States, and the Philippines.* Chapel Hill, NC: University of North Carolina Press.

Kubota, R. (1998). Ideologies of English in Japan. *World Englishes, 17*(3), 295–306.

Kubota, R. (2019). A critical examination of common beliefs about language teaching: From research insights to professional engagement. In F. Fang & H. P. Widodo (Eds.), *Critical perspectives on global Englishes in Asia: Language policy, curriculum, pedagogy and assessment* (pp. 10–26). Bristol: Multilingual Matters.

Kubota, R., & Lin, A. (2006). Race and TESOL: Introduction to concepts and theories. *TESOL Quarterly, 40*(3), 471–493.

Kumaravadivelu, B. (2008). *Cultural globalization and language education.* New Haven, CT: Yale University Press.

Lin, A. (2004). Introducing a critical pedagogical curriculum: A feminist reflexive account, In B. Norton & K. Toohey (Eds.), *Critical pedagogies and language learning* (pp. 271–290). Cambridge: Cambridge University Press.

Lorente, B. P. (2012). The making of "workers of the world": Language and the labor brokerage state. In A. Duchêne, A. & Heller, M. (Eds.), *Language in late capitalism* (pp. 193–216). New York, NY: Routledge.

Lorente, B. (2013). The grip of English and Philippine language policy. *The politics of English: South Asia, Southeast Asia and the Asia Pacific,* 187–204.

Mangila, B. B. (2018). Are IMs culturally relevant?" A critical analysis of the instructional materials used in mother tongue-based multilingual education programs. *Asia Pacific Journal of Multidisciplinary Research, 6*(2), 53–60.

Martens, M., Rinnert, G. C., & Andersen, C. (2018). Child-centered design: Developing an inclusive letter writing app. *Frontiers in Psychology, 9*, 22–77.

Martin, I. P. (2014). English language teaching in the Philippines. *World Englishes, 33*(4), 472–485.

Martin, I. P. (Ed.). (2018). *Reconceptualizing English education in a multilingual society. English in the Philippines*. Singapore: Springer.

Menard-Warwick, J. (2008). 'Because she made beds. Every day'. Social positioning, classroom discourse, and language learning. *Applied Linguistics, 29*(2), 267–289.

Metila, R. A. (2009). Decoding the switch: The functions of codeswitching in the classroom. *Education Quarterly, 67*(1), 44–61.

Miller, K. (2020). *Effectively enabling translanguaging in the classroom. School of Education student capstone projects.* Retrieved from https://digitalcommons.hamline.edu/hse_cp/515

Morgan, B. (1992). Teaching the Gulf war in an ESL classroom. *TESOL Journal, 2*, 13–17.

Nye, J. (2017). Soft power: The origins and political progress of a concept. *Palgrave Communications, 3*(1), 1–3.

Oliver, R., Wigglesworth, G., Angelo, D., & Steele, C. (2021). Translating translanguaging into our classrooms: Possibilities and challenges. *Language Teaching Research, 25*(1), 134–150.

Ortega, L. (2019). SLA and the study of equitable multilingualism. *The Modern Language Journal, 103*, 23–38.

Osborn, T. (2000). *Critical reflection and the foreign language classroom.* Westport, CT: Bergin & Garvey.

Osborn, T. (2006). *Teaching world languages for social justice.* Mahwah, NJ: Lawrence Erlbaum.

Otheguy, R., Garcia, O., & Menken, K., (n.d.). *Translanguaging guides.* Retrieved from https://www.cuny-nysieb.org/translanguaging-resources/translanguaging-guides/

Pangket, W. F. (2019). Oral English proficiency: Factors affecting the learners' development. *International Journal of Science and Management Studies (IJSMS) E-ISSN,* 2581–5946.

Parba, J. (2018). Teachers' shifting language ideologies and teaching practices in Philippine mother tongue classrooms. *Linguistics and Education, 47*, 27–35.

Parba, J., & Morikawa, T. (2022). "Fun place and hospitable people": (Post)colonial gaze towards the Philippines on webpages for Japanese learners of English. In B. Sharma & S. Gao. (Eds.), *Intercultural communication in tourism: Critical perspectives* (pp. 81–103). Abingdon: Routledge.

Park, J. S-Y. (2011). The promise of English: Linguistic capital and the neoliberal worker in the South Korean job market. *International Journal of Bilingual Education and Bilingualism, 14*, 443–455.

Paterno, M. G. (2009, August 16). *Designing worksheets for critical language practice.* Retrieved from http://blog.nus.edu.sg/eltwo

Pennycook, A. (1999). Introduction: Critical approaches to TESOL. *TESOL Quarterly, 33*(3), 329–348.

Pennycook, A. (2001). *Critical applied linguistics: A critical introduction.* Mahwah, NJ: Lawrence Erlbaum Associates.

Pennycook, A., & Otsuji, E. (2016). Lingoing, language labels and metrolingual practices. *Applied Linguistics Review, 7*(3), 259–277.

Perfecto, M. R. G. (2020). English language teaching and bridging in mother tongue-based multilingual education. *International Journal of Multilingualism,* 1–17.

Phillipson, R. (1992). *Linguistic imperialism.* Oxford: Oxford University Press.

Quijano, C. A. (2012). *Philippines: The role of language and education in globalization*. Retrieved from https://files.eric.ed.gov/fulltext/ED567190.pdf

Racca, R. M. A. B., & Lasaten, R. C. S. (2016). English language proficiency and academic performance of Philippine science high school students. *International Journal of Languages, Literature and Linguistics, 2*(2), 44–49.

Reagan, T., & Osborn, T. (2002). *The foreign language educator in society: Toward a critical pedagogy.* Mahwah, NJ: Lawrence Erlbaum Associates.

Ryoo, N. E. (2017). *Understanding translanguaging and identity among Korean bilingual adults* (Unpublished doctoral dissertation). University of San Francisco, San Francisco, USA.

Salonga, A. O. (2010). Language and situated agency: An exploration of the dominant linguistic and communication practices in the Philippine offshore call centers (Unpublished doctoral dissertation). National University of Singapore, Singapore.

Salonga, A. O. (2015). Performing gayness and English in an offshore call center industry. In R. Tupas (Ed.), *Unequal Englishes: The politics of Englishes today* (pp. 130–142). Basingstoke: Palgrave Macmillan.

Shin, J. K., & Crookes, G. (2005). Exploring the possibilities for EFL critical pedagogy in Korea: A two-part case study. *Critical Inquiry in Language Studies, 2*(2), 113–136.

Shor, I. (1992). *Empowering education: Critical teaching for social change.* Chicago, IL: University of Chicago Press.

Shor, I. (1996). *When students have power: Negotiating authority in a critical pedagogy.* Chicago, IL: University of Chicago Press.

Smokotin, V. M., Alekseyenko, A. S., & Petrova, G. I. (2014). The phenomenon of linguistic globalization: English as the global lingua franca (EGLF). *Procedia-Social and Behavioral Sciences, 154*, 509–513.

Steele, G., Avila, J., Miller, D., & Britain, G. (2014). Ending extreme poverty in the Philippines through urban-led growth. *Development, 48*(11), 1629–1648.

Stillar, S. (2013). Raising critical consciousness via creative writing in the ESL classroom. *TESOL Journal, 4*(1), 164–174.

Takayama, K. (2009). Progressive struggle and critical education studies scholarship in Japan: Toward the democratization of critical education studies. In M. W. Apple, W. Au, & L. A. Gandin (Eds.), *The Routledge international handbook of critical education* (pp. 354–367). New York, NY: Routledge.

Terasawa, T. (2015). "Nihonjin to eigo" no shakai gaku: Naze eigo kyôiku wa gokai darake nano ka [*Sociology of English for the Japanese: Fallacies of the discourses of English language teaching*]. Tokyo: Kenkyûsha.

Tullao, T. S. (Ed.). (2003). *Education & globalization.* Makati: Philippine APEC Study Center Network.

Tupas, R. (Ed.). (2015a). *Unequal Englishes: the politics of Englishes today*. New York, NY: Springer.

Tupas, R. (2015b). Inequalities of multilingualism: Challenges to mother tongue-based multilingual education. *Language and Education, 29*(2), 112–124.

Tupas, R. (2019). Entanglements of colonialism, social class, and unequal Englishes. *Journal of Sociolinguistics, 23*(5), 529–542.

Tupas, R., & Salonga, A. (2016). Unequal Englishes in the Philippines. *Journal of Sociolinguistics, 20*(3), 367–381.

Tupas, R., & Tabiola, H. (2017). Language policy and development aid: A critical analysis of an ELT project. *Current Issues in Language Planning, 18*(4), 407–421.

Valderama, T. (2019, November 18). Pinoys' English proficiency declines sharply. *The Manila Times*. Retrieved from https://www.manilatimes.net/2019/11/18/opinion/columnists/topanalysis/pinoys-english-proficiency-declines-sharply/656784/

Valdés, G. (2020). Sandwiching, polylanguaging, translanguaging, and codeswitching: Challenging monolingual dogma in institutionalized language teaching. In J. MacSwan & C. Faltis (Eds.), *Codeswitching in the classroom: Critical perspectives on teaching, learning, policy, and ideology* (pp. 114–147). London and New York: Routledge.

Valdez, P. N. (2012). Actualizing critical English language teaching: A classroom experience in the Philippines. *Asia-Pacific Education Researcher (De La Salle University Manila), 21*(2), 279–285.

Vandrick, S. (1995). Privileged ESL university students. *TESOL Quarterly, 29*(2), 375–381.

Watts, R. J. (2011). *Language myths and the history of English*. Oxford: Oxford University Press.

Wei, L. (2011). Moment analysis and translanguaging space: Discursive construction of identities by multilingual Chinese youth in Britain. *Journal of Pragmatics, 43*(5), 1222–1235.

Wei, L. (2018). Translanguaging as a practical theory of language. *Applied Linguistics, 39*(1), 9–30.

West, G. B. (2019). Navigating morality in neoliberal spaces of English language education. *Linguistics and Education, 49*, 31–40.

Young, R. (1992). *Critical theory and classroom talk*. Clevedon: Multilingual Matters.

7

EFL TEACHERS' EXPERIENCES WITH NEURODIVERSE STUDENTS AND SELF-EFFICACY FOR INCLUSIVE PRACTICE IN JAPANESE UNIVERSITIES

Jennifer Yphantides, Soka University, Japan

ABSTRACT

This narrative research study explores English foreign language teachers' experiences with neurodiverse students (those with dyslexia, ADHD and autism) at the tertiary level in Japan and their reported levels of self-efficacy for inclusive practice. Bandura's (1977) theory of self-efficacy, which examines teachers' mastery of experience, vicarious experience, social persuasion and emotional states, was used as a framework for interpreting teachers' interview data. Findings indicate that English language teachers at the tertiary level in Japan lack training for working with neurodiverse students, their self-efficacy for creating inclusive classrooms is relatively low, and they lack communication with other institutionally-based professionals who could support them. The practical implications of this study are that English-as-a-foreign-language teachers in the Japanese context should be afforded additional training. They require the establishment of direct communication with counselling/special needs offices on campus, and issues related to the stigma of neurological differences need to be addressed to facilitate discussions between teachers and students about curricular accommodations or modifications.

KEYWORDS

Neurodiversity, inclusion, self-efficacy, Japanese higher education.

1. INTRODUCTION

In the Japanese context, an increasing number of neurodivergent students are attending post-secondary schools (Kayama & Haight, 2013). As a result, more special needs students are required to take basic English-as-a-foreign-language (EFL) courses as part of their graduation requirements. This narrative research study explores English foreign language teachers' experiences with neurodiverse students and their reported levels of self-efficacy for inclusive practice in Japanese higher education. Several previous studies have examined Japanese teachers' attitudes and self-efficacy towards inclusive practice and found that while Japanese educators are especially concerned about their neurodiverse students, their self-efficacy for inclusive education is low and they report receiving little centralised support for developing inclusive practices (Forlin, Kawai, & Higuchi, 2015; Song, 2016; Yada & Savolainen, 2017). However, no research conducted to date examines EFL teachers' experiences working with neurodiverse students at the tertiary level or sense of self-efficacy for working with these students. This article attempts to fill this gap. It provides readers with an overview of inclusive education policy and practice with an emphasis on how the Japanese education system is somewhat behind the rest of the developed world. It also provides an explanation of the concept of neurodiversity and how that construct can fit in with inclusive education, particularly in the EFL domain. The article then outlines the theoretical framework, Bandura's (1997) construct of self-efficacy, and provides support for the use of this theory as an analytical tool applied to the data collected. The analysis of data is separated into four sections, based on the framework, and the article concludes with concrete steps for taking a more inclusive agenda forward.

2. INCLUSIVE EDUCATION: INTERNATIONAL MANDATES AND THE JAPANESE LAG

The inclusion of children with physical and mental disabilities in mainstream classrooms to study alongside their peers is a worldwide trend that has been gaining traction over the past two and a half decades due to UNESCO's Salamanca Statement on inclusive practices (Sharma, Loreman, & Forlin, 2011). In developed countries, legislation and educational policies, based on United Nations guidelines, have been developed in recent years to guarantee inclusion, and teacher training programmes have provided pre-service teachers with instruction on inclusive practices (Song, 2016). However, inclusion is not simply about placing children with disabilities in mainstream classrooms. Rather, it implies a change in mindset on the part of teachers and administrators, a fundamental shift towards a new type of practice in which students' needs are not seen as a problem to be solved but an opportunity to prompt the reshaping of the education system to suit all learners' needs (Sharma, Loreman, & Forlin, 2011). Japan has been following this international trend towards developing inclusive policies, albeit at a slower pace than other developed countries (Forlin, Kawai, & Higuchi, 2015).

In the 1950s, a process of *normalisation* began in Japanese education that made school compulsory for students with disabilities. Ideally, their education was to take place in a mainstream classroom with a resource teacher removing students for individualised support when necessary (Takahashi & Matsuzaki, 2014). However, this process of normalisation was not supported by additional legislation that stipulated the particulars of how inclusive education was to be realised in the post-Salamanca classroom (Forlin, Kawai, & Higuchi, 2015). In fact, only in 2014 did the Japanese Ministry of Education put forward a proposal for legislation guaranteeing in-class accommodations and modifications to materials for special needs students (Forlin, Kawai, & Higuchi, 2015). Despite this proposed move forward, the reality is that teachers lack the necessary training to realise inclusive education in their classrooms (Forlin, 2013). Nagano and Weinberg (2012) have identified the three principle barriers to implementing inclusive practices in Japan: proposed legislation that does not become law, a lack of parental awareness of the legal rights that do exist, and the limited practical support available in the school system. Added to this are the voices of teachers who feel they did not receive the appropriate pre-service training for inclusion or sufficient structural support (Forlin, 2012).

3. INCLUSIVE PRACTICE, NEURODIVERSITY AND FOREIGN LANGUAGE TEACHING

Inclusive practice is rooted in an educational philosophy that all people are entitled to an education that meets their unique needs and facilitates their success (Yada & Savolainen, 2017). If students face challenges, it is due to the classroom environment rather than any inherent learning deficit. While dyslexia, ADHD and ASD have traditionally been described by the professional community as disorders and people living with these conditions are usually seen as problems that needed to be fixed, the neurodiversity movement, like the philosophy of inclusion, has prompted a shift in perception (Silberman, 2017). The term neurodiversity, a portmanteau of the words neurology and diversity, was coined by Judith Singer in the late 1990s. She used the term to describe people with dyslexia, ADHD and autism, and her goal was to alter the discourse surrounding these conditions from a medical model, where these terms are a pathology, to a social model. In the social model, the conditions are recognised and respected as naturally occurring phenomena in human diversity that may require teachers and other support personnel to take alternative approaches for neurodiverse students or make modifications or accommodations to the materials they use (Silberman, 2017).

Language teachers are in a unique position to recognise and support neurodiverse students for several reasons. First, instead of lecturing to large groups, they tend to teach small classes where students are often engaged in communicative activities. This allows for easier identification of students that may need additional support both in and out of the classroom or students that require modifications or accommodations in order to succeed academically. Second, because language teachers usually teach small groups, they can contribute to the support and inclusion of neurodiverse students by nominating them to speak or by carefully monitoring their group work, thereby maintaining a more equal level of class participation. As Motschenbacher (2016) notes, teachers may employ a variety of strategies to support their neurodiverse students by prompting them to speak and giving them additional thinking time before responding to questions. Third, the most common presentations of neurodiversity are dyslexia, ADHD and autism, and all of these conditions significantly alter how languages are learnt. Due to this fact, language teachers need to be particularly aware of how neurodiversity impacts upon language learning and devise methods, in cooperation with students and support staff, to overcome the challenges. For example, dyslexia is a fairly common brain difference that affects approximately 15-20 per cent of the population, and evidence collected during neuroimaging procedures demonstrates that dyslexic people have differences in grey matter structure, which governs speech, and in white matter, which controls neurological responses to the printed word (D'Mello & Gabrieli, 2018). Dyslexic students not only face difficulty with reading, but also with other key aspects of foreign language acquisition, including distinguishing between new words, memorisation and retrieval of vocabulary, pronunciation, and developing the confidence necessary to use a foreign language (Dal, 2008). Possible support mechanisms could include using dyslexic-friendly fonts and a variety of multimodal games to facilitate the acquisition of new vocabulary.

Less common than dyslexia is ADHD, which is diagnosed in about 10 per cent of children according to the Center for Disease Control and Prevention. The primary challenges for foreign language students with ADHD are the working memory required to learn a new language and the executive functioning necessary to cope with many of the usual tasks students are presented with in the classroom (Leons, Herbert, & Gobbo, 2009). Working memory refers to the capacity to hold temporary information, which impacts upon reasoning and decision-making behaviour, while executive function is defined as a cognitive process that governs the monitoring of behaviour and organisation of thought. Because students with ADHD have trouble with working memory and executive functioning, learning new vocabulary is difficult and these students often find activities that require a good deal of organisational power to be challenging. These would include anything ranging from task-based group activities to organisation of an outline for a piece of academic writing. Language teachers can support students with ADHD by having more visual guidance in the classroom and by aiding in executive functioning tasks with graphic organisers or other similar organisational support.

Autism affects approximately 1-2 per cent of the world population, according to the Center for Disease Control and Prevention, but other experts suggest that many more students, approximately one in thirty, may be somewhere on the autism spectrum but do not have a formal diagnosis (Silberman, 2017). The core feature of autism is difficulty with language acquisition and with developing an understanding of what is pragmatically appropriate (Tager-Flusberg, Paul, & Lord, 2005). Autistic students may also have difficulty with pair and group work, another staple feature of the communicative language classroom, due to the anxiety that may come as a result of social interaction or the lack of social skills required to communicate with neurotypical students (Tager-Flusberg, Paul, & Lord, 2005). In order to support all students with communication difficulties, language teachers are in a unique position because modelling communicative competence is a standard part of their role in the classroom.

4. SELF-EFFICACY

Self-efficacy (Bandura, 1977), the theoretical framework used to shape this study, is primarily concerned with examining a person's belief in their ability to maintain control over their functioning and their ability to react constructively to events. Bandura (1977) outlined four key factors that influence the development of self-efficacy. First is *mastery experiences*. When an individual is forced to confront a challenging situation on repeated occasions and is able to cope successfully, mastery of experience is gained. This mastery of experience is translated into high self-efficacy in the challenging domain. The second, *vicarious experiences*, refers to situations in which a person watches a peer successfully cope with a challenging situation. This vicarious experience also allows for a measure of self-efficacy to develop, although not as great as the mastery of experience. Third, *social persuasion*, or receiving positive feedback when coping with challenges is an additional driver supporting the development of high self-efficacy. Finally, *emotional states*, or a person's psychological condition when coping with a challenging situation, can also influence self-efficacy. When an individual suffers from anxiety, anger or frustration while dealing with a challenging task, it becomes more difficult to develop a high sense of self-efficacy.

Self-efficacy is crucial in education because, as Bandura (1977) argued, people's beliefs about their abilities have a profound effect on their performance. While ability is a fluid construct and there is great variability in how people perform tasks, those who have a strong feeling of self-efficacy tend to be more resilient. Even in the face of failure, they approach tasks with a problem-solving mindset (Bandura, 1977). The development of high self-efficacy has been linked with numerous benefits such as increased ability to cope with adversity and stress, improved performance, increased motivation, and a higher level of educational achievement (Domenech-Betorat, Abellan-Rosello, & Gomez-Artiga, 2017).

5. QUALITATIVE REPORTS ON INCLUSIVE PRACTICES AND SELF-EFFICACY

Quantitative investigations into teacher self-efficacy are still the norm while qualitative research in this area is still relatively rare (Wyatt, 2015). However, there are a number of good reasons to support a qualitative inquiry into teacher self-efficacy and inclusion. First, quantitative researchers tend to view teacher self-efficacy as a relatively stable construct (Tschannen-Moran & Johnson, 2011), but others argue that this is an overly simplistic way of examining teacher experience in the classroom (Wyatt, 2015). While teachers may experience a high degree of self-efficacy when dealing with daily classroom issues that they have grown accustomed to, they may simultaneously experience low levels of self-efficacy when problems arise with students that face learning challenges. For this reason, the present study uses qualitative methods. A second reason why qualitative research is useful for self-efficacy studies is because some quantitative studies have been criticised for their lack of practical applications to real world problems faced by teachers because they look at breadth rather than depth (Wheatley, 2005). In this study, qualitative research was chosen as the method in order to attempt to circumvent this issue by digging deeply into teacher experiences and self-reports of their feelings of efficacy. Teachers participating in this study were also invited to generate potential solutions to the problems they experienced in the classroom, thereby adding their own voices to the final section of this article on the implications for practice.

6. RESEARCH METHODS

This narrative study involved one-on-one interviews with eight participants who were known to the author and purposively selected because they had either attended workshops on supporting EFL students facing learning challenges or discussed their concerns about supporting special needs students in the EFL classroom with the author. Of the eight individuals interviewed, four were Japanese teachers of English (all female) and four were non-Japanese teachers of English (two female and two male). All were employed in post-secondary institutions in Japan and had three years of teaching experience at a minimum. Interviews lasted between 30 and 60 minutes and were recorded and transcribed. Transcriptions were manually coded, and codes were organised into thematic categories, based on Bandura's (1977) construct of self-efficacy development, including mastery of experience, vicarious experience, social persuasion and emotional states.

7. RESEARCH FINDINGS

The findings of this study indicate that EFL teachers at the tertiary level in Japan tend to report lower levels of self-efficacy for working with students who face learning challenges. In many cases, they feel they lack the knowledge and skills necessary to best accommodate learners with learning differences and they do not have much access to professionals for consultation. They also lack communication with diversity-and-inclusion office personnel who could advise teachers on how to support students who face learning challenges in the EFL classroom. The lack of communication is due to several factors: linguistic and cultural barriers, stigma, and simply not knowing how to contact these professionals. Despite this, some teachers interviewed were particularly resourceful in seeking out opportunities to liaise with the support staff available on campus. However, their resourcefulness indicates an overall lack of infrastructure that links teachers with special needs support personnel.

7.1 MASTERY EXPERIENCES

Having the opportunity for mastery experiences is the most important factor in the development of high self-efficacy (Bandura, 1997). However, EFL teachers working with neurodiverse students lack mastery experiences for a number of reasons. First, they have not been equipped with the necessary skills to approach students who they think may be struggling to communicate with others during class, and thus allow them opportunities to practise using those skills. While they report that they usually have "one student in every class" that seems to be isolated from the others or exhibits learning challenges that seem to be related to a potential neurologically-based difference, they recount that they are not sure how to speak to these students about the issues they have noticed in the classroom.

For example, one teacher interviewed made a statement that highlighted the social strain caused by this problem. She said:

> I really can't tell a student that I think they're different and that I think they need counselling.
> Any conversation I have with a student, no matter how PC (politically correct) it might be,
> amounts to my saying that I think they're different and need help.

Another teacher also expressed hesitation to communicate with students about the difficulties they have in class, which the teacher believes are a symptom of developmental disability. She stated: "[t]here is a stigma when it comes to disability, and I don't want to be the person who has to bring the subject up with a student. I don't know how they will react, but I guess they will be offended." Because teachers lack the necessary skills to start these conversations, they in turn lose opportunities for mastery of experience. This situation can be particularly acute in the Japanese context where teachers are viewed as strong authority figures and the power distance between teachers and students tends to be high. In this setting, it perhaps becomes more difficult for teachers to broach personal topics with students than in other contexts.

While teachers lack the skills necessary to address learning issues with students and this leads to limitations on opportunities for mastery of experience, teachers also provided a second reason for having a lack of mastery experiences. They said they felt that a lack of communication with other professionals reduced their chances for the development of a positive sense of self-efficacy. For example, one teacher recounted: *"I know there is some sort of disability support office on campus but I'm not sure where it is or who works there."* Other teachers were more aware of the support services available but they said that even in contexts where they did have contact with counsellors or learning support personnel, the specific diagnosis of some of their students remained shrouded in mystery. Because of laws that protect the privacy of students, teachers do not always have access to important information that may help them to better understand the behaviour of their students, how to modify materials, or how to plan for accommodations in assessment. One teacher reported that she is told at the beginning of each semester which students she needs to *"pay special attention to"* but she is not told why or what exactly is expected of her in terms of modification. Another related issue that teachers recounted were situations in which students were clearly struggling with developmental disabilities such as autism and ADHD but no formal diagnosis had yet been made, or if it had, it was not shared with the university. Students are not obliged to share any formal diagnosis with the institutions they study at and even if they do, the teachers are unlikely to ever receive clear information about that diagnosis, how the diagnosis presents itself in that particular individual, or how to best work with the student in question.

A third reason teachers have difficulty developing mastery experiences is because, even when they are told of a student's specific diagnosis, they often do lack knowledge of what the diagnosis means. For example, one teacher explained:

> *I am trained as an educator, not as a counsellor or psychologist. I have little to no knowledge of what it means to have autism or ADHD. When I was growing up, I didn't see these kinds of kids in my school and there was just very little awareness. Things are not much better now.*

In addition to this lack of knowledge is a sceptical sentiment expressed by some teachers about neurological differences. As one participant recounted:

> *Nowadays, some teachers still believe that these are made-up diagnoses and that every little difference or problem has become a pathology. They are simply unwilling to acknowledge there are neurological differences and assume the problems students experience boil down to a self-discipline issue. They expect that students who are accepted to university should be able to keep up with their work by getting outside support when necessary. It should not be the responsibility of the university to provide support.*

Indeed, in the Japanese context, many parents send their children to after-school, commercial programmes geared towards providing them with additional support with academic work. It is perhaps due to this well-accepted cultural norm that teachers feel it is not incumbent upon them or universities to provide additional support.

As a result of these three factors highlighted in the paragraphs above, opportunities for mastery experiences simply do not present themselves. Instead, teachers report feeling a sense of hesitation to initiate conversations about learning challenges with students and they also state that they feel cut off from access to important information about their students because of privacy laws that could be rooted in social stigmas of developmental differences. However, if there is a cultural shift within a department on how to address and support special needs students, some teachers may feel a stronger sense of self-efficacy and be afforded more opportunities for mastery experiences.

7.2 VICARIOUS EXPERIENCE

Vicarious experience, or experiencing the success of peers, is another important factor in developing self-efficacy. However, the teachers interviewed did not report vicariously experiencing the success of their fellow teachers in helping support students with special learning needs or communicative differences. Instead, the communication they had with their colleagues could be characterised as negative and indicated a sense of frustration and fear amongst staff. Most teachers reported private discussions with their colleagues about students' difficulties and remarked on how these discussions quickly took on a negative tone. For example, one teacher recounted that whenever she spoke to colleagues about a certain *"problematic"* student they shared in class, the teachers *"lamented that nothing significant could really be done to help him because no one knew what to do."* Other teachers mentioned that their conversations with colleagues were not fruitful because there was no protocol in place to reach out for help. While the teachers expressed their gratitude for being able to talk to each other about their students, and thus *"voice their concerns and blow off a bit of steam"* the discussions did not progress beyond that because teachers did not know who to turn to for more specific direction.

While teachers reported private discussions with colleagues that were either negative or unfruitful, they also described interactions at faculty meetings when students facing challenges were discussed in a more formal manner. During these meetings, teachers were not afforded opportunities to increase their self-efficacy through vicariously experiencing the success of their co-workers in coping with challenged students. Rather, they witnessed the extent of the distress of their fellow teachers. For instance, one teacher recounted that in a faculty meeting, her colleague was asked to explain why she had chosen to call learning support personnel to the classroom to remove an autistic student who had put his head down on the desk during class, refusing to work with classmates. This teacher felt that in this meeting, they were being held responsible for:

> making the wrong decision, meaning a decision that the department head didn't approve of,
> despite the fact that she did not have any special training and was not given any prior

instructions on how to support this student or to help him to cope when he was experiencing difficulty in front of the class.

Another teacher told a story about a faculty meeting during which members of the special needs learning support centre made a presentation about the signs teachers should look for to help identify and support neurodiverse students who either do not have a formal diagnosis or do not want to share their diagnosis with the university. At the meeting, one of the teacher's colleagues complained to the support personnel that EFL teachers *"are not trained to deal with special needs students" and that "the jobs of special needs teachers should not be pushed off on to us."*

These examples indicate the mixed feelings of teachers; one is nervous about how she might be treated by her superiors for having tried and failed to support a student and another expressing the opinion that he does not and should not need to take responsibility for students with learning differences. Self-efficacy can develop when teachers see their peers successfully cope with a challenging situation in the classroom. However, it seems that when teachers conduct private conversations with one another, or more publicly discuss special needs students at faculty meetings, there is little opportunity for self-efficacy development. Rather, it seems to be the case that teachers taking part in these conversations and meetings would continue to experience low self-efficacy as a result of hearing about their colleagues being unable to cope with the classroom challenges presented to them in an effective manner.

7.3 SOCIAL PERSUASION

Another potential avenue for the development of teacher self-efficacy is social persuasion, or the verbal encouragement provided to teachers by others when they have successfully coped with a challenging task. One reason why there is little verbal encouragement, and therefore limited opportunities to develop self-efficacy, is because teachers often work alone. All of the teachers participating in this study taught solo in their classrooms and, as a result, lacked opportunities to be observed while working with students that were facing learning challenges due to developmental differences.

Although there is a lack of social persuasion among teachers, there are possibilities for social persuasion when working with support personnel. The participants in this study are employed by universities that are equipped with counselling centres and support staff are available to liaise and consult with teachers. However, despite this opportunity for verbal encouragement, there is little communication between teachers and professional support staff. For example, the non-Japanese teachers participating in this study voiced concern that language and cultural barriers between themselves and support staff impeded communication. To illustrate, one teacher said that, because he and his colleagues are not able to use Japanese proficiently and the support staff are not fluent in English, they hesitate to approach support staff for consultation. As for cultural barriers, another teacher stated that:

> [t]*here is more of a focus on diagnosis and labelling in the West that does not appear in the Japanese context. It seems that the Japanese counsellors are less willing to label students*

with this or that kind of diagnosis. This could be because there are no real benefits to having a diagnosis. There are no rules at the university about how to provide accommodations for certain students and the label is seen as more of an embarrassment than anything else.

Another teacher reiterated this point in his interview and stated:

[t]here is a strong stigma around mental issues in Japan and mental illness is often mixed up with developmental difference. No one here wants to be different, you know that expression, 'the nail that sticks out gets hammered down.' Well, that's exactly the problem, no one wants a label proving the fact they're different from others.

The comments of these teachers indicate that there are several issues at play in their situations ranging from stigma to language barriers to a lack of structured support mechanisms. In terms of structured support mechanisms, it seemed as if teachers who were involved with support personnel expected clear rules. Because support for students often needs to be negotiated on a regular basis by the student, the teacher and the support staff, it may be difficult for universities to provide clear-cut rules for accommodations, something Japanese teachers in particular may find frustrating due to the rather rule-oriented nature of educational administration in this context.

While Japanese EFL teachers did not voice their concerns about language or culture barriers between themselves and the support staff, they did discuss a lack of opportunities to communicate with them and, therefore, a lack of opportunity for some kind of positive feedback or social persuasion. For example, one of the Japanese teachers interviewed stated, similar to one of her colleagues quoted in the previous section: *"I know there is some kind of support service available for students, but I have no idea where it is or how to refer students there."* Another Japanese teacher shared that while counsellors had contacted her on behalf of a student on one occasion, it was an extreme situation and that, in her nearly 30 years of teaching, she had only communicated with support staff on this isolated occasion. These statements highlight the willingness of the universities to provide support and the fact that appropriate staff are in place to provide the support. However, the key barrier here is communication between teaching staff and support personnel. It is reasonable to assume that it is difficult for teachers to help students in class without contact with external support staff who provide them with information about the student's specific needs. It is also reasonable to think that it would be difficult for support personnel to adequately do their jobs without communicating with teachers about their course and their assessments of students. Because of this lack of connection between professionals, there are very few opportunities for teachers to get feedback and, therefore, few chances to develop self-efficacy.

7.4 EMOTIONAL STATES

Emotional states were identified by Bandura (1977) as a final factor that influences the development of self-efficacy. Emotional states refer to the psychological condition teachers are in when performing tasks. Stress and anxiety can negatively affect performance, and thereby impact upon self-efficacy, while positive mental states can improve performance and increase self-efficacy. In this study, the teachers' comments clearly demonstrate a pattern of anxiety when working with students facing learning challenges caused by developmental differences. Part of the reason may be that teachers are not sure what is causing what one of them characterised as the peculiar behaviour of some of their students. When asked about their TESOL training, none of the teachers interviewed had taken a course that addressed special needs in the foreign language classroom, nor had any of their courses touched upon the subject. Furthermore, none of the teachers participating in this study had attended more than a couple of workshops on supporting special needs students, if any at all. The teachers that had attended workshops stated that they had sought out opportunities to participate in these professional development opportunities through local teacher organisations or at conferences they attended. No workshops were provided by teachers on-site or through their institutions.

Possibly because of this lack of training, teachers feel anxiety when trying to reach out to students who show challenging behaviour in class such as withdrawing from the group, refusal to participate in class discussions, or not responding at all during class. Some quotes collected from the teachers highlight this anxiety and lack of training particularly well. For example, one teacher said: *"I am really uncomfortable talking with students directly because I'm afraid I might open the floodgates so to speak and then find myself in a situation that is out of control."* Another teacher stated that:

> [i]t is really tough to work with these students. It's stressful and I feel really frustrated because I just don't know what to do. It's like they're in a little bubble and it's really difficult to get through to them and understand what is going on in their heads.

Confusion seemed to be another emotional state experienced by teachers when in the classroom with students showing behavioral differences like refusal to communicate. When asked what they think caused such behaviours, some teachers responded that these students just have different personalities from others and that that is at the root of their challenges in class. For example, one teacher said she thought these students were *"suffering from communication problems caused by an awkward personality that don't go away even when they speak Japanese."* She followed up on this by saying that: *"[s]ome people are just really shy and withdrawn from society, probably due to bullying or negative past experiences at school. They also might have some personal problems or family issues."*

Taken together, the general picture that emerges from the data is one of anxiety, frustration and confusion on the part of teachers when they try to support students that have obvious developmental challenges. Because of these negative emotions, teachers seem to perpetually experience low self-efficacy when working with these students and, as one of them noted, because they are in a position of authority in the class and other students are looking for them for social cues on how to behave with these students, they feel additional pressure to perform but they are not sure how to cope with the situation. This sometimes results in other students further isolating a peer that has communication difficulties.

7.5 ATTITUDES TOWARDS INCLUSION

The data analysed using Bandura's (1977) theory of self-efficacy do illuminate the challenges teachers face in supporting their neurodiverse students and their relatively low levels of self-efficacy due to a lack of experience, a lack of vicarious experience, little social persuasion (positive feedback) and negative emotional states. However, what the data do not capture is the resilience expressed by the research participants and their hope that they might be able to develop the skills necessary to build a more inclusive classroom. For example, one participant said that he was particularly interested in trying to reach out to students who looked like they needed support to communicate with their peers during classroom tasks. While he expressed his lack of experience and professional training and stated that he had never taught a student *"with a formal diagnosis,"* he showed his enthusiasm for supporting all the students in his class. He attributed this attitude to being a foreigner in Japan and regularly experiencing communication difficulties outside the classroom. He also said that *"teaching is a constant process of shifting to meet the needs of all students."* He further stated that he had been raised in a particularly *"compassionate home"* and that he was a student in a Montessori school where he experienced what he described as a *"more inclusive"* kind of education.

Other teachers also expressed their interest in advocating for workshops to be held on campus and for greater contact with professional support staff. One teacher recounted a story in which she accompanied her students on a field trip and one student who had always seemed a bit *"fragile"* and *"withdrawn"* in class reached out to the teacher and told her that she needed a break from the activities because she was feeling *"overwhelmed."* While the teacher was able to accommodate this request at the time, it made her reflect on other situations when students were not able to communicate their feelings to her. She stated that while she was able to support this one student on this isolated occasion, she felt the need to be able to support others in a similar way but by using a more systematic approach, alongside professionals that were specially trained to support neurodiverse students.

8. CONCLUSION AND IMPLICATIONS

The findings of this study indicate that EFL teachers report experiences that are similar to those of Japanese elementary and high school teachers; they are concerned about the rising number of special needs students in their English language classes but their self-efficacy for inclusive practice is relatively low. This is due in part to the fact that they report few opportunities to develop the necessary skills through facilitated experiences with special needs students. Additionally, they report a lack of communication with other institutionally-based professionals responsible for the inclusion and accommodation of these students, which impacts on the chances afforded to them to develop more positive self-efficacy. The implications of this study are that EFL teachers in the Japanese context need more training and greater institutional support in order to create a more inclusive classroom setting for students with developmental differences or other special learning needs. Particularly, teachers want more direct communication with diversity and inclusion offices on campus and greater input from those specially trained in inclusive education practices. Teachers also need to be supported as they discuss issues with their special needs students because of the stigma around developmental differences.

According to the findings of this study, probably the most significant step a university can take to support the inclusion of special needs students is to train the teachers who work with those students on a daily basis. In the context of Japanese higher education, where many first-year students are required to take EFL classes, English teachers are in a unique position to identify students who might need more individualised support throughout their time at university. However, according to the teachers participating in this study, they and their colleagues are hesitant to address learning challenges with students partly because they are not trained to do so. In order to remedy this problem, awareness-raising workshops could be held at the beginning of each academic year or semester in order to help teachers to identify students who may need more support, to help them to broach the topic with students, and to make teachers aware of the avenues they have for additional support which may include counselling centres or diversity and inclusion offices.

Connected to this, many teachers in this study reported that they and their colleagues have little contact with support personnel at their universities. As a result, it may be worth exploring possibilities to increase communication between teachers and staff that are especially trained to work with students facing learning challenges. For instance, at the beginning of the semester, students who have diagnoses could be encouraged to share this information with their teachers in the presence of a counsellor who is facilitating the meeting between the teacher and student. At this meeting, the teacher could ask questions of both the student and the counsellor about what kind of support the student might need and they could cooperatively devise a support plan for the semester. In this way, a line of communication would simultaneously be opened between the teacher and the student, between the teacher and the counsellor, and between the student and the counsellor.

In the Japanese context, however, there are many students who lack a formal diagnosis or who do not want to share their diagnosis with the university. These students may not want to visit counselling centres or learning support offices due to the stigma of a label that may come as a result of the visit. Because of this stigma, these students are often unable to benefit from formal classroom accommodations, like additional time to take exams, which may help them to succeed academically. However, even with this barrier, teachers, along with these students, can devise support plans at the start of the semester that do not make use of a schedule of formal accommodations or outside support, provided that teachers are trained to approach these students in order to arrange this private support plan.

Another possibility for developing more inclusive practice is making teachers more aware of Universal Design for Learning (UDL) guidelines. These guidelines help teachers to focus on three areas: engagement, representation and expression. Teachers are encouraged to provide students with multiple ways to engage in class, a variety of ways of presenting materials to them, and different methods to allow students to express what they know.

Finally, a key theme that arose in the data that has an important implication for practice is stigma. Teachers fear talking to students due to stigma and students also fear sharing important information about themselves that impacts on their ability to perform academically due to pressure to conform to others around them. The challenge of overcoming stigma seems insurmountable. However, it is possible to take small, concrete steps to reduce stigma in one's own department within the university. At the foundation of inclusive education is the recognition that diversity is important to growth and development. In order to exploit diversity, stigma needs to be reduced by changing the culture around difference. It is possible to imagine a university which embraces students with learning differences, that empowers teachers to support students by establishing firm ties between counselling centres, teachers, and students. Additionally, it is possible to reduce stigma by having teachers act as role models of inclusion. Neurotypical students also lack skills to work collaboratively with those who are different from them. In order for those in the EFL classroom to embrace diversity and benefit from it, not only teachers need to be supported and trained, but also neurotypical students who are called on to work collaboratively with all kinds of classmates. In order to facilitate this process, teachers, with the proper support and training, can serve as models for inclusion in their classrooms and lead students to develop mutually-beneficial skills that they can take with them outside the classroom and into the wider world.

REFERENCES

Bandura, A. (1977). Self-efficacy: Toward a unifying theory of behavioral change. *Psychological Review, 84* (2), 191–215.

Bandura, A. (1997). *Self-efficacy: The exercise of control*. New York, NY: Freeman.

Dal, M. (2008). Dyslexia and foreign language learning. In G. Reid, A. Fawcett, F. Manis, & L. Siegel (Eds.), *The Sage handbook of dyslexia* (pp. 439–454). London: Sage.

D'Mello, A. M., & Gabrieli, J. D. (2018). Cognitive neuroscience of dyslexia. *Language, Speech, and Hearing Services in Schools, 49*(4), 798–809.

Doménech-Betoret, F., Abellán-Roselló, L., & Gómez-Artiga, A. (2017). Self-efficacy, satisfaction, and academic achievement: The mediator role of students' expectancy-values and beliefs. *Frontiers in Psychology, 8*, 1193.

Forlin, C. (2012). Diversity and its challenges for teachers. In C. Forlin (Ed.), *Future directions for inclusive teacher education* (pp. 83–92). Oxford: Routledge.

Forlin, C. (2013). Issues of inclusive education in the 21st century. *Journal of Learning Science, 6*, 67–81.

Forlin, C., Kawai, N., & Higuchi, S. (2014). Educational reform in Japan towards inclusion: Are we training teachers for success? *International Journal of Inclusive Education, 19*(3), 314–331.

Kayama, M., & Haight, W. (2013). Disability and stigma: How Japanese educators help parents accept their children's differences. *Social Work, 59*(1), 24–33.

Leons, E., Herbert, C., & Gobbo, K. (2009). Students with learning disabilities and ADHD in the foreign language classroom: Supporting students and instructors. *Foreign Language Annals, 42*(1), 42–54.

Motschenbacher, H. (2016). Inclusion and foreign language education: What linguistics can contribute. *ITL - International Journal of Applied Linguistics, 167*(2), 159–189.

Nagano, M., & Weinberg, L. (2012). The legal framework for the inclusion of students with disabilities: A comparative analysis of Japan and the United States. *International Journal of Special Education, 27*(1), 128–143.

Sharma, U., Loreman, T., & Forlin, C. (2012). Measuring teacher efficacy to implement inclusive practices. *Journal of Research in Special Educational Needs, 12*(1), 12–21.

Silberman, S. (2017). *Neurotribes: The legacy of autism and how to think smarter about people who think differently*. London: Atlantic Books.

Song, J. (2016). Inclusive education in Japan and Korea: Japanese and Korean teachers' self-efficacy and attitudes towards inclusive education. *Journal of Research in Special Educational Needs, 16*(S1), 643–648.

Tager-Flusberg, H., Paul, R., & Lord, C. (2005). Language and communication in autism. In F. Volkmar, R. Paul, A. Klin, & D. Cohen (Eds.), *Handbook of autism and pervasive developmental disorders* (pp. 335–364). New York, NY: Wiley.

Takahashi, J., & Matsuzaki, H. (2014). The changes and problems in inclusive education. *The Bulletin of the Faculty of Human Development and Culture, 19*, 13–26.

Tschannen-Moran, M., & Johnson, D. (2011). Exploring literacy teachers' self-efficacy beliefs: Potential sources at play. *Teaching and Teacher Education, 27*(4), 751–761.

Wheatley, K. F. (2005). The case for reconceptualizing teacher efficacy research. *Teaching and Teacher Education, 21*(7), 747–766.

Wyatt, M. (2015). Using qualitative research methods to assess the degree of fit between teachers' reported self-efficacy beliefs and their practical knowledge during teacher education. *The Australian Journal of Teacher Education, 40*(1), 117.

Yada, A., & Savolainen, H. (2017). Japanese in-service teachers' attitudes toward inclusive education and self-efficacy for inclusive practices. *Teaching and Teacher Education, 64*, 222–229.

THE EUROPEAN JOURNAL OF APPLIED LINGUISTICS AND TEFL

8 USING THE MULTISENSORY STRUCTURED TEACHING APPROACH TO HELP LEARNERS WITH DYSLEXIA IN ACQUIRING A SECOND/ADDITIONAL LANGUAGE

Bimali Indrarathne, University of York, UK

ABSTRACT

The Multisensory Structured Language Teaching (MSLT) approach uses visual, auditory, tactile and kinaesthetic pathways in combination. This combined approach particularly aids learners' memory, as it integrates sensory activities. MSLT is widely used when teaching second or additional languages to learners with dyslexia. It is believed that the approach can provide additional support that learners with dyslexia need in learning languages. A recent teacher training initiative in Sri Lanka on teaching learners with Specific Learning Difficulties has also highlighted that English language teachers find MSLT a useful approach in teaching not only learners with dyslexia, but any learner. This article provides an overview of dyslexia, its consequences and the MSLT approach. It provides some examples of multisensory activities that teachers can use in the language classroom and discusses empirical findings relating to the approach. In addition, it highlights teacher perceptions on using the MSLT approach with children with and without dyslexia.

KEYWORDS

MSLT, dyslexia, EFL learners, inclusive education.

1. INTRODUCTION

Dyslexia is one of several Specific Learning Difficulties (SpLDs) which is usually identified as a reading difficulty (e.g., Lyon, Shaywitz, & Shaywitz, 2003). However, learners with dyslexia show several other difficulties, such as lower working memory capacity, spelling difficulties, lower attention span and difficulties in information processing. In addition, each learner with dyslexia may show unique issues, and demonstrate various strengths and weaknesses. The severity of these issues can also vary from mild to strong. Usually, learners with dyslexia encounter numerous challenges in learning languages, including their first language (L1). In particular, they may face issues when learning a second/additional language (L2), especially if it differs from their first language to a greater extent.

Due to the challenges learners with dyslexia face in learning languages, several teaching methods/approaches are used to enhance their learning. The Multisensory Structured Language Teaching (MSLT) approach is one of them. It was originally developed by Sparks et al. (1991), based on the Orton-Gillingham (OG) approach (Gillingham & Stillman, 1960), and since then has been adapted by many others. It has been subjected to several empirical studies which investigated its effectiveness in teaching learners with dyslexia.

This article provides an overview of the problems faced by learners with dyslexia when learning a second/foreign language and how teachers can use the MSLT approach to assist them. It also discusses empirical evidence on the MSLT approach and provides findings of an empirical study which investigated English language teachers' perceptions of and experiences with the MSLT approach.

2. DYSLEXIA AND LANGUAGE LEARNING

The International Dyslexia Association (2002, n.d.) defines dyslexia as:

> a specific learning disability that is neurobiological in origin. It is characterized by difficulties with accurate and/or fluent word recognition and by poor spelling and decoding abilities. These difficulties typically result from a deficit in the phonological component of language that is often unexpected in relation to other cognitive abilities and the lack of provision of effective classroom instruction. Secondary consequences may include problems in reading comprehension and reduced reading experience that can impede growth of vocabulary and background knowledge.

As the definition highlights, reading comprehension issues that learners with dyslexia face are secondary, and the primary difficulties include issues in spelling, decoding abilities and accurate and fluent word recognition. In order to understand how these difficulties cause reading comprehension issues, it is important to understand how we learn to read. According to Frith (1986), there are three stages in the process of learning to read. In the first stage called the *logographic stage*, children learn to read a few words together. However, in this stage, they do not visually process the words. In the second, or *alphabetic stage*, children learn to segment words into letters and combine letters to create sounds. This stage is where phonological processing takes place. In the third, or *orthographic stage*, children focus on larger units such as syllables.

According to the phonological deficit hypothesis (Stanovich, 1988), reading difficulties are caused by impaired phonological awareness. Those who have impaired phonological awareness show issues in syllabic and phonemic knowledge. For example, they may show inability to segment words into syllables and combine them to form words, due to impaired syllabic knowledge. They may also be unable to identify and differentiate sounds in words, combine sounds to form words and add/delete sounds from words if they have reduced phonemic knowledge. Learners with dyslexia show deficits in syllabic and phonemic knowledge. Therefore, in the alphabetic stage, they may find it difficult to segment words and understand how to combine letters to form sounds. In the orthographic stage also, they may find it difficult to process larger units such as syllables. Such phonological processing difficulties influence not only reading, but also writing, speech perception and production (Kormos & Smith, 2012). In addition to these issues, learners with dyslexia may show difficulties in naming speed and processing speed (Pennington, 2006). Reading difficulties are also caused by word decoding problems and insufficient attention paid in sentence and text level processing (Perfetti, 2007).

Working memory capacity is an influential factor in reading comprehension. Baddeley and Hitch (1974) explain that working memory consists of a storage capacity and a processing capacity. According to them, there are three main components to working memory: a central executive and two slave systems. The two slave systems are the phonological loop and the visuospatial sketchpad. The phonological loop is said to process information related to speech and visuospatial imagery information is processed by the visuospatial sketchpad. Another component called episodic buffer was later added to this model. According to Baddeley (2015), the function of the central executive is to coordinate the subsidiary memory systems, retrieving information, switching attention, inhibiting irrelevant information and manipulating information in the phonological loop and the visuospatial sketchpad. In reading comprehension, one needs to keep the already processed information active, receive new and update the existing information, monitor comprehension, and inhibit irrelevant information (Cain, 2006). Thus, lower working memory capacity observed in learners with dyslexia negatively influences their reading comprehension ability.

Automaticity is another important aspect that needs discussion under reading comprehension. It refers to the "fast, accurate and effortless word identification at the single word level" (Hook & Jones, 2004, p. 17). Since one has limited attention resources as well as a limited working memory capacity, automaticity is important to maintain reading speed. In other words, it is necessary to process the incoming information quickly to be ready to receive the following information. In doing so, one needs to process the known words/information automatically without much effort. Then, the available attention resources can be directed to process the new information. Because of the word/letter/sound recognition difficulties that learners with dyslexia face, they may not develop automaticity in reading, which slows down their reading comprehension.

In summary, learners with dyslexia face several linguistic and non-linguistic problems (Kormos & Smith, 2012). The former includes "problems in segmenting words into phonological units, problems with phoneme-grapheme correspondences, problems in word-recognition, slow reading speed, difficulties in spelling, smaller ranges of vocabulary, slow word retrieval, slow speech, articulation problems and problems in keeping verbal material in the phonological short-term memory" (p. 32). The latter includes a "smaller span of working memory, problems with arithmetic and memorising multiplication tables, difficulties with handwriting, gross motor-coordination problems, problems with sustained attention, difficulties in time-management and organising work, and difficulties in automatising new skills" (p. 33).

The above discussion highlights that it is inaccurate to recognise dyslexia solely as a reading difficulty. Therefore, remedial measures should also focus on the specific difficulties that learners face. In particular, they need help in identifying sounds, letters and their correspondences and in processing information. They also need assistance in enhancing their memory and organising information. Therefore, the teaching approach used to teach learners with dyslexia should address numerous issues that such learners face.

3. THE MULTISENSORY STRUCTURED LANGUAGE TEACHING APPROACH (MSLT) AND ITS APPLICATIONS

As explained in the previous section, learners with dyslexia face numerous challenges, particularly when learning second/additional languages. Thus, Rawson (International Dyslexia Association, 2000a, p. 1) emphasises that:

> dyslexic students need a different approach to learning language from that employed in most classrooms. They need to be taught, slowly and thoroughly, the basic elements of their language – the sounds and the letters which represent them – and how to put these together and take them apart. They have to have lots of practice in having their writing hands, eyes, ears, and voices working together for conscious organization and retention of their learning.

The MSLT approach has been recognised as a suitable method that fulfils those needs and can be used to teach additional languages to learners with dyslexia. The approach was first proposed by Sparks et al. (1991) based on the OG approach (Gillingham & Stillman, 1960), which places importance on direct, diagnostic, sequential and prescriptive ways of teaching literacy (Orton-Gillingham, 2018). It also encourages one-on-one teacher-student instruction. However, small group teaching is also commonly used. Its diagnostic nature allows teachers to take individual strengths and weaknesses into consideration and cater to specific learner needs.

Based on the OG approach, Sparks et al. (1991, p. 108) provide a daily lesson plan to teach phonology and syntax. It contains five steps. The first is blackboard drills to teach phonology and grammar. They emphasise that only one new sound should be taught per day at the blackboard drill stage. Frequent review of previously learnt sounds is also important. They recommend presenting vowels first, then consonants which are similar in the first and the target languages, the consonants which are different in the two languages as the third step and finally, special combinations of sounds in the target language. The second stage is the oral sound drill stage, which is used to review the sounds that learners learnt in the first stage. In this stage, corresponding graphemes are used in a flash card format. The third step involves introducing and reviewing grammatical concepts where explicit grammar teaching takes place with revision of previously learnt grammar structures. Acting out the language is also recommended in this stage. Vocabulary teaching, that is introduction of new vocabulary which contains new and previously learnt sounds comes as the fourth step. Vocabulary is taught using visuals. The vocabulary items should be chosen based on the phonemes that students have already learnt. Finally, reading or communicative activities should be used to provide opportunities to practise *real* communication in the target language. As communicative activities, Sparks et al. (1991) propose listening, speaking, reading and writing activities which allow learners to practise phonological, syntactic and semantic systems of the target language.

One of the key features of the MSLT approach is that it makes use of visual, auditory, kinaesthetic and tactile pathways simultaneously. Sparks et al. (1991) emphasise the importance of providing learners with the opportunity to see, hear and do the language simultaneously in order to enhance their ability to "unlock and crack the code of a foreign language" (p. 106). For example, when teaching a vocabulary item, teachers would repeat the same word several times providing auditory information. Then, pictures would be used to provide visual information related to the word. Finally, students would be asked to act it out, to provide kinaesthetic information. The concept behind using visual, auditory, kinaesthetic and tactile pathways simultaneously is to aid memory by using several sensory channels. Some learners may find it difficult to process phonological information presented in one channel, for example, verbally. In such instances, presenting information using a different sensory channel (e.g., visually) helps them to learn the same vocabulary item in an alternative way.

Another key feature of the MSLT approach is that it emphasises the importance of teaching a small amount of material at a given time and making learners master it. This means that there should be extensive practice on the language items in different settings until such items become automatic (Kormos & Smith, 2012). In other words, extensive practice helps increase automaticity. Since some learners do not have the capacity in their working memory to hold the amount of information that their peers would be able to, presenting a small amount of material and extensive practice can aid them. As previously discussed, drilling is also regularly used in the MSLT approach, in particular, with varying contexts. This also ultimately aids the memorisation and automatisation of rules.

According to Schneider and Crombie (2003), the use of language learning strategies is also an important aspect of the MSLT approach. For example, learners with dyslexia may benefit from understanding and applying learning strategies which aid memorisation. Therefore, it is important for teachers to demonstrate and ensure learners practise language learning strategies. For example, when teaching reading, teachers can make learners aware of reading strategies such as predicting content from illustrations or titles. Using mnemonic devices to remember words is another strategy that learners may find useful. Learners should be made aware of such strategies and encouraged to use them regularly.

Explicit teaching of language related concepts is found to be useful for learners with dyslexia (International Dyslexia Association, 2020). Using the L1 to provide grammar explanations and comparisons is found to be useful (Cambridge University Press, 2019). This may help learners to understand the regularities and irregularities between the L1 and L2. Both synthetic and analytic instruction are needed in using the MSLT approach (International Dyslexia Association, 2000a/b). In the former, parts of language are taught separately, learners are shown how different parts work to form a whole. For example, in the former, letter-sound correspondence of individual items such as "b," "a," and "t" can be taught separately, and learners blend those sounds/letters to form words. In the latter, the whole is presented, and students are shown how it can be broken down into parts (e.g., the word "bat" is presented to learners who already know, for example, "rat" and "cat" as they can apply this to the new phoneme combination of "b" + "at").

Logical sequencing of materials to be presented to learners is another requirement of the MSLT approach (International Dyslexia Association, 2000a, 2000b). It emphasises the importance of sequencing the easiest and most basic first and progressing to more difficult ones. In addition, each concept/item taught should be based on the previously learnt items and regular review is needed to strengthen memory. Continuous student-teacher interaction should be maintained through direct instruction and there should be continuous monitoring and assessment of students' learning and their needs (International Dyslexia Association, 2000b). Based on the diagnosis, the teacher should adapt methods and use flexible and individualistic teaching.

In summary, the key features of the MSLT approach are the use of visual, auditory, kinaesthetic and tactile pathways simultaneously, ample practice, frequent drilling of language items, frequent revision, explicit teaching, presenting a small amount of material at a time with a carefully structured order and teaching learning strategies. In the following sections, I will briefly discuss how the MSLT approach can be used in teaching grammar, vocabulary and the four skills.

3.1 TEACHING SOUNDS AND SPELLING

It is important to explain the spelling rules and how to pronounce sounds to learners with dyslexia and use several MSLT activities for this purpose (see Pearson English, 2014, and Future Learn and Lancaster University Dyslexia and Foreign Language Teaching MOOC for detailed descriptions of the activities described below). In particular, when the sounds do not correspond with the letters, learners with dyslexia may find it difficult to understand and process the variations. For example, in English, /b/ is silent in *debt*. In such instances, it may be beneficial to provide an explicit explanation to learners that /b/ is silent. The teacher can demonstrate it and learners can practise pronouncing it. Mnemonic activities and sound/syllable segmenting, adding and deleting activities are also beneficial in teaching sounds and spelling. In the activity shown in Figure 1 (based on Pearson English, 2014), the sound /tʃ/ is used in word-initial and word-final positions. Also, it is spelt in two different ways (<ch> and <tch>). In addition, colour coding emphasises the position of the sound in different places of the words. Through this activity, learners receive practice on how to use the /tʃ/ sound in different positions of words and practise different spellings of the same sound. They will understand that the sound /tʃ/ can be deleted from or added to words – either at the beginning or at the end. As can be seen in the figure, learners are able to move the <ch> part, which gives them kinaesthetic/tactile input. Colour coding provides the visual input. Both the teacher and learners can pronounce the words, which provides auditory input.

Sparks and Miller (2000) provide a sequence of teaching phonology/orthography to help learners with dyslexia. In this sequence, the teacher first models the sound or in other words the phoneme while writing the corresponding letter/grapheme on the board. Then, the students are asked to repeat the word and they are expected to look at the letter which is repeating. Students then write down the letter while pronouncing the sound aloud. This sound-symbol relationship is practised several times and reviewed in the following lessons. These sounds and letters are then added to a flash card deck. Learners can write the letter in their notebook, on a chalkboard or in the air. Sparks and Miller emphasise the importance of providing extensive practice on this sound-letter correspondence to aid learner memory.

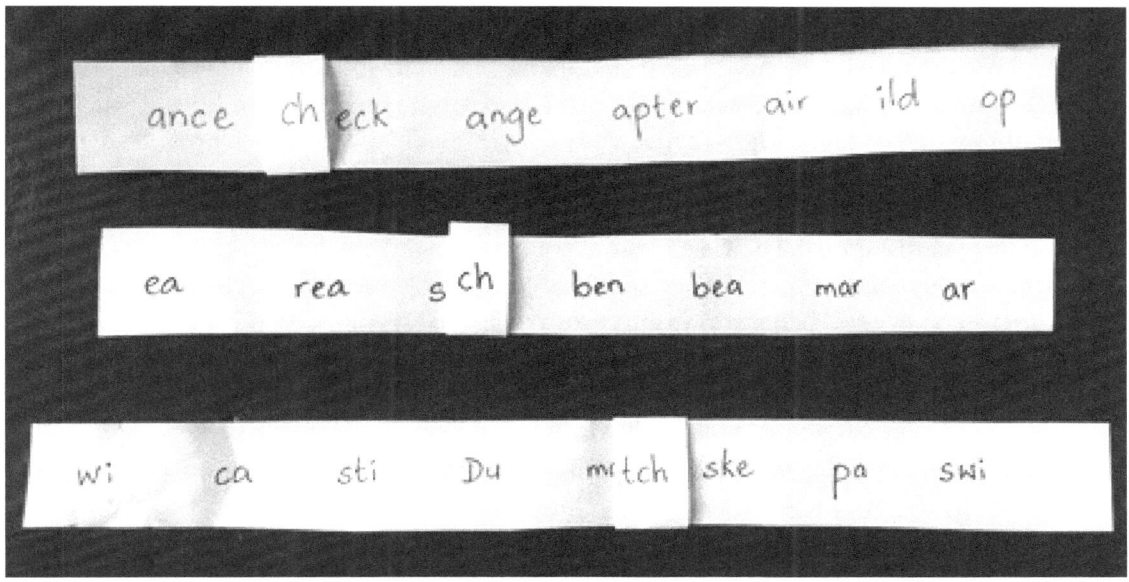

Figure 1. A sound and spelling activity (Indrarathne, 2017, p. 14, activity was prepared based on Pearson English, 2014).

3.2 TEACHING VOCABULARY

It is recommended that a limited number of new words should be taught at a time – a maximum of six to eight (Kormos & Smith, 2012). Explicitly teaching the words, frequent practice and revision, teaching similar sounding words and words with a similar meaning separately, teaching sound-meaning correspondences before teaching other related aspects, such as spelling and the use of the MSLT techniques, are important in vocabulary teaching. Figure 2 illustrates a sample MSLT vocabulary activity to teach minimal pairs (activity developed based on DysTEFL2, 2016, and Future Learn / Lancaster University, n.d.). With the words, pictures are used to provide visual input and help the learners. Colour coding is used to separate letters and letter combinations with different sounds (similar spelling/sounds are in one colour). These are used as letter/picture cards and students are expected to form words from the letters and then match the words with the pictures (kinaesthetic/tactile input). The teacher can provide auditory information by pronouncing the words.

Schneider and Ming (2019) propose "multisensory structured metacognitive language (MSML) strategies to foster students' mastery of prefix-root-suffix (PRS) vocabulary in reading and writing tasks" (p. 101). According to them, this approach has three phases. In the first phase, the teacher introduces PRS patterns and shows learners how to memorise and recall them. PRS cards are used for this purpose. In the second phase, students engage in three-to-five-minute activities practising pronunciation, meaning and spelling. They also prepare for contextualising PRS patterns in the next phase. The third phase is a series of short reading,

147

writing and speaking tasks where PRS patterns are contextualised. In this approach, PRS patterns are introduced with their pronunciation, meaning and spelling, using gestures.

According to Schneider and Ming (2019), the steps of the process include: (1) displaying two or more words in the learners' active vocabulary containing the chosen prefix/suffix, (2) asking learners to form meaningful sentences using those words and predict their meaning (images explaining the words can also be provided), and (3) showing the learners the chosen affix on large cards or on the board and pronouncing the word pattern, while learners are asked to repeat several times. They also trace spellings on the desk, on a sheet of paper or on a board. In the next step (4), the teacher shows the gesture that corresponds with the chosen affix.

Then (5), a discussion takes place on the meaning of the word pattern with the chosen affix. Learners are asked to repeat the gesture while stating the meaning of the affix aloud. Thereafter (6), learners prepare PRS cards which contain the chosen affix, its meaning, corresponding image/gesture, words that contain the affix and sample sentences. The new cards are then added to the existing cards. In the next stage (7), students perform short tasks such as Bingo, Pictionary, and Memory Match using the PRS cards to automatise pronunciation and spelling. This practice would be helpful to internalise word meaning. In the last phase (8), students listen to and/or read texts which contain the previously learnt PRS patterns. Authentic materials such as TV reports, podcasts and newspaper articles can be used for this purpose. Then, students revisit the texts to identify the previously learnt PRS patterns in them. Word charts can be used to record the new vocabulary that students find in these texts. Contextualised spoken and written language practice is also provided in which students use the newly learnt vocabulary in short speaking (e.g., mini story) and writing tasks (e.g., journal entry).

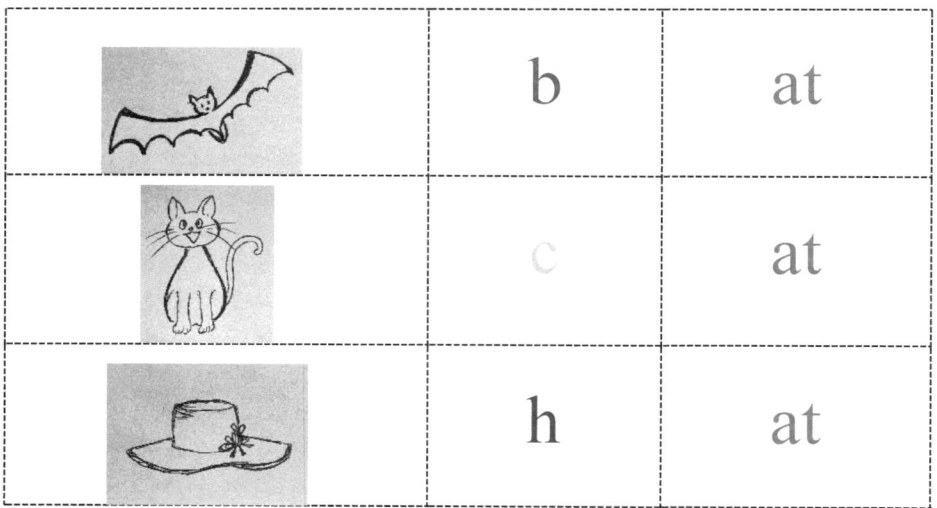

Figure 2. A vocabulary activity (adapted from Indrarathne, 2017, p. 38, developed based on DysTEFL2, 2016, and Future Learn / Lancaster University, n.d.).

3.3 TEACHING GRAMMAR

According to Sparks and Miller (2000), direct instruction is extremely important in teaching grammar to learners with dyslexia. Presenting grammar in context and avoiding technical jargon to explain it (e.g., nouns, adjectives) is also crucial (Kormos & Smith, 2012). Grammar teaching should take place from simple to complex structures, with ample opportunities to practise the structures until they get automatised. When it comes to grammar, controlled practice should precede freer practice. It is helpful for learners with dyslexia if oral practice is provided before any writing takes place. Constant revision and building upon learners' existing knowledge are also important. Sparks and Miller (2000) recommend providing grammar rule explanations in the L1 first, and then in the L2 with modelling. Thereafter, multisensory drills are recommended. In the activity shown in Figure 3 (activity adapted from DysTEFL2, 2016, and Future Learn / Lancaster University, n.d.), the MSLT approach is used to introduce and practise the target structure. Colour coding helps learners to differentiate between the subject, verb and object (visual pathway). It allows the teacher to avoid using the actual grammatical terms. When learners are exposed to this type of activity for a long period, they will understand what each colour represents. For example, blue represents the agent of the action. In order to add other pathways, the teacher can pronounce sentences and encourage drilling (auditory pathway) to automatise the structures. The words can be separately used as word cards and learners form sentences using them (kinaesthetic/tactile pathways). All these variations encourage learners to practise the structures which will aid memory and automatisation of them.

He	is	playing	soccer
She	is	writing	poems
It	is	drinking	milk
They	are	watching	movies

Figure 3. A grammar activity (developed based on DysTEFL2, 2016, and Future Learn / Lancaster University, n.d.).

3.4 TEACHING READING

Kormos and Smith (2012) provide several tips for teaching reading. As learning to read can be very challenging for learners with dyslexia, it is important to start reading lessons with short texts and gradually increase the length. If longer texts are to be taught, it would be helpful to separate them into smaller sections. Reading texts should be compatible with learners' proficiency levels. There should be only a few unfamiliar words and a limited number of unfamiliar syntactic structures per text. Providing a glossary for the unknown words, pre-teaching unfamiliar words and pre-reading activities are very helpful for learners with dyslexia. It is important to note that learners with dyslexia should not be asked to read aloud. Short activities such as quizzes, discussions, diagrams and flowcharts for different sections of the reading text may aid reading comprehension. This also provides learners with the opportunity to process sections of the text one at a time, understand the content in the sections and move on to the next. The teacher can ask learners to illustrate or act out what they have read to help them understand the meaning of the text. Reading strategies such as predicting content from illustrations/titles/sub-titles and guessing word meaning from the context and co-text are useful for learners with dyslexia. Therefore, explicit teaching of such strategies is needed.

3.5 TEACHING LISTENING

Kormos and Smith (2012) also illustrate several techniques that can be used to teach listening. Using short pieces of listening texts at a time and having only a few similar sounding words in a lesson are beneficial for learners with dyslexia. The length and complexity of the listening texts should be gradually increased. It would be useful to provide visual support with the oral texts using pictures and videos and provide pre-listening activities. Learners with dyslexia may find it difficult to engage in two tasks simultaneously (e.g., listening and writing). Therefore, they should be given the opportunity just to listen to the text first without having to complete another task. Completing tasks while listening can also be challenging. Therefore, they should be given time to complete them after listening. MSLT activities such as listening and drawing and listening and acting out can also aid listening comprehension. As in reading, learning listening strategies such as predicting content from the topic will enhance listening comprehension.

3.6 TEACHING SPEAKING

According to Kormos and Smith (2012), teaching speaking should start with simple activities such as responding with short answers to questions. Pronunciation activities will be helpful to memorise pronunciation and intonation. Multisensory activities such as speaking and acting out also aid speaking. Learners should be given ample speaking practice opportunities. Instructions on how to perform and structure tasks, revision of vocabulary and syntactic structures needed for speaking tasks and providing planning time are beneficial. Before making learners speak to a larger audience, it is essential to provide them with opportunities to perform the tasks in small groups. Providing visual and textual support such as flash cards and PowerPoint presentations while speaking can also be helpful and reduce anxiety related to forgetting.

3.7 TEACHING WRITING

Kormos and Smith (2012) illustrate several activities that can be helpful to teach writing to learners with dyslexia. As in all other skills teaching, writing should start with short and less complex activities. Writing can be particularly challenging for learners with dyslexia. Therefore, they can be asked to complete simple tasks such as filling in missing information when they start learning to write. Scaffolding and help should be provided regularly. Allowing learners to type on the computer instead of writing is a good alternative for students who struggle with handwriting. Allowing brainstorming, planning, providing a model text, using colour codes to highlight essential information in models and reviewing vocabulary and syntactic structures needed for writing tasks are beneficial. Organising ideas can be challenging for learners with dyslexia. Therefore, providing visual help with templates such as that in Figure 4 would be useful. Learners can organise ideas on the template first, and then refer to the template when writing. Mind maps are very helpful for learners with dyslexia, as they provide them with the opportunity to brainstorm ideas. In addition, mind maps can provide visual help for learners to understand the whole picture of a task/topic (e.g., a mind map can be drawn for an essay topic and by looking at it, learners will understand how to structure different paragraphs and the content of the whole essay).

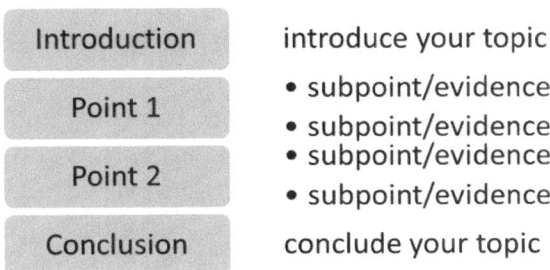

Figure 4. A template for organising ideas.

4. EMPIRICAL EVIDENCE

So far, we have discussed how the MSLT approach can be used in teaching second/additional languages to learners with dyslexia. It is also important to understand if the approach is beneficial for other learners.

Several studies conducted by Sparks and others show a positive impact of the MSLT approach. For example, Sparks et al. (1992) compared foreign language and native language aptitude of three groups of learners: those who received MSLT instruction in both English and

Spanish, MSLT instruction only in Spanish and a traditional type teaching with no MSLT instruction. The non-MSLT group did not show any pre/post-test gains while the MSLT groups demonstrated gains in different aptitude tests. A follow-up study conducted by Sparks and Ganschow (1993) demonstrated that the participants in the Sparks et al. (1992) study were able to maintain their initial gains in both the native language and the foreign language aptitude measures. The new cohort of participants in this study, who received MSLT instruction in both English and Spanish, were able to demonstrate significant gains on native language aptitude tests. Ganschow and Sparks (1995) compared the at-risk participants who received MSLT instruction in the 1992 and 1993 studies with the not-at-risk group who received traditional instruction. Both groups showed significant gains in the aptitude measures. However, the at-risk group which received MSLT instruction showed significantly greater gains.

Sparks et al. (1998) compared four groups of which three were at-risk and one was not-at-risk. The three at-risk groups received (1) MSLT Spanish instruction (2) traditional textbook Spanish instruction and both groups were in a special self-contained class. Group (3) received traditional textbook instruction in a regular Spanish class. Among the three groups, the MSLT group demonstrated significant gains in the aptitude measures. The MSLT group and the fourth group which was not-at-risk showed significantly greater gains in the native language measures compared to the other two at-risk groups which did not receive MSLT instruction. No significant difference was observed between the MSLT at-risk group and the not-at-risk group on foreign language proficiency measures. The most important finding of this series of studies is the fact that at-risk groups who received MSLT instruction were able to demonstrate similar gains to the participants in not-at-risk groups, highlighting that the MSLT approach has been beneficial in teaching learners with learning difficulties such as dyslexia.

Warnick and Caldarella (2016) compared a group of learners who received multisensory phonic reading instruction with a group who received standard reading instruction. The pre/post-test comparison showed that those who received multisensory instruction demonstrated significant gains in norm-referenced reading measures compared to the other group. In Stewart's (2011) study, a group who received multisensory phonic instructions was compared with a group who received traditional basal reading instruction. Both groups consisted of struggling readers. Word attack and word recognition ability was measured in a pre/post-test design. The findings highlighted a significant increase in word decoding skills among those who received multisensory instruction. Joshi et al. (2002) also compared a basal instruction group with a multisensory instruction group and found that the multisensory group showed statistically significant gains in phonological awareness, decoding and reading comprehension compared to the basal instruction group which showed significant gains only in reading comprehension. Korkmaz and Karatepe (2018) studied the reading comprehension performance of two groups of fourth graders in Turkey. One group was taught reading using multisensory techniques, whereas the other group received traditional reading instruction. A reading achievement test was used in the pre/post and delayed post-tests. Statistically significant gains in the reading test were demonstrated by learners who received multisensory instruction compared to the other group in both the post and delayed-post tests. In addition to these, some other studies such as Downey et al. (2000), Denton et al. (2003) and Ritchey and Goeke (2006) found a positive impact of multisensory instruction.

5. TEACHER PERCEPTIONS: A STUDY

The research evidence discussed so far is based on studies that compared learners who received multisensory instruction with those who received other types of instruction. It is also important to discuss teachers' experience with using the MSLT approach to analyse the positive aspects as well as challenges they face in using the approach. The following is a discussion of a study that investigated teacher perceptions of MSLT instruction. This was conducted as part of the project discussed in Indrarathne (2019).

5.1 CONTEXT

In Sri Lanka, English is taught as a second language to all children from grade three (starting from the age of about eight years) and is a compulsory subject in the General Certificate of Education (Ordinary Level) examination, which is a national examination equivalent to GCSE in the UK. However, students' performance in the English language in this examination is poor (Perera, 2010), and many students reach only the A2 proficiency level (CEFR-Common European Framework of Reference) by the end of secondary school (Shepherd & Ainsworth, 2018). In addition to the overall poor performance among students, learners with dyslexia seem to be at a disadvantage, as SpLDs are not really addressed in the mainstream education system in the country. There is very limited attention to providing comprehensive knowledge on SpLDs in the existing pre- and in-service teacher training programmes in Sri Lanka.

A teacher training programme was conducted in 2017 to raise English language teachers' awareness of dyslexia, its features and consequences. In addition, the programme attempted to raise their awareness of how to accommodate learners with dyslexia in the English language classroom. In this programme, several workshops were conducted for English language teacher trainers, language policy planners, textbook and assessment writers and a group of English language teachers from the mainstream education system and private institutes. Two-day workshops were conducted for teacher trainers and one-day workshops were conducted for the rest of the participants. The content covered in the workshops included: main features of dyslexia, identifying learners with dyslexia in class, inclusive classroom techniques, the MSLT approach and its application in teaching language skills and systems, and assessing learners with dyslexia. Workshop materials were designed based on the content covered in Kormos and Smith (2012) and DysTEFL project materials (DysTEFL2, 2016).

Immediately after the workshops, participant feedback was obtained to assess teacher perception of the content covered in the workshops. Several semi-structured interviews were conducted a few months after the workshops to assess the effectiveness of the training and to understand teachers' experience of using the MSLT approach in their classrooms.

5.2 PARTICIPANTS

One hundred teacher trainers, 172 teachers and 19 policy planners/textbook writers/ language assessment writers took part in the workshops. The teacher trainers had more than ten years of experience in English language teaching and represented all districts of the country – both rural and urban areas. Their teaching experience varied from three to 38 years. The other participants such as the curriculum developers, policy planners, textbook writers and language test developers had more than 15 years of teaching experience. This analysis uses data collected from these workshop participants on two occasions (1) immediately after they completed the training (2) two to three months after the training. Eight teacher trainers and ten teachers took part in the semi-structured interviews conducted in the second phase.

5.3 INSTRUMENTS

A questionnaire was used to collect immediate feedback from the participants after the workshops. There was one specific question asking them to comment on the teaching techniques that they had learnt in the workshop. In the semi-structured interviews, participants were particularly asked to comment on their use of the MSLT approach in teaching learners with and without learning difficulties. They were asked to comment on their use of the teaching techniques taught in the workshops in their real classroom teaching. They were also asked to comment on challenges that they had encountered when using the MSLT approach in class.

5.4 PROCEDURE

Anonymous questionnaire responses were collected from the workshop participants immediately after each workshop. Semi-structured interviews were conducted individually, and each took approximately 15 minutes. Interviews were conducted via Skype and phone or face-to-face. All interviews were conducted in English. Collected data were analysed using the thematic analysis approach (Bryman, 2012). Transcriptions were done only for the content; all paralinguistic features were ignored as those were irrelevant to the study.

5.5 RESULTS

In the post workshop feedback, many participants commented on the perceived usefulness of the MSLT approach. Ninety-eight per cent of the teachers and teacher trainers commented that they would be able to use the MSLT approach in their classroom. Three teachers said:

> *Yes, we can adapt* [the] *MSLT method even with* [students without dyslexia] [Extract 1: T16]

> *Using the MSLT approach, not only* [students with dyslexia] *but other slow learners too* [can] *be identified and it is good to simplify some lessons in any class* [Extract 2: T14]

154

> *Some methods can be applied in a normal classroom too. Specially colour coding, divide the text into chunks, sounds with small changes* [Extract 3: T6]

The above quotes highlight that the participants presumed that the MSLT approach can be used with learners who do not have dyslexia type difficulties too. There were no negative comments or concerns on the use of the MSLT approach in class. When asked if they assumed that they would find any difficulties in using inclusive classroom techniques, most comments concerned a lack of resources and time to prepare visual aids. The following comment summarises the only concern given by most participants to the question of whether they would face any difficulties:

> *...preparation of visual materials, cards, and the durability of the materials for all time use* [and] *using them with students where the classes are bigger.* [Extract 4: T8]

When the semi-structured interviews took place two to three months after the workshops, teachers had had the opportunity to trial some of the MSLT techniques in their class. One teacher mentioned that she used flashcards with struggling learners and had observed changes. The teacher mentioned that two struggling learners were given time to complete the task on their own using the flashcards before making them join the other students. This initial preparation stage seemed to have assisted them to perform the follow-up task with the non-struggling learners successfully.

The following is a quote from another teacher who used multisensory activities to help a struggling reader in class. The student who told the teacher he had a problem with reading at a stretch or reading long sentences because he did not see them clearly, seemed to have benefited from the colour coding used in reading. The teacher said:

> *I select colour text for him he told me that colour texts reading is easier than reading black and white texts* [Extract 6: TT4I]

The teacher also mentioned that:

> *I don't give him long paragraphs to read actually I break the long paragraphs to small pieces, and I ask him to read* [Extract 6: TT4I]

Several participant teachers also commented on how the MSLT approach made positive changes to their students. The following is a summary of changes that a teacher noticed after providing multisensory instruction to struggling learners.

> *Yeah...they were so into the lesson...while I bring something different to the class and what's more [the materials are] visually friendly for them...they were into the lesson like specially the* [students with dyslexia]*...like I have two to handle...they were more into what's happening in the class than the normal lessons* [Extract 7: T8I]

The participants were also asked to comment on any problems that they faced when using the MSLT approach in class. Unlike the feedback given in the post workshop questionnaire, teachers had identified some other issues when implementing the MSLT approach in class. The main issue is the negative attitudes of their colleagues. It seems a lack of training provided to teachers on topics such as dyslexia and the MSLT negatively influences the way they treat learners. It may also be difficult to make changes in the classroom without the help of colleagues. As one teacher mentioned, language teachers are not class teachers so if the classroom setting is too distracting for learners with dyslexia, for example, if there are too many posters around the blackboard, language teachers alone may not be able to change it:

> *I asked them not to paste too many posters around the blackboard and all and some listened to me and some* [did] *not...because actually they don't have the training* [Extract 8: T7I]

Similar to the issues highlighted in the post-workshop questionnaire, one teacher commented on the problem of lack of resources and that they have to prepare materials when using the MSLT approach:

> *because in our classrooms normally we don't have much of the resources...like to use multimedia and IWBs [interactive white boards] and all...so that would be a problem...because it's a lot for the teacher before coming to the class...like preparing visual aids and all...so that would be a small issue...other than that I haven't come across anything* [Extract 10: T8]

In summary, this study of teacher perceptions of the usefulness of the MSLT approach and the challenges in applying it in the classroom highlights that the MSLT approach helps all learners, in particular learners with dyslexia or slow learners to cope with the work in the language classroom. More importantly, the approach seems to have assisted learners with dyslexia to be on a par with those who do not have dyslexia type difficulties in terms of participating in classroom activities. However, teachers seem to need explicit training on the approach and resources to prepare materials to successfully implement the method in class.

6. CONCLUSION

As pointed out previously, learners with dyslexia face challenges in learning second/foreign languages due to various difficulties that they encounter. The main difficulties that they face are in phonological processing, memory, accurate and fluent word recognition, spelling and decoding. As a result, their performance in reading, listening, speaking and writing can vary and they may need additional help from the teacher.

The existing research evidence highlights that the MSLT approach can be successfully used in teaching second/foreign languages to learners with dyslexia. Teachers should consider the main features of the MSLT approach: providing input and practice in auditory, visual, kinaesthetic and tactile pathways. Extensive practice through drills, frequent revision of learnt items, building up new items based on previously learnt items, teaching learning strategies and presenting a small amount of work at a given time are important aspects to be taken into consideration. There is research evidence that the MSLT approach is suitable not only for learners with dyslexia, but also for those who do not have dyslexia type difficulties. Therefore, it can be used as an inclusive classroom approach in any second/foreign language classroom.

REFERENCES

Baddeley, A. D. (2015). Working memory in second language learning. In Z. Wen, M. Borges, & A. McNeill (Eds.), *Working memory in second language acquisition and processing* (pp. 17–28). Bristol: Multilingual Matters.

Baddeley, A. D., & Hitch, G. (1974). Working memory. In G. H. Bower (Ed.), *The psychology of learning and motivation: Advances in research and theory* (Vol. 8, pp. 47–89). New York, NY: Academic Press.

Cain, K. (2006). Individual differences in children's memory and reading comprehension: An investigation of semantic and inhibitory deficits. *Memory, 14*, 553–569.

Cambridge University Press. (2019). *The use of L1 in English language teaching.* Retrieved from https://languageresearch.cambridge.org/images/CambridgePapersInELT_UseOfL1_2019_ONLINE.pdf

Downey, D., Snyder, L., & Hill, B. (2000). College students with dyslexia: Persistent linguistic deficits and foreign language learning. *British Journal of Dyslexia, 6*, 101–111.

Denton, C. A., Foorman, B. R., & Mathes, P. G. (2003). Perspective: Schools that "beat the odds." *Remedial and Special Education, 24*, 258–261.

DysTEFL2. (2016). *Dyslexia for teachers of English as foreign language.* Retrieved from www.dystefl.eu

Frith, U. (1986). A developmental framework for developmental dyslexia. *Annals of Dyslexia, 36*, 69–81.

Future Learn / Lancaster University. (n.d.). Dyslexia and Foreign Language Teaching MOOC. Retrieved from https://www.futurelearn.com/courses/dyslexia

Ganschow, L., & Sparks, R. (1995). Effects of direct instruction in Spanish phonology on the native language skills and foreign language aptitude of at-risk foreign language learners. *Journal of Learning Disabilities, 28*, 107–120.

Gillingham, A., & Stillman, B. W. (1960). *Remedial training for children with specific disability in reading, spelling and penmanship.* Cambridge, MA: Educators Publishing Service.

Hook, P. E., & Jones, S. D. (2002). The importance of automaticity and fluency for efficient reading comprehension. *Perspectives, 28*(1), 9–14.

Indrarathne, B. (2017). Dyslexia and English language teaching in Sri Lanka: A teacher training guide. Retrieved from http://www.dyslexiaprojectsl.com/wp-content/uploads/2017/01/guide-book-final-copy.pdf

Indrarathne, B. (2019). Accommodating learners with dyslexia in English language teaching in Sri Lanka: Teachers' knowledge, attitudes, and challenges. *TESOL Quarterly, 53*(3), 630–654.

International Dyslexia Association. (n.d.). *Definition of dyslexia*. Retrieved from https://dyslexiaida.org/definition-of-dyslexia/#:~:text=%E2%80%9CDyslexia%20is%20a%20specific%20learning,poor%20spelling%20and%20decoding%20abilities

International Dyslexia Association. (2000a). *Multisensory teaching fact sheet #69-01/100*. Retrieved from http://ma.dyslexiaida.org/wp-content/uploads/sites/7/2016/03/Multisensory_Teaching.pdf

International Dyslexia Association. (2000b). *Orton-Gillingham-based and/or multisensory structured language approaches fact sheet # 68 – 05/02*. Retrieved from https://www.dys-add.com/resources/Myths/IDA.OG.Fact.Sheet.pdf

International Dyslexia Association. (2020). *Structured literacy: Effective instruction for students with dyslexia and related reading difficulties*. Retrieved from https://dyslexiaida.org/structured-literacy-effective-instruction-for-students-with-dyslexia-and-related-reading-difficulties/

Joshi, R. M., Dahlgren, M., & Boulware-Gooden, R. (2002). Teaching reading in an inner-city school through a multisensory teaching approach. *Annals of Dyslexia, 52(*1), 229–242.

Korkmaz, S. C., & Karatepe, C. (2018). The impact of multisensory language teaching on young English learners' achievement in reading skills. *Novitas-ROYAL, 12*(2), 80–95.

Kormos, J., & Smith, A. M. (2012). *Teaching languages to students with specific learning differences*. Bristol: Multilingual Matters.

Lyon G. R., Shaywitz, S. E., & Shaywitz, B. A. (2003). A definition of dyslexia. *Annals of Dyslexia, 53*, 1–14.

Orton-Gillingham Academy. (2018). *What is the Orton-Gillingham approach?* Retrieved from https://www.ortonacademy.org/resources/what-is-the-orton-gillingham-approach/

Pearson English. (2014). Dyslexic learners in the EFL classroom. https://www.youtube.com/watch?v=ofDMOmuG4GQ

Pennington, B. F. (2006). From single to multiple deficit models of developmental disorders. *Cognition, 101*(2), 385–413.

Perera, M. (2010). *Coping with the student heterogeneity in the English language classroom*. Colombo: National Education Commission.

Perfetti, C. A. (2007). Reading ability: Lexical quality to comprehension. *Scientific Studies of Reading, 11*, 357–383.

Ritchey, K. D., & Goeke, J. L. (2006). Orton-Gillingham and Orton-Gillingham-based reading instruction: A review of the literature. *Journal of Special Education, 40*, 171–183.

Schneider, E., & Crombie, M. (2003). *Dyslexia and foreign language learning*. London: David Fulton Publisher.

Schneider, E., & Ming, K. (2019). Masters of morphology: Explicit multisensory structured metacognitive language strategies to foster adolescent learners' content vocabulary. *The Clearing House: A Journal of Educational Strategies, Issues and Ideas, 92*(3), 101–111.

Shepherd, E., & Ainsworth, V. (2018). *English impact: An evaluation of English language capability – Sri Lanka*. Colombo: British Council.

Sparks, R., Artzer, M., Patton, J., Ganschow, L., Miller, K., Hordubay, D., & Walsh, G. (1998). Benefits of multisensory structured language instruction for at-risk foreign language learners: A comparison study of high school Spanish students. *Annals of Dyslexia, 48*, 239–270.

Sparks, R., & Ganschow, L. (1993). The effects of a multisensory structured language approach on the native and foreign language aptitude of at-risk foreign language learners: A follow-up and replication study. *Annals of Dyslexia, 43*, 194–216.

Sparks, R., Ganschow, L., Kenneweg, S., & Miller, K. (1991). Use of an Orton-Gillingham method to teach a foreign language to dyslexic learning-disabled students: Explicit teaching of phonology in a second language. *Annals of Dyslexia, 41*, 96–118.

Sparks, R., Ganschow, L., Pohlman, J., Artzer, M., & Skinner, S. (1992). The effects of a multisensory, structured language approach on the native and foreign language aptitude skills of at-risk foreign language learners. *Annals of Dyslexia, 42*, 25–53.

Sparks, R., & Miller, K. (2000). Teaching a foreign language using multisensory structured language techniques to at-risk learners: A Review. *Dyslexia, 6*, 124–132.

Stanovich, K. E. (1988). Explaining the differences between the dyslexic and the garden-variety poor readers: The phonological-core variable-difference model, *Journal of Learning Disabilities, 21*, 590–612.

Stewart, E. D. (2011). The impact of systematic multisensory phonics instructional design on the decoding skills of struggling readers (Doctoral dissertation). Retrieved from ProQuest Dissertations and Theses database (Publication No. 3443911).

Warnick, K., & Caldarella, P. (2016). Using multisensory phonics to foster reading skills of adolescent delinquents. *Reading & Writing Quarterly, 32*(4), 317–335.

9

EXPLORING VIRTUAL SIMULATIONS TO DEVELOP TEACHERS' ABILITY TO SUPPORT ENGLISH LANGUAGE LEARNERS' SOCIAL-EMOTIONAL DEVELOPMENT

Sharen Bertrando, National University, USA

ABSTRACT

As federal and state initiatives and educational policy institutes continue to promote social-emotional learning (SEL) for K-12 students in public schools within the United States, innovative approaches play a key role for both future and current teachers to keep up with existing research and best practices to prepare them to support the linguistic, cultural and social-emotional needs of English language learners (ELLs). Although "on the ground" fieldwork before candidates enter the profession has long been the traditional means for future teachers to learn and practise classroom teaching, just as professional development has been for current teachers, limited options alone do not customise training experiences, offer safe environments to learn or optimise learning spaces. As dynamic spaces afforded by technological advances beyond the traditional settings (e.g., brick and mortar instruction and practice), virtual simulations can depict a wide range of student characteristics and novel scenarios to help teachers to perfect their skills without the risk of harm to students, allow for flexible anytime/anywhere access to learning, and the ability to transfer their theoretical knowledge into action through repeated trials. The argument for using virtual simulated teaching environments to complement real-time training to support the social-emotional development with the advancement of language acquisition of ELLs is addressed.

KEYWORDS

English language learners, social-emotional learning, virtual simulations.

1. INTRODUCTION

Recent contributions from neuroscience and the sciences of learning and development affirm that major domains of human development (social, emotional and academic) are deeply intertwined in the brain and behaviour and, therefore, all are central to learning (Darling-Hammond & Cook-Harvey, 2018; Farrington et al., 2012; Immordino-Yang, Darling-Hammond, & Krone, 2018). As a result, there is growing interest to transition from an academic achievement standardised test score focus to a *whole child* approach to education in the United States. Co-authors of a recent report from the Learning Policy Institute, Darling-Hammond and Cook-Harvey (2018), argue that educating the whole child "supports students' growth across all the developmental pathways – physical, psychological, cognitive, social and emotional" (p. v) that have long-lasting positive outcomes to prepare young people for success in college, careers and life. This newly discovered interconnectedness of co-cognitive factors has influenced education policy-making decisions to adopt social and emotional learning (SEL) instruction alongside academic learning (Beyer, 2017; Hough, Kalogrides, & Loeb, 2017; Schonert-Reichl, Kitil, & Hanson-Peterson, 2017).

While various means to promote students' academic, social and emotional learning currently exist and are evolving, a generic approach to address SEL competences does not meet the needs of English language learners (ELLs). ELLs in American classrooms come from diverse racial, cultural and linguistic backgrounds. They have different lived experiences than their English-proficient peers. As federal and state initiatives and educational policy institutes continue to promote SEL in schools, training plays a key role for both current and future teachers to keep up with existing research and best practices to prepare them to support the linguistic, cultural and social-emotional needs of ELLs. Although fieldwork, also known as practicum, has long been the traditional means for future teachers (i.e., education and training before candidates enter the field) to learn and practise classroom teaching, just as professional development has been for current teachers (i.e., ongoing professional development), they are not always customised training experiences, safe environments to learn, or optimal learning spaces that afford repeated practice.

The increasingly complex skills and knowledge required for teachers to address SEL for ELLs calls for novice approaches to learn and practise teaching. As dynamic spaces afforded by technological advances beyond the traditional settings (e.g., brick and mortar instruction and practice), virtual simulations can depict a wide range of student characteristics and novel scenarios to help teachers to perfect their skills without the risk of harm to students and allow for flexible anytime/anywhere access to learning. This article explores the use of virtual simulations to complement real-time training to support social-emotional development with the advancement of language acquisition of ELLs.

2. SOCIAL EMOTIONAL LEARNING

Social-emotional learning is a framework for students to improve academic performance, social behaviours, and decrease emotional distress (Durlak et al., 2011). Comprehensive, systematic pedagogical efforts of social, emotional, ethical and cognitive learning were created to increase effectiveness and foster progress through empirical and theoretical research (Collaborative for Academic, Social, and Emotional Learning [CASEL], 2019). As defined by CASEL (2019) in 1994, social-emotional learning is:

> the processes in which students acquire and effectively apply the knowledge, attitudes, and skills necessary to understand and manage emotions, set and achieve positive goals, feel and show empathy of others, establish and maintain positive relationships, and make responsible decisions ("What is SEL?", para. 1).

CASEL identified the following five core interrelated competence components that support student cognitive and affective success: (1) *self-awareness*: the ability to recognise one's emotions and values as well as one's strengths and challenges; (2) *self-management*: the ability to manage emotions and behaviours to achieve one's goals; (3) *social awareness*: the ability to show understanding and empathy for others; (4) *relationship skills*: the ability to form positive relationships, work in teams and deal effectively with conflict; and (5) *responsible decision making*: the ability to make ethical, constructive choices about personal and social behaviour (Denham & Brown, 2010; Zins, Bloodworth, Weissberg, & Walberg, 2007). The SEL competences are manifested in *behaviours* (e.g., class attendance, participation in class and completing assignments), *perseverance* (e.g., performing the best to one's ability), *mindsets* (e.g., attitudes and beliefs about oneself), *learning strategies* (e.g., strategies one uses to aid in remembering and thinking), and *social skills* (e.g., collaboration, responsibility and empathy) (Farrington et al., 2012). SEL interventions that address these core competences have been shown to increase students' academic performance; improve classroom behaviour; increase their ability to manage stress and depression; and increase positive attitudes about themselves, others and school (Durlak et al., 2011).

3. SEL MOVEMENT

As state and federal policies acknowledge the positive outcomes of research in social and emotional development to improve student outcomes, SEL is becoming a major focus in K-12 public education in the United States. The Every Student Succeeds Act (ESSA, 2015) provided an important opportunity for states to broaden the definition of student success to include measures of students' social-emotional, as well as academic development. ESSA requires state accountability systems to include indicators of school quality and student success in addition to indicators of academic outcomes. Federal funds can be used to include training in classroom instruction and schoolwide initiatives that enable students to acquire the knowledge, attitudes and skills most conducive to social and emotional competence. SEL competences are students' capacity to integrate skills, attitudes and behaviours to deal effectively with daily tasks and challenges (CASEL, 2018).

As more states adopt policies and mandate state-level SEL standards, it is critical to consider how SEL initiatives impact ELLs and training to support future and current teachers. According to the National Clearinghouse for English Language Acquisition (2018), there are almost five million ELLs acquiring English in the public school system throughout the United States, representing almost 10 per cent of the population. Based on the data from the National Center for Education Statistics (2019), it is predicted that by the year 2025 approximately 25 per cent of all public-school students in the United States will have a primary language background other than English. As the number of ELLs in our country continues to grow, proactive measures to identify how these adoptions will affect them and how they can be tailored to better meet the unique needs are essential.

4. SEL NEEDS OF ELLS

As teachers face the increased diversity of students in their classrooms, they are required to understand the social-emotional development of all their students. While ELLs in the US public school system come from diverse racial, cultural and linguistic backgrounds as refugees, immigrants, adoptees and US born children of non-English-speaking parents, they frequently share common experiences of isolation, discrimination and acculturation, which can negatively impact social and emotional development (Beyer, 2017).

Researchers Castro Olivo et al. (2013) and Halle et al. (2014) contend that ELLs frequently endure higher levels of stress due to marginalisation, social alienation, acculturation stress, trauma and encounter negative academic outcomes combated with minimal social-emotional competences. These shared experiences can negatively impact positive academic outcomes combated with marginal social and emotional development (Beyer, 2017).

Medley (2012) argues that without exposure to some type of healing from distress, ELLs will be hindered from learning another language. As Butvilofsky, Escamilla, Soltero-González, & Aragon (2012) point out, second language learning is a complex phenomenon that includes several aspects such as linguistic, cognitive, sociocultural, psychological and emotional, reminding teachers of the psychological and emotional daily demands of being a second language learner and the stress involved in having his/her intelligence and ability judged in a language he/she is still learning.

5. RESEARCH ON SEL WITH ELLS

In general, SEL has been shown to address and assuage social-emotional obstacles for K-12 public school children by providing them with emotional coping skills, relationship-building skills and self-advocacy skills (Durlak et al., 2012). However, there is a dearth of research devoted to the impact of embedding SEL into the curriculum specifically for ELLs. The following are recent SEL studies that exemplify the significance of ELLs' social-emotional well-being.

Niehaus and Adelson (2014) conducted a study focusing on elementary-aged students' self-concept as an aspect of SEL with Spanish-speaking (87%) and Asian (6%) language background ELLs asserting that self-concept has a significant impact on academic performance, on physical and on social-emotional well-being. They identified specific environmental stressors that can negatively impact ELLs such as trauma and displacement because of immigration, family separations, poverty, discrimination and cultural conflicts between home and school (2013). They concluded that ELLs with limited English proficiency tend to have lower interpersonal skills and higher internalisation of problems, higher externalising problems, and fewer adaptive skills than English-speaking peers. They attributed language acquisition and socio-economic status to these higher risk factors. They concluded that when ELLs' anxiety in the classroom increased, their level of academic achievement decreased.

In another study, Brown and his colleagues (2012) focused on how to best support and promote SEL and prevent violence in Latino youth due to the various risk factors that they may experience such as poverty, racial discrimination, acculturation and stress. They evaluated the school-wide effects of Second Step in pre-school through fourth grade for a predominantly Latino ELL population. (Second Step is a violence prevention curriculum that aims to promote a positive school environment and decrease school violence.) They found significant increases in social and emotional knowledge in Latino students from low socio-economic backgrounds. The findings are important because individuals from minority groups and low SEL backgrounds may be at greater risk for being negatively affected by detrimental outcomes.

While the results of these two studies demonstrate the need to attend to the social-emotional learning of ELLs, further interpretation is warranted. In the study conducted by Niehaus and Adelson (2014), when data were disaggregated between the two different ELL groups, differences were found. Spanish-speaking ELLs acquired language at a slower rate and almost twice the number fell into poverty when compared to their Asian ELLs. Although Asian language ELLs had a lower risk of externalising problems, they rated themselves significantly lower on peer relationships, experienced difficulties making friends, felt not liked by peers or had fewer friends when compared to Spanish-speaking ELLs. Although Spanish-speaking ELLs and Asian-speaking ELLs share common experiences, detangling the data indicates further analysis is needed before prescribing one-size-fits-all SEL interventions.

Furthermore, Brown et al. (2012) caution limitations for interpreting the results of their study. They noted that ELLs received the curriculum in English. Therefore, self-reported post-intervention assessment increases for both non-readers and readers may have been due to improvements in language proficiency due to participation in language acquisition programmes. The authors explain that not all students may have had sufficient language proficiency to completely understand the curriculum depending on their stage of language acquisition. Teaching ELLs in the classroom calls for a deep foundational understanding of language development along with cultural diversity to identify and comprehend the unique social-emotional development of ELLs. As such, researchers advocate for teachers to be cognizant of the social-psychological situation of the ELL students they teach (Medley, 2012).

Findings from the research of these studies highlight the fact that identifying the needs of the social-emotional development of ELLs is complex (Beyer, 2017). ELLs are not a monolithic group. As such, a one-size-fits-all approach to SEL will not work. As the number of ELLs enrolled in classrooms across the United States continues to rise, the accountability of teacher preparation training programmes and professional development to prepare them to reach the needs of ELLs in their classrooms requires immediate attention.

6. SEL TRAINING FOR TEACHING ELLS

Identifying what to address and how to implement SEL programmes for ELLs is unclear due to the nascent research on the connection between SEL and ELLs. A policy brief from the American Youth Policy Forum suggested incorporating SEL during English-as-a-second-language instruction (ESL) (Beyer, 2017). As required by federal and state laws, ELLs in the United States are provided ESL instruction and assessed annually to monitor their growth in language proficiency and to determine the continued need for support with English language development. The amount and duration of ESL instruction may decrease as the student's language proficiency increases.

For ELLs, evidence points to three distinct ways to build social and emotional competences during ESL instruction: (a) intentional changes to classroom culture, (b) explicit SEL instruction, and (c) implementation of ELL evidence-based practices in school and cultural structuring (Beyer, 2017; Byrne, 2013; Herrmann, 2013). However, there are several types of ESL instruction throughout the United States. Some ESL options include *push-in*, *pull-out*, *sheltered instruction*, and *bilingual* programmes. Push-in instruction occurs when the ELL teacher collaborates and co-instructs with the general education teacher. Pull-out occurs when the ELL teacher removes ELLs from a mainstream class for targeted English language development instruction. Sheltered instruction requires ELLs to learn the general education curriculum in a separate room with an ELL teacher. Bilingual education occurs when the entire school has an established curriculum that is taught in both the native and target languages. The type of ESL instruction delivered as well as the composition of ELLs calls for variations of SEL implementation. Providing explicit training to identify the needs of the social-emotional development of the increasing number of ELLs presents challenges (Beyer, 2017; Hammond, 2015) and reasons to seek novel ways to prepare teachers.

7. VIRTUAL SIMULATIONS

Made possible through emerging technologies, simulations have proven to be an effective way to teach, develop and evaluate the skills in the fields of aviation, business, military training and medicine (Dieker et al., 2014). In their review of literature, Kaufman and Ireland (2016) found support for simulations in the following fields: in aviation for practice and evaluation such as crisis and response through scenarios; in business to support hiring decisions; for a range of training purposes in the military where the soldier assumes a role and performs tasks; and in medicine during residency where the intern is presented problem-based scenarios where virtual patients represent actual patient problems. However, the literature around simulations for teachers in the field of education is nascent (Clarke, 2013).

The use of simulations in the field of pre-service training and in-service training for teachers has recently gained attention across the globe (e.g., in Australia, Canada, Greece, the Philippines, Puerto Rico, South Korea, the United Arab Emirates, the United Kingdom and the United States) to enhance pedagogical practice (Cheong, 2010; Collum, Christensen, Delicath, & Johnston, 2019; Dieker et al., 2014; Dieker et al., 2015; Kim & Blankenship, 2013; Medula, 2017; Park, Ryu, & McChesney, 2019; Stavroulia, Makri-Botsari, Psycharis, & Kekkeris, 2016; Tyler-Wood et al., 2015). In fact, several institutes of education require time spent in virtual simulations as part of the screening process, coursework and fieldwork (Dieker et al., 2014). For example, Stanford University uses a simulation to screen potential second-language teacher assistants to evaluate their language fluency and communication skills, and Teach for America, a non-profit agency, requires candidates to teach simulated classes as part of their final interviews before hiring (Kaufman & Ireland, 2016). Utah State University uses simulations in special education teacher preparation programmes as a blended course approach combining online with face-to-face instruction (Dieker et al., 2014).

Virtual simulations are dynamic models of reality implemented as a system (Badiee & Kaufman, 2015). They have distinctive characteristics from games as they do not involve competition (Kaufman & Ireland, 2016). Effective simulations produce a sense of realism (Dieker et al., 2014) where users are active participants rather than passive observers (Badiee & Kaufman, 2015). They can provide relevant and authentic scenarios for practising and refining the transfer of newly learnt theory and skills, based on trials, feedback and reflection (Badiee & Kaufman, 2015; Gundel, Piro, Straub, & Smith, 2019). In simulations, users interact with virtual students taking on the role of teachers. Users are offered a variety of tools and resources to use such as a menu of choices to make decisions about how to modify instruction to enhance student progress by interpreting students' performance and behaviour. Through repeated cycles of practice and reflection afforded by the technology, users can analyse classroom decision making, and draw on theory introduced in class, and relate theory back to practice (Tyler-Wood et al., 2015).

8. ADVANTAGES OF SIMULATIONS

Although simulations are not replacements for real-time classroom experiences, they can enhance real-life experiences (Aldrich, 2004; Driver, Zimmer, & Murphy, 2018). Due to technology applications, simulated environments have proven to offer multiple advantages. Simulations can customise training experiences, offer safe environments to learn, optimise learning experiences and allow for repeated practice (Badiee & Kaufman, 2015; Dieker et al., 2014; Dieker et al., 2015; Park, Ryu, & McChesney, 2019).

8.1 CUSTOMISATION

As evident by the unprecedented COVID-19 pandemic, flexible environments for learning and growth presented challenges for teacher training (e.g., limited or no access to students and transitioning to hybrid or remote teaching). Teachers encounter multiple types of students. Therefore, training should be geared to meet teachers' needs and goals. Typical problems with traditional field experience addressed in recent studies included finding enough placement locations so that pre-service teachers could interact with students whose primary language is other than English from multiple countries (Garmon 2004; Lin & Lucey, 2010; McCabe, 2011; Milner, 2006). Furthermore, the pre-service teachers' geographical locations might make working directly with students from multiple languages impossible. Arnett and Freeburg (2008) found that fieldwork did not duplicate authentic situations and was not often meaningful and insightful to pre-service teachers. As a result, they left them with an inaccurate perception of the duties of teaching.

Virtual classrooms can be designed to control the diversity of students (e.g., range of ages, abilities and behaviours), school culture and curriculum to match the variables encountered in the field (Dieker et al., 2014). They can be customised to allow learners to choose what they need to meet their goals (e.g., practise teaching where students with disabilities receive instruction in the general education classroom, try out specific instructional strategies to heighten language proficiency in ELL students, and explore classroom management strategies). In addition, the features of some simulations include the ability to control the level of complexity depending upon the level of the expertise of the user. Customised learning platforms could provide teachers with the means to learn critical skills needed for their success and for the success of the students they teach or will teach (Dieker et al., 2014; Landon-Hayes, Peterson-Ahmad, & Frazier, 2020).

8.2 SAFE DOMAIN

Field experiences can have harmful or negative impacts on students. Cheong (2010) claims that unintended mistakes made by teachers in a classroom may negatively impact students because mistakes cannot be undone. Cheong proposed that an adoption of a safe, easy and effective way to provide teaching practice, to enhance their sense of self-efficacy about teaching, would be valuable.

In virtual settings, users have the freedom to learn from mistakes without harming students. Within safe, controlled environments, teachers can experience the consequences of making complex decisions in the classroom, and how they affect student behaviour, engagement and achievement, to repeatedly practise their teaching skills without negative impact on students (Badiee & Kaufman, 2015; Dieker, et al., 2014). Users reported that they felt comfortable trying out strategies with simulated students without fear of serious consequences on the learning of actual students (Christensen et al., 2011; Dieker et al., 2014).

8.3 OPTIMAL SPACES

Virtual environments are boundless in space and time. Space and time are critical components for adult learners that need to continually stay current with their careers but are hindered to do so in traditional bricks and mortar "seat time" or "credit hour" settings. Learners can work at their own pace, any time, and anywhere to ensure mastery of skills.

Simulations can provide unrestricted access giving learners more time to review and practise their skills when needed, allowing for acceleration or mediation, which builds self-efficacy (one's confidence to complete a task) (Badiee & Kaufman, 2014; Christensen, Knezek, Tyler-Wood, & Gibson, 2011; Gundel et al., 2019). Users claimed that they saw a great benefit in being able to access the simulation lesson multiple times, allowing the ability to transfer their theoretical knowledge into action through repeated trials (Dieker et al., 2014).

9. SIMULATIONS IN TEACHER EDUCATION

The following are the descriptions of four prominent simulation-based learning models currently used to train pre-service and in-service teachers using virtual environment platforms. Included are studies that address training for teachers of ELLs.

9.1 ClassSim

ClassSim, awarded through a grant by the Australian Research Council and developed by the Faculty of Education at the University of Wollongong, is a classroom simulation developed to provide pre-service teachers with access to additional classroom experience in a virtual environment (Carrington, Kervin, & Ferry, 2006). It is based upon a "literacy block" representing authentic classroom teaching lessons or "episodes" that can link in a variety of ways according to the learning needs of its users (Ferry et al., 2005). The user takes on the role of an elementary teacher of a typical class of diversified students during literacy lessons, known as a literacy block. The classroom includes three targeted students: a refugee child from Afghanistan with limited English, the student's friend, whose primary language is English, and a student with Attention Deficit Hyperactivity Disorder (ADHD). During the episodes, the user is faced with a number of decisions, including relating to the relationship between an English language learner and her friend. In tandem during the lessons, the user is required to make decisions about classroom management and organisational steps to deliver instruction. A unique feature is a "thinking space" where pre-service teachers can reflect on their experiences during the lessons (Ferry et al., 2005).

ClassSim was developed in response to a reported number of limitations of pre-service teacher programmes in Australia regarding the quality of the practicum and the generalisability of course work to authentic application in the field (Carrington et al., 2006). Findings revealed that pre-service teachers felt that the "thinking space" provided a framework where they could build connections between theory, their training and practical experiences, and a space to provide a rationale for their decision making (Ferry et al., 2005).

9.2 SECOND LIFE

Second life, developed by Linden Labs in 2003, is an online three-dimensional (3D) virtual environment, where players take on the role of online avatars as personal manifestations of themselves, to interact with other players (Dieker et al., 2014; Inman, Wright, & Hartman, 2010). The 3D virtual platform allows students and teachers to collaborate simultaneously via voice and typing to exchange ideas and information, working towards lesson objectives (Dieker et al., 2014; Aldosemani & Shepherd, 2014).

Several studies have been conducted using Second Life to reform teacher preparation. Kim and Blankenship (2013) utilised Second Life for English as a collaborative tool for candidates in the English for Speakers of Other Languages (ESOL) pre-service teacher programme, promoting the idea of reconceptualising teachers to receive training to keep up with the trends of professional development. They argue that teacher training should reflect and support future students in a digital society. A study by Aldosemani and Shepherd (2014) used Second Life to explore the use of 3D virtual spaces to build multicultural knowledge for pre-service and in-service teachers. The researchers concluded that Second Life's three-dimensional platform could serve as a space to grow multicultural knowledge through culturally represented locations, artefacts and communications. In a study by O'Brien and Levy (2008, as cited by Aldosemani & Shepherd, 2014), German language students interacted with others in virtual worlds to learn about the culture of the target language. Muir, Allen, Rayner and Cleland (2013) found Second Life to be valuable to enhance the understanding of classroom management within a diverse classroom. A study by Cheong (2010) found it to be useful in regard to pre-service teacher efficacy.

9.3 SIMSCHOOL

SimSchool is a classroom simulation programme that supports the rapid accumulation of teachers' experience in analysing student differences, adapting instruction to individual learner needs, gathering data about the impacts of instruction, and seeing the results of their teaching (simSchool, 2013). It is an Internet-based classroom simulation programme, where users have the opportunity to practise teaching to a group of diverse learners. It provides opportunities for pre-service and in-service teachers to make decisions that are personalised and provides feedback on decisions made within the virtual platform. Each simulated student has an individualised profile that contains information about his/her personality and academic achievement, and teacher reflections modelled after real student profiles. Users access as preset (system generated) simStudents or custom generated simStudents when preparing a classroom to teach. The user must choose from a menu of dropdown tasks and conversational exchanges that best fit the students' needs. In return, the students respond through body language, facial expressions, and brief "chat-typed" responses. The goal is for users to make appropriate decisions to encourage students to successfully complete given tasks (Badiee & Kaufman, 2015).

SimSchool was established through a grant from the Preparing Teachers to Teach with Technology programme of the US Department of Education. The simulated teaching environment has been used in a multitude of studies for a variety of educational purposes. Stavroulia et al. (2016) used the classroom simulation to train Greek pre-service teachers in classroom and behaviour management strategies. Other studies using simSchool showed promising results focusing on teaching in inclusive classrooms with special populations such as students with disabilities (Christensen et al., 2011) and developing teacher self-efficacy to gain a deeper appreciation of diversities represented in classrooms (Bush, Hall, Scott-Simmons, & Saulson, 2012).

9.4 TLE TeachLivE™

TLE TeachLivE™ was developed at the University of Central Florida (UCF), located in Orlando. It is used in over 48 US universities (Kaufman & Ireland, 2016). TLE TeachLivE™ is a mixed reality classroom simulation in the field of education. Pre-service teachers practise, as avatars, the teaching methodologies, and classroom management skills that they have learnt in coursework. Targeted content areas include mathematics, language arts, science, social studies, classroom management, teacher-student relationships, teacher behaviours, students with autism spectrum disorders, and English language learners.

EL TLE TeachLivE™ is a classroom simulation specifically in the field of English learner education. Pre-service teachers as avatars practise the teaching methodologies and classroom management skills that they have learnt in coursework. Users can present new content, review previous work, and test a specific teaching strategy to English language learners and non-native English learners. The programme is used to close the gap between teacher preparation programmes from what they learn in class to their fieldwork in the field (Dieker et al., 2014).

10. DRAWBACKS TO ADOPTION

For virtual simulations to be recognised as viable training opportunities in the discipline of education, they must be seen as valuable and credible by their users. Beyond the issues of the high technical requirements of virtual worlds such as Internet bandwidth, computer processing, and memory, requirements for virtual worlds (e.g., time delay lag associated with environment rendering and complex avatar controls), common drawbacks regarding the educational uses of virtual environments reported by participants in several research studies included usability and suspension of disbelief (Aldosemani & Shepherd, 2014; Badiee & Kaufman, 2015; Christensen et al., 2011; Dieker et al., 2014).

As defined by Badiee and Kaufman (2015), "usability, or the ease with which users are able to carry out tasks using the software" (p. 3). Pre-service and in-service teachers have various technical skills and learning experiences (e.g., using search engines, manipulating objects, marking locations), which, in turn, can affect their level of confidence and comfort using and adopting technology tools. Similarities between study participants reported technical hindrances such as lack of training time to familiarise themselves with application-related and navigation-related tasks in order to become comfortable with the system processes and feedback prior to beginning the activity and technical support (Aldosemani & Shepherd, 2014; Badiee & Kaufman, 2015). User recommendations included scaffolding the learning activities by first focusing on virtual world navigation and slowly transitioning into teaching activities (Aldosemani & Shepherd, 2014). Macedo and Morgado (2010) advised creating collaborative learning environments among users to support each other to work around technical difficulties. Mitigating technology issues to ensure programme familiarity is essential when implementing virtual worlds in education.

According to Dieker et al. (2014), a virtual simulation must provide a sense of real presence so that each user believes it is real and simultaneously feels a sense of personal responsibility for improving his or her practice grounded in a process of critical reflection. Through the use of both hardware and software applications, it is anticipated that users will immerse themselves in virtual worlds to perceive them in some sense as real ones, in other words, a suspension of disbelief. Suspension of disbelief requires a high level of stimulation between the user and technology for learner engagement (Dede 2009, as cited by Dieker et al., 2014). Since teachers may value different activities and objectives of any given system, the design principles of a simulation may hinder or support its viability as a form of professional growth beyond offering face-to-face training. In a study conducted by Badiee and Kaufman (2015), a large number of participants identified several design options which hindered their ability to suspend their disbelief: (a) inappropriate, limited or unrealistic options for conversation and interaction with students; (b) inability to allow users to create their own comments for interactions with students; and (c) general ease of use (e.g., navigation). These results are consistent with previous research (Aldosemani & Shepherd, 2014). A virtual model may be technically functional but will lack relevance to learners in other ways that no amount of technology can fix.

11. CONCLUSION

The purpose of this article was to explore the use of virtual classroom simulations to complement traditional training practices to prepare pre-service and in-service teachers to support the linguistic, cultural and social-emotional needs of ELLs. As the number of ELLs served in the US public school system continues to grow, new approaches for teachers to learn and practise teaching them are essential. Virtual spaces can provide a variety of training experiences and opportunities that are not available in real-world settings. As advances in technology continue in the fields of aviation, business, military training and medicine, it is time to consider its place in education.

REFERENCES

Aldosemani, T., & Shepherd, C. (2014). Second life to support multicultural literacy: Pre- and in- service teachers' perceptions and expectations, *Techtrends, 58*(2), 46–58.

Badiee, F., & Kaufman, D. (2015). Design evaluation of a simulation for teacher education. *SAGE Open, 5*(2), 215824401559245. Retrieved from https://doi.org/10.1177/2158244015592454

Beyer, L. (2017). *Social and emotional learning and traditionally underserved populations: Policy brief.* Retrieved from http://www.aypf.org/wp-content/uploads/2017/10/SEL-Special-Populations_Final.pdf

Brown, J. A., Jimerson, S. R., Dowdy, E., Gonzalez, V., & Stewart, K. (2012). Assessing the effects of school-wide Second Step implementation in predominately English language learner, low SES, Latino sample. *Psychology in the Schools, 49*(9), 864–875.

Bush, L., Hall, J., Scott-Simmons, W., & Saulson, J. (2012). The impact of simSchool on teachers' sense of efficacy. In T. Bastiaens & G. Marks (Eds.), *Proceedings of E-Learn 2012 World Conference on E-Learning in Corporate, Government, Healthcare, and Higher Education 1* (pp. 1755–1760). Montréal, Quebec: Association for the Advancement of Computing in Education (AACE).

Butvilofsky, S. A., Escamilla, K., Soltero-González, L., & Aragon, L. (2012). Promoting reflective teaching through simulation in a study in Mexico program. *Journal of Hispanic Higher Education, 11*(2), 197–212.

Carrington, L., Kervin, L. K., & Ferry, B. (2006). Cognitive tools of ClassSim: Building connections between theory and practice. Australian Association for Research in Education Conference 36th Annual Conference (pp. 1–10). Melbourne: Australian Association for Research Education.

Castro-Olivo, S. M., Tran, O. K., Begum, G. F., Arellano, E. M., Garcia, N. M., & Tung, C. Y. (2013). A comprehensive model for promoting resiliency and preventing violence in schools. *Contemporary School Psychology, 17*(1), 23–24.

Center for Academic, Social, and Emotional Learning [CASEL]. "What is SEL?" Retrieved from http://www.casel.org/what-is-sel/

Cheong, D. (2010). The effects of practice teaching sessions in second life on the change in pre-service teachers' teaching efficacy. *Computers & Education, 55*(1), 868–880.

Christensen, R., Knezek, G., Tyler-Wood, T., & Gibson, D. (2011). SimSchool: An online dynamic simulator for enhancing teacher preparation. *International Journal of Learning Technology, 6*(2), 201–220.

Clarke, L. (2013). Virtual learning environments in teacher education: A journal, a journey. *Technology, Pedagogy, and Education, 22*, 121–131.

Collum, D., Christensen, R., Delicath, T., & Johnston, V. (2019). SimSchool: SPARCing new grounds in research on simulated classrooms. In K. Graziano (Ed.), *Proceedings of Society for Information Technology & Teacher Education International Conference* (pp. 733–739). Las Vegas, NV: Association for the Advancement of Computing in Education (AACE).

Darling-Hammond, L., & Cook-Harvey, C. M. (2018). *Educating the whole child: Improving school climate to support student success*. Palo Alto, CA: Learning Policy Institute. Retrieved from https://learningpolicyinstitute.org/product/educating-whole-child-report

Dieker, L., Hynes, M. C., Hughes, C. E., Hardin, S., & Becht, K. (2015). TLE TeachLivE™: Using technology to provide quality professional development in rural schools. *Rural Special Education Quarterly, 34*(3), 11–16.

Dieker, L. A., Rodriguez, J. A., Lignugaris, B., Kraft, B., Hynes, M. C., & Hughes, C. E. (2014). The potential of simulated environments in teacher education: Current and future possibilities. *Teacher Education and Special Education, 37*(1), 21–33.

Driver, K., Zimmer, K. E., & Murphy, K. M. (2018). Using mixed reality simulations to prepare preservice special educators for collaboration in inclusive settings. *Journal of Technology and Teacher Education, 26*(1), 57–77.

Durlak, J. A., Weissberg, R. P., Dumnicki, A. B., Taylor, R. D., & Schellinger, K. B. (2011). The impact of enhancing students' social and emotional learning: A meta-analysis of school-based universal interventions. *Child Development, 82*(1), 405–432.

ESSA. (2015). *Every student succeeds*. Act, Pub. L. No. 114-95, § 1112(b)(1)(D), 129 Stat. 1802. Retrieved from https://www.ed.gov/essa

Farrington, C. A., Roderick, M., Allensworth, E., Nagoka, J., Keyes, T. S., Johnson, D. W., & Beechum, N. O. (2012). *Teaching adolescents to become learners. The role of noncognitive factors shaping school performance: A critical literature review*. Chicago: University of Chicago Consortium on Chicago School Research. Retrieved from https://files.eric.ed.gov/fulltext/ED542543.pdf

Ferry, B., Kervin, L. K., Cambourne, B. L., Turbill, J. B., Hedberg, J., & Jonassen, D. (2005). Incorporating real experience into the development of a classroom-based simulation. *Journal of Learning Design, 1*(1), 22–32.

Gay, G., & Kirkland, K. (2003). Developing cultural critical consciousness and self-reflection in preservice teacher education. *Theory into Practice, 42*(3), 181–187.

Gundel, E., Piro, J. S., Straub, C., & Smith, K. (2019). Self-efficacy in mixed reality simulations: Implications for preservice teacher education. *The Teacher Educator, 54*(3), 244–269.

Halle, T. G., Whittaker, J. V., Zepeda, M., Rothenberg, L., Anderson, R., Daneri, P., Wessel, J., & Buysse, V. (2014). The social-emotional development of dual language learners: Looking back at existing research and moving forward with purpose. *Early Childhood Research Quarterly, 29*(4), 734–749.

Hough, H., Kalogrides, D., & Loeb, S. (2017). *Using surveys of students' social-emotional learning and school climate for accountability and continuous improvement*. Stanford, CA: Policy Analysis for California Education [PACE]. Retrieved from https://edpolicyinca.org/sites/default/files/SEL-CC_report.pdf

Immordino-Yang, M., Darling-Hammond, L., & Krone, C. (2018). *The brain basics for integrated social, emotional, and academic development*. Aspen, CO: The Aspen Institute. https://www.aspeninstitute.org/publications/the-brain-basis-for-integrated-social-emotional-and-academic-development/

Kaufman, D., & Ireland, A. (2016). Enhancing teacher education with simulations. *Tech Trends, 60*, 260–267.

Kim, D., & Blankenship, R. J. (2013). Using "second life" as a virtual collaborative tool for pre-service teachers seeking English for speakers of other languages endorsement. *Journal of Educational Computing Research, 48*, 19–43.

Landon-Hays, M., Peterson-Ahmad, M. P., & Frazier, A. D. (2020). Learning to teach: How a simulated learning environment can connect theory to practice in general and special education educator preparation programs. *Education Sciences, 10*(7), 184–201.

Lucas, T., Villegas, A. M., & Freedson-Gonzalez, G. (2008). Linguistically responsive teacher education. *Journal Teacher Education, 59*, 361–373.

Macedo, A., & Morgado, L. (2010). Learning to teach in second life. Retrieved from https://www.academia.edu/23580579/LEARNING_TO_TEACH_IN_SECOND_LIFE

Medley, M. (2012). A role for English language teachers in trauma healing. *TESOL Journal, 3*(1), 110–125.

Medula, T. C. (2017). Simulated apprenticeship for pre-service Filipino teachers. *World Journal on Educational Technology: Current Issues, 9*(2), 89–97.

Melnick, H., & Martinez, L. (2019). *Preparing teachers to support social and emotional learning. A case study of San Jose State University and Lakewood Elementary School.* Palo Alto, CA: Learning Policy Institute. Retrieved from https://learningpolicyinstitute.org/sites/default/files/product-files/SEL_CaseStudies_SJSU_Lakewood_REPORT.pdf

Muir, T, Allen, J. M., Rayner, C. S., & Cleland, B. (2013). Preparing pre-service teachers for classroom practice in a virtual world: A pilot study using Second Life. *Journal of Interactive Media in Education 1*(3), Art. 3.

National Center for Education Statistics. (2018, April). *The condition of education.* Retrieved from https://nces.ed.gov/pubs2018/2018144.pdf

National Clearinghouse for English Language Acquisition. (2018). *Fast facts.* Retrieved from https://americanenglish.state.gov/resources/national-clearinghouse-english-language-acquisition

National Research Council. (2010). Preparing teachers: Building evidence for sound policy. Retrieved from http://www.nap.edu/catalog.php?record_id=12882

Niehaus, K., & Adelson, J. L. (2014). School support, parental involvement, and academic and social-emotional outcomes for English language learners. *American Educational Research Journal, 51*(4), 810–844.

Park, S., Ryu, J., & McChesney, K. (2019). Collaborative studio experiences between South Korean and American pre-service teachers: A case study of designing culturally-responsive virtual classroom simulation. *TechTrends, 63*, 217–283.

Schonert-Reichl, K. A., Kitil, M. J., & Hanson-Peterson, J. (2017). To reach the students, teach the teachers: A national scan of teacher preparation and social and emotional learning. A report prepared for the Collaborative for Academic, Social, and Emotional Learning (CASEL). Vancouver, BC: University of British Columbia. Retrieved from https://files.eric.ed.gov/fulltext/ED582029.pdf

SimSchool. (2013). About simSchool. Retrieved from https://www.simschool.org/home/simschool/#about

Stavroulia, K., Makri-Botsari, E., Psycharis, S., & Kekkeris, G. (2016). Using simulations as a tool to enhance classroom management practice. *The International Journal of Information and Learning Technology, 33*(3), 172–185.

Tyler-Wood, M., Estes, M., Christensen, R., Knezek, G., & Gibson, D. (2015). SimSchool: An opportunity for using serious gaming for training teachers in rural areas. *Rural Special Education Quarterly, 34*(3), 17–20.

Zins, J. E., Bloodworth, M. R., Weissberg, R. P., & Walberg, H. J. (2007). The scientific base linking social and emotional learning to school success. *Journal of Educational and Psychological Consultation, 17*(2-3), 191–210.

10 INCLUSIVE COMMUNICATIVE LANGUAGE TEACHING: HIDDEN CONTRADICTIONS AND OVERT PRACTICAL ISSUES

Joanna Pfingsthorn, University of Bremen, Germany

ABSTRACT

The last few decades of foreign language education have been heavily impacted by the pedagogical approach of communicative language teaching and, on some level, influenced by insights from debates within inclusive education. Although the basic theoretical assumptions behind these two teaching philosophies to foster participation and communication within and among societies have by now been accepted as sensible, and are thus hardly ever questioned, their joint practical execution in educational settings is less than straightforward. While inclusive education postulates that teaching practice needs to accept a wide spectrum of learner profiles, communicative language teaching seems to, at least to a degree, favour structured, reflective, autonomous, and open communicators. This article demonstrates how (pre-service) EFL teachers approach such theoretical contradictions in their conceptualisations of teaching practice and, more specifically, in their evaluation of diverse learner personality traits, cognitive styles, preferences and potential deficits that can occur in language learning contexts. In this sense, the article investigates the extent to which foreign language teachers who are trained to teach communicatively resonate with the basic premise of inclusive education to accommodate all learners.

KEYWORDS

Inclusion, diversity, CLT, teacher education.

1. INTRODUCTION

From around 1970, the dominant view in the field of foreign language (FL) education has started to rest on the assumption that becoming proficient in an FL is equivalent to developing functional (intercultural) communicative competence, or the ability to participate actively in real-life communication. While this change in teaching perspective, which some have somewhat hastily likened to an actual paradigm shift (Jacobs & Farrell, 2003), did not seem to resemble a massively radical move comparable to the shift to the Direct Method a hundred years earlier, it gradually established a different core concern of language teaching. The focus emphasised the establishment of correct language habits through rehearsal and repetition in favour of their confident and purposeful use in the real world (Howatt & Smith, 2014). The new approach thus favoured the use of communicative and interactive activities in the classroom, such as "role-plays, improvisation, simulation and cooperative problem-solving or task-based work" (Howatt & Smith, 2014, p. 90). By extension, this implied that students who, for example, develop strategies to keep a conversation going, experiment with language freely, are able to vary their language use flexibly and, according to the needs of the situation, exhibited the desirable profiles that make the learning process more effective (Nunan, 1995).

While attempts to identify learner traits, techniques or strategies that enhance the attainment of communicative competence in an FL certainly have pragmatic merits, they also establish categories of "desired" and "less desired" abilities, choices, attitudes, or behaviour patterns in learning an FL. Such "less-desired" qualities and abilities of students can be perceived as their deficits, which leads to students themselves becoming the source of the problem (Thomas & Loxley, 2007). This is troublesome from the standpoint of inclusive education, which, in its purest form, calls for a radical restructuring of educational systems so that they accommodate all learners (Clough & Corbett, 2000; Frederickson & Cline, 2002) and make participation and engagement in education accessible to all (Smith, 2008). Seen from this perspective, "less-desired" qualities or learning difficulties should be perceived as socially constructed barriers, whose causes should be attributed to the environment and not individuals themselves (Riddick, 2001).

In this sense, the traditional approach of communicative language teaching, which implicitly favours particular abilities, strategies, learner profiles and behavioural patterns over others in the language classroom, stands in opposition to the idea(l)s that underlie inclusive educational settings. This article examines the extent to which pre-service English-as-a-Foreign-Language (EFL) teachers categorise various learner traits, needs, behavioural patterns and learning strategies as desirable and facilitating in the context of EFL education. By extension, the article also examines the degree to which pre-service EFL teachers perceive them as potential barriers to learning EFL. Thereby, the article attempts to uncover hidden contradictions of two prevailing teaching perspectives, inclusive education and communicative language teaching, and reflects upon the practical implications of these insights.

2. THEORETICAL BACKGROUND

In this section, a primarily cognitive and learner-centred perspective is assumed to explain a wide range of individual differences that FL learners may exhibit and investigate some conceptualisations of "good" and "poor" FL learners proposed in the literature. I then investigate guiding principles of inclusive education and illustrate the ways in which they can contradict the basic assumptions of communicative language teaching.

2.1 "GOOD" AND "POOR" LANGUAGE LEARNERS

Communicative competence can be considered a complex and multidimensional construct, as it encompasses several further extensive sub-competences. These include linguistic competence, which covers the use of lexical, phonological, and syntactic knowledge applied in various modalities. They also encompass sensitivity to social conventions of language use, for example in terms of politeness, situationally appropriate use of various language forms and functions as well as intercultural competence, that is, the "knowledge, motivation and skills needed to interact effectively and appropriately with members of different cultures" (Wiseman, 2002, p. 8; see also Canale, 1983; Celce-Murcia, 2007). The fact that this list of various competences, types of knowledge and affective variables that play a role in the language learning process is quite long makes it reasonable to assume that an FL cannot be learnt easily by everyone in a straightforward and comparable manner.

Individual observable differences between language learners have indeed spurred interest in "discovering and disseminating information about successful activities or practices" (Norton & Toohey, 2001, p. 307) and have encouraged efforts to investigate profiles of good language learners. Learners identified or labelled as "good" were perceived as models of desirable constellations of personality traits, cognitive styles, attitudes or learning experiences as well as techniques, strategies and activities that differed from those of "less successful" learners (Brown, 2001; Naiman, Fröhlich, Stern, & Todesco, 1978; Norton & Toohey, 2001; Nunan, 1995; Rubin, 1975; Ushioda, 2008). As Fillmore et al. (1979, p. 221) show, success at learning was often attributed to the intrinsic make-up of a learner: "The secret of Nora's spectacular success as a language learner can be found in the special combination of interests, inclinations, skills, temperament, needs and motivations that comprised her personality."

While some scholars recognised the role of context and "conversations in their communities" that impact learners' success at learning (Norton & Toohey, 2001, p. 310), the very focus on listing the features of a "good learner" remained prevalent until the 1990s and 2000s, which were marked by research efforts to view learner strategies through the perspective of learner preferences (Oxford, 2003). The early focus on "good learner" features revealed that patterns of cognition, affect and behaviour that "good learners" were believed to exhibit included, for example, taking an active approach to the task of language learning. "Good learners" were also believed to be able to notice and exploit the systematic nature of language, to use the language they were learning for communication and interaction, to manage their own affective difficulties with language learning, and to monitor their own language learning performance (Naiman et al., 1978). Other qualities included the ability to develop strategies to keep a conversation going, learn different styles of speech to vary one's language according to the needs of the situation, make intelligent guesses, use one's linguistic knowledge of the mother tongue, other languages and the world to help oneself through the learning process, be creative and experiment with language, also outside the classroom, or exercise human agency and rely on social resources within social networks (Norton & Toohey, 2001; Nunan, 1995).

By extension, FL learners who do not qualify as "good" experience less success or even some degree of learning difficulties in several areas. In fact, substantial research attention has been given to populations of learners classified as "low-achieving," "poor," or "at-risk for learning" (e.g., Ganschow & Sparks, 1995). Some of the learning patterns observed among these populations can be associated with Sparks and Ganschow's (1991) Linguistic Coding Differences Hypothesis. It proposes that if problems with certain language rule systems occur in the mother tongue, they will carry over onto the FL because of their neurological, behavioural, cognitive, and environmental complexity linked to phonological awareness, speed of processing and working memory. A common learning difference of this kind is dyslexia, which has indeed been shown to act as a barrier in the FL learning process (e.g., Brady & Shankweiler, 1991; Nijakowska, 2008; Ramus et al., 2003). Learners experiencing such difficulties will most likely show lower performance in reading rate, accuracy, comprehension, and fluency. They may also fare worse on spelling, grammar and punctuation accuracy as well as the clarity of written expression (American Psychiatric Association, 2013). In addition, they may be unable to identify phonemes and discriminate between them, struggle to memorise and use grammatical structures, independent of the amount of practice. Not uncommon among learners experiencing this form of learning difference are difficulties with rapid retrieval of words and possibly due to problems with automatisation of cognitive processes. Learners with dyslexia may struggle with multitasking, become tired quicker and require clear instructions (Daloiso, 2017).

It has also been shown that there is a considerable overlap between this type of learning difficulty and a number of others, such as high-functioning autism as well as attention deficit hyperactivity disorder (Oxford University Press Experts, n.d.). Neurodiverse learners placed on the Autism spectrum may show "persistent deficits in social communication and social interaction across multiple contexts" (American Psychiatric Association, 2013, p. 50). These can manifest as problems with social-emotional reciprocity, such as failures in typical turn-taking within a conversation, or in initiating and responding to social interactions (American Psychiatric Association, 2013, p. 50). Furthermore, neurodiverse learners placed on the Autism spectrum can experience difficulties in non-verbal communicative behaviours used for social interaction, including eye contact and the use of gestures. Learners on the Autistic spectrum may also experience problems adjusting their behaviour to suit the needs of various social contexts and with participating in imaginative play. This can be traced to inflexibility with respect to the adherence to routines, structures and ritualised patterns of verbal and non-verbal behaviour (American Psychiatric Association, 2013, p. 50).

It has also been suggested that learners with social, emotional and behavioural difficulties, which can be linked to specific learning difficulties or external factors such as trauma, may find the social interaction component of communicative FL classrooms more challenging than others, and hence be less prone to success (Oxford University Press Experts, n.d.). Some investigations suggest that FL learners who are less likely to succeed tend to lack positive appreciation of their abilities and chances of success or self-confidence (Bandura, 1986; Masgoret & Gardner, 2003). Students experiencing learning difficulties tend to lose their motivation to learn languages (Kormos & Csizer, 2010) and develop symptoms of language anxiety (Sparks & Ganschow, 1991). Language anxiety, due to worry and intrusive thoughts, has also been shown to negatively affect working memory capacity and consequently reduce the processing of input and production of output (Eysenck & Calvo, 1992). Moody (1988) additionally demonstrates that language students pursuing a degree in a foreign language tend to show personality traits typically associated with introversion, for example, being oriented towards the inner world and considering deeply before acting to a lesser degree than other college samples.

2.2 INCLUSIVE EDUCATION VS. COMMUNICATIVE LANGUAGE TEACHING

Seen from the perspective of "good" vs. "poor" language learner profiles, learners who experience any of the challenges described above would classify as "poor", as they exhibit constellations of features that are not linked with high degrees of success in FL classrooms. Yet, assigning evaluative labels to psychological profiles, styles, preferences, and dispositions raises the danger of creating artificial divisions that can lead to lowered expectations and potential discrimination against students with disabilities, impairments, or general learning differences. There is some indication that this is what happens in educational institutions when learners face assessment performed by qualified professionals whose goal is to diagnose the potential disability or specific learning difficulty present in the individual. In such situations, students can fall prey to what Wickenden (2019, p. 123) describes as "disabled versus nondisabled binarism" (see also Kormos & Smith, 2012). Such a segregating approach can be challenging or counterproductive, as Emanuelsson (2001, p. 135) points out:

> Once children are identified as 'different' they become problematic to mainstream schools and teachers. From within the categorical perspective the process of labelling children as 'having difficulties', has the effect of investing the source of any difficulty or problem within the child.

Seen from this perspective, operating with the term "good language learner" and/or relying on the very notion that it is possible to identify constellations of FL learner traits and tendencies that are particularly promising is not correct.

Booth and Ainscow (2003, p. 1) suggest the expression "barriers to learning and participation," which is aimed at providing an alternative to the categorical concept of "special educational needs" and encompasses all aspects of the educational experience, including what happens in students' communities, the interaction between them as well as what is taught and how. This line of reasoning represents inclusive education, which in its purest form calls for a radical restructuring of educational systems so that they accommodate all learners (Clough & Corbett, 2000; Frederickson & Cline, 2002) and make participation and engagement in education accessible to all (Smith, 2008). The underlying principle here is one of equity, which means that each learner is provided with what they need. Equity can be contrasted with equality, which implies that everyone receives the same treatment, for example, modelled on the basis of an extremely successful learner.

Over the last two decades, inclusion, as opposed to integration, or what Dyson (2001) calls "responsible inclusion," has become a pivotal perspective in the international arena and even obtained the status of a "global descriptor" (Vislie, 2003, p. 18). Yet, this widespread nod of acknowledgement has yet to result in the establishment of "formally fixed" or "stable" terminology pertaining to the topic (Vislie, 2003, p. 2). Nor has it been able to create enough momentum in teaching practice that would lead to the recognition of the inclusive principle as more than "something that we are taking steps toward" (Allan, 2005, p. 27). However, it is recognised at the education policy level. The operational principles put forward for the implementation of structures and procedures within inclusive education systems by the European Agency for Special Needs and Inclusive Education (https://www.european-agency.org) highlight the need to raise the achievements of learners through the recognition of their talents as well as through the meeting of their individual learning needs and interests, ensuring that all stakeholders value diversity. They also underline that all stakeholders involved in educational processes need to align their attitudes, beliefs, understanding, skills and knowledge with the goals and principles of inclusive education systems through systematic reflection. This is also true for the German teacher education system. Here, educational policy makers highlight that (Hochschulrektorenkonferenz, 2015, p. 3):

> [a]ll teachers should be educated and continuously trained in a way that will allow them to acquire fundamental transferable competences in general teaching and in special needs education. This should also enable them to develop a professional approach to dealing with diversity in schools, particularly in the areas of educational diagnostics and special programmes to foster and support their pupils.

The main premise of inclusive education can also, to some extent, be observed at the European FL education policy level. On the one hand, the Common European Framework of Reference (CEFR) (Council of Europe, 2001) echoes the consensus within FL education to perceive communicative competence in its full complexity as the ultimate goal of FL learning:

> Communicative language competence can be considered as comprising several components: linguistic, sociolinguistic and pragmatic. Each of these components is postulated as comprising, in particular, knowledge and skills and know-how. (Council of Europe, 2001, p. 13)

> There does appear in practice to be a wide, though by no means universal, consensus on the number and nature of levels appropriate to the organisation of language learning and the public recognition of achievement. (Council of Europe, 2001, p. 18)

This operationalisation of communicative competence as a construct seems quite robust and deterministic. On the other hand, the CEFR also recognises the individuality of the learning process, thereby acknowledging learner diversity: "the process of language learning is continuous and individual. No two users of a language, whether native speakers or foreign learners, have exactly the same competences or develop them in the same way" (Council of Europe, 2001, p. 17).

The recently published companion volume to the CEFR (Council of Europe, 2018, p. 36) recommends a more pragmatic approach to defining the desirable goal of learning that is based on the needs relevant to particular groups of learners and, by extension, their preferences and possibly dispositions:

> The reason the CEFR includes so many descriptor scales is to encourage users to develop differentiated profiles. Descriptor scales can be used firstly to identify which language

> activities are relevant for a particular group of learners and then secondly to establish which
> level those learners need to achieve in those activities in order to accomplish their goals.

In this sense, the CEFR does encourage some form of reflection of the relation between various forms of learner diversity and feasibility of the achievement of highest proficiency levels, or the necessity to strive for it. At the same time, the CEFR explicitly avoids specific methodological discussions of its implications for teaching, leaving the question how to organise FL teaching so that it addresses the principles of inclusive education largely unanswered:

> In accordance with the basic principles of pluralist democracy, the Framework aims to be not
> only comprehensive, transparent and coherent, but also open, dynamic and non-dogmatic.
> For that reason, it cannot take up a position on one side or another of current theoretical
> disputes on the nature of language acquisition and its relation to language learning, nor should
> it embody any one particular approach to language teaching to the exclusion of all others.
> (Council of Europe, 2018, p. 18)

While research in the field has delivered more practical suggestions that offer helpful and promising insights into inclusive FL teaching (e.g., Daloiso, 2017; Kormos & Smith, 2012; Oxford University Press Experts, n.d.), the question under what conditions FL teachers actually incorporate these into their classroom practice remains unanswered. As does the question how FL teachers make sense of the contradicting suggestions to, on the one hand, foster learner qualities that promise success at learning and, on the other, to accommodate all forms of learner diversity. In other words, it remains unclear in how far FL teachers manage to perceive various forms of learner diversity as equally favourable in the context of the FL classroom if they rest their worldview on the assumption that language learners with certain neurocognitive, affective, linguistic and personality profiles are predisposed to succeed more than others.

3. METHOD

The investigation was conducted among 25 pre-service EFL teachers, pursuing their MEd degree in Germany, in the state of Bremen. At the time of the study, about 80 per cent of the participants were in an advanced stage of their bachelor's degree and aiming to become secondary school teachers. About 20 per cent of the sample were studying with the goal of becoming a primary school teacher.

The participants filled out an online questionnaire that consisted of open-ended questions as well as numerous statements, which were evaluated on a five-point Likert scale (Table 1). The two open-ended questions aimed to capture the extent to which the participants' agreed that it is possible to speak of "good FL learners." Should this be the case, the participants were then asked to elaborate on their concepts of a "good" and a "poor" FL learner.

In the quantitative part of the questionnaire, the participants evaluated the degree to which they thought that examples of learner personality traits, cognitive styles, mental processes, aspects of social communication and interaction as well as learners' need for structure and organisation are representative of "good" FL learners in an institutionalised teaching context. The selection of items was largely based on the following sources that delineate various qualities, techniques, strategies and traits of learners or individuals:

1. The Learning Style Survey suggested by Cohen, Oxford and Chi (2006), which was developed in order to capture the dimensions of cognitive style, personality traits and perceptual styles that seem to have the most relevance to language learning (Cohen & Weaver, 2006).

2. The Diagnostic and Statistical Manual of Mental Disorders, Fifth Edition (DSM-5) (American Psychiatric Association, 2013), a diagnostic and taxonomic tool that provides an overview of individual traits associated with a number of disabilities and disorders. Particular attention was paid to diagnostic criteria relevant to communication (for example language disorder, speech sound disorder, childhood-onset fluency disorder, social (pragmatic) communication disorder and Autism spectrum).

Table 1

Examples of Items Used in the Quantitative Part of the Questionnaire

personality traits	"Good" learners: enjoy interacting with others; try things out first, even though they do not yet fully understand them; prefer individual activities or games; are often quiet and listen when they are part of a larger group; are often exhausted after working in a larger group.
cognitive styles	"Good learners": form utterances before speaking or writing; ignore details that are not relevant; find it sufficient to understand the rough idea; focus on accuracy before speaking or writing.
communication and interaction	"Good learners": communicate effectively, despite limited vocabulary/grammar; communicate effectively, despite difficulties with coherence; can participate in social interactions; can initiate social interactions; have no difficulties with non-verbal communication.
need for structure and organisation	"Good learners": need detailed and clear instructions; require detailed and clear task descriptions; show flexibility in school routines and rules; are well organised.

The obtained data were anonymised. A random number was assigned to each participant. For example, PN20 meant participant number 20.

4. RESULTS

4.1 CONCEPTUALISATIONS OF "GOOD" LEARNERS IN THE OPEN-ENDED QUESTIONS

The analysis of the two open-ended questions revealed that pre-service EFL teachers were generally in agreement that it is in fact possible to speak of "good" FL learners and were able to identify several traits, qualities, attitudes, or behavioural patterns that, from their perspective, determine the mental set-up of language learners predestined for success. The most prevailing argumentation that the participants used referred to affective or dispositional traits of "good" FL learners: they emphasised the role of motivation, attention and readiness and willingness to learn, also outside of the language classroom. The participants also mentioned having a positive attitude towards and interest in language learning, foreign cultures and mentalities. For example, three participants stated that:

> I think that there are in fact good FL learners. I don't think that this refers to the ability, but to the motivation and attitude towards the FL. (PN 20)

> I believe that what distinguishes good FL learners is that they always show an interest in the language and not only during the lessons. In other words, they are also interested in the language outside the classroom, watching programmes in the language, talking, learning vocabulary, etc. (PN 25)

> A good FL learner is open and motivated by the content presented by the teacher. He/she is also attentive and tries to learn the language in other, non-teaching contexts (for example reading, social media, etc.). (PN 27)

For some participants, discipline and self-organisation on the part of FL learners seemed to be a crucial component that distinguishes "good" FL learners. They seemed to associate "good" FL with actions undertaken by learners themselves to facilitate their learning process. Two comments included:

> Strong will to acquire the language, discipline in learning vocabulary, certain interest in the English-speaking world, communicative. (PN 50)

> Good FL learners are self-motivated, active and ask for help when they do not understand something. (PN 34)

It thus seems that "good" learners are imagined as individuals with a relatively strong sense of self-regulation, which allows them to monitor and manage their emotional states and behaviour actively and in a way that increases their learning.

Pre-service EFL teachers also highlighted the ability to deal with activities that require integration of multiple skills as a trait that distinguish "good" FL learners. In addition, they stressed the importance of metalinguistic skills and a solid grasp of linguistic basics. Three participants made the following observations:

Good FL learners have a fundamentally positive attitude towards FL learning. They also respond well to tasks that require individual or multiple skills. (PN 45)

In my opinion, one can speak of "good" FL learners when there is a high motivation to learn the respective FL. In addition, previous experience, for example in the acquisition of the first language and (written) linguistic competence play an important role. (PN 52)

Yes, in my opinion, one can speak of "good" FL learners, but one should not let oneself be restricted by the term. Characteristics: generally open to other cultures and ways of thinking (are reflected in language), willingness to learn a language, experience with other languages (multilingual if necessary), able to speak meta-linguistically about language, prior knowledge of linguistics. (PN 51)

Only two participants expressed some reservation with respect to the concept of a "good" learner:

I would not necessarily speak of "good" learners, but I do think that a certain enthusiasm for a language can make children "better" learners. (PN 24)

I think it always depends on the context. Accordingly, it is difficult to define what "good" means. Does it mean only to communicate in a foreign language, i.e., even with very little knowledge of the foreign language, or should grammar and so on also correspond to the level of a native speaker. (PN 26)

Many pre-service teachers who accepted the notion of a "good" learner rejected the idea that their counterparts are in fact "poor" learners. For instance, two participants stated the following:

No, if then there are bad preconditions/starting conditions for individual learners (for example a lack of concentration, a lack of motivation, a lack of support, unsuitable learning material etc.). (PN 27)

Bad FL learners do not exist in the ultimate sense. The attributes that were listed when the good FL learners were addressed are allowed not to be present. This does not mean, however, that the learner is a bad FL learner, only that the starting conditions are not optimal. (PN 45)

The participants who were not opposed to operating with the label "poor" learners referred to affective variables such as lack of motivation and the "wrong" attitude to learning and learning strategies as well as to the interest in what goes on in the classroom, their active participation and openness to new methods. Interestingly enough, some participants did not attribute the lack of success or being a poor learner to the learner themselves but did acknowledge the role of external factors such as the teacher. Three participants noted:

Clearly, poor FL learners are unmotivated and have the wrong attitude as well as the wrong learning strategy. However, I also find that it often depends on the learner's teacher. I have noticed this for myself. (PN 3)

Poor FL learners are those who actually have no desire to learn the language. Because of the time span in which the language is learnt, it can come to a change of interests etc., this can also be reversed quickly and with the emerging motivation the bad FL learner changes to a good FL learner. (PN 20)

They do not take part in teaching and do not learn on their own, they are unmotivated and not interested, they close themselves to new teaching methods. (PN 34)

4.2 PRE-SERVICE TEACHERS' PERCEPTIONS OF "GOOD" LEARNERS' TRAITS, STYLES, PROCESSING AND COMMUNICATION TENDENCIES

Cohen and Weaver (2006, p. 13) describe extroverted learners as "energized by the outside world, active, interaction-oriented and outgoing," with broad interests. Introverted learners are the opposite: they are "energized by the inner world, prefer concentration, focus on thoughts and concepts, have fewer interests, but deep ones, like to be reflective" (Cohen & Weaver, 2006, p. 13). When asked to what extent they agree that extrovert and introvert traits characterise "good" language learners, German pre-service EFL teachers tended to favour extrovert traits over introvert ones (Figure 1 and Figure 2). They (strongly) agreed that "good" FL learners try things out and experiment with language, even if they do not fully understand the new material (M=3.98, SD=1.06). They were also of the opinion that "good" learners enjoy interacting with others (M=3.81, SD=1.16) and are happy to take part in classroom discussions (M=4.17, SD=1.07). They were less convinced that "good" learners require the presence of others and learn better in groups than individually.

The participants of the study generally did not perceive introvert traits as representative of how they conceive "good" language learners (Figure 2). Here, they expressed little agreement with the statement that "good" language learners attempt to understand things well before they try them out (M=2.76, SD=1.06). The participants were generally sceptical with respect to the ideas that "good" learners are quiet and listen when being a part of a larger group (M=2.16, SD=1.24), that they can experience exhaustion after working in a larger group (M=2.01, SD=1.28), focus strongly on particular interests (M=2.24, SD=1.28), prefer activities that allow for individual work (M=2.58, SD=1.27) and focus on their "inner world" (M=2.48, SD=1.53).

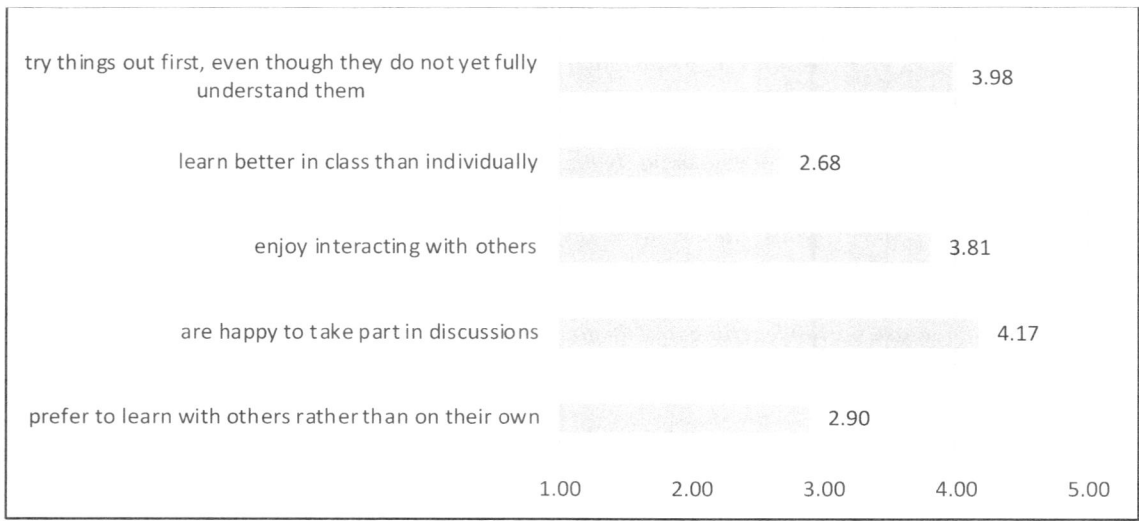

Figure 1. The estimate of extrovert traits being representative of "good" learners on a Likert scale (1= "I completely disagree," 2= "I disagree," 3= "I neither disagree nor agree," 4= "I agree," 5= "I completely agree"). Mean scores.

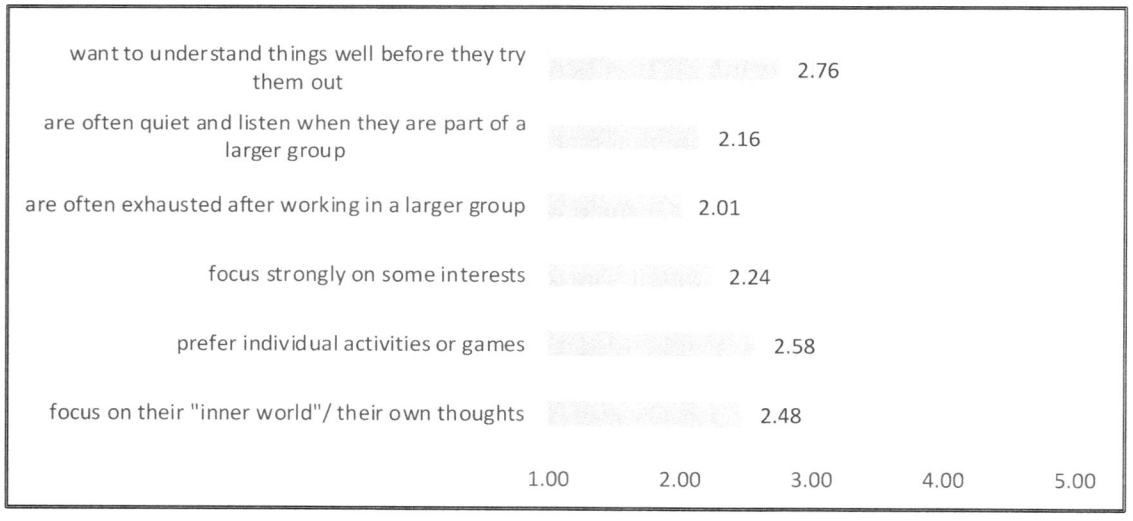

Figure 2. The estimate of introvert traits being representative of "good" learners on a Likert scale (1= "I completely disagree," 2= "I disagree," 3= "I neither disagree nor agree," 4= "I agree," 5= "I completely agree"). Mean scores.

Pre-service teachers of English as an FL showed a similar preference for extrovert-type of traits or tendencies, when asked to evaluate various aspects of communication and social interaction that can prove difficult in the context of several neurodevelopmental disorders as delineated in the DSM-5. There was strong agreement among the participants that "good" language learners can initiate (*M*=4.53, *SD*=0.62) and participate (*M*=4.50, *SD*=0.7) in social interactions. The participants also generally agreed that "good" FL learners have no difficulty in taking turns in a conversation (*M*=4.06, *SD*=0.65), communicate effectively despite limited vocabulary and/or grammar (*M*=3.94, *SD*=0.99) and despite problems with coherence (*M*=3.71, *SD*=1.04), have no difficulties with non-verbal communication (*M*=3.56, *SD*=1.46), understand humour and irony in the target language (*M*=3.94, *SD*=0.87), and cope well with ambiguity in the target language (*M*=3.94, *SD*=9.99). The participants were somewhat less convinced that "good" learners typically like to take part in role-plays (*M*=3.18, *SD*=1.18).

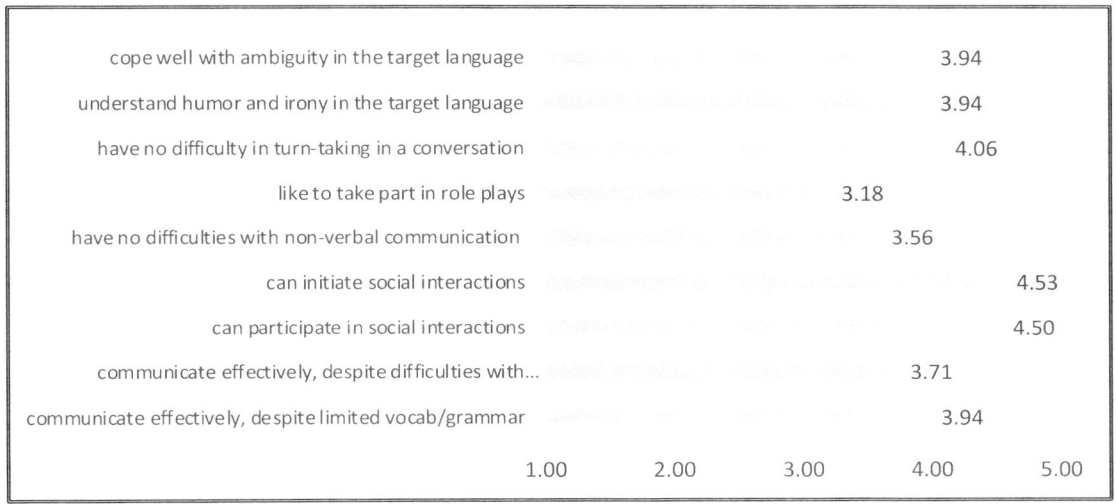

Figure 3. The estimate of how various communicative strategies and preferences are representative of "good" learners on a Likert scale (1= "I completely disagree," 2= "I disagree," 3= "I neither disagree nor agree," 4= "I agree," 5= "I completely agree"). Mean scores.

The participants were also asked to evaluate the extent to which they associate different cognitive styles with the image of a "good" language learner. The questionnaire focused on the distinction suggested by Cohen and Weaver (2006, p. 14) between global and particular learning styles. While the latter refers to learners who require "specific examples to understand fully, pay attention to specific facts or information" and are "good at catching new phrases or words," the former describes learners who "enjoy getting the main idea and are comfortable communicating even if they do not know all the words or concepts" (Cohen & Weaver, 2006, p. 14). The questionnaire also focused on some qualities of reflective learners, who – according to Cohen and Weaver (2006, p. 14) – "process material at low speed with high accuracy" and "avoid risks and guessing" as well as field-independent learners, who are "able to handle the language parts as well as the whole without being distracted" and "good at juggling numerous language elements at once without dropping the ball."

The participants did not seem to strongly agree that learners who need time to focus on accuracy (*M*=3.15, *SD*=1.06) or to formulate their utterances before they start speaking or writing (*M*=2.61, *SD*=1.03) could be characterised as "good" FL learners. Neither were they very convinced that "good" learners would typically express the need to be given concrete ideas in order to understand things completely (*M*=2.56, *SD*=1.15), forget some details (*M*=2.40, *SD*=1.05), be satisfied with a rough understanding of things (*M*=2.58, *SD*=0.79) or ignore details that are not relevant (*M*=4.50, *SD*=0.7) (Figure 4).

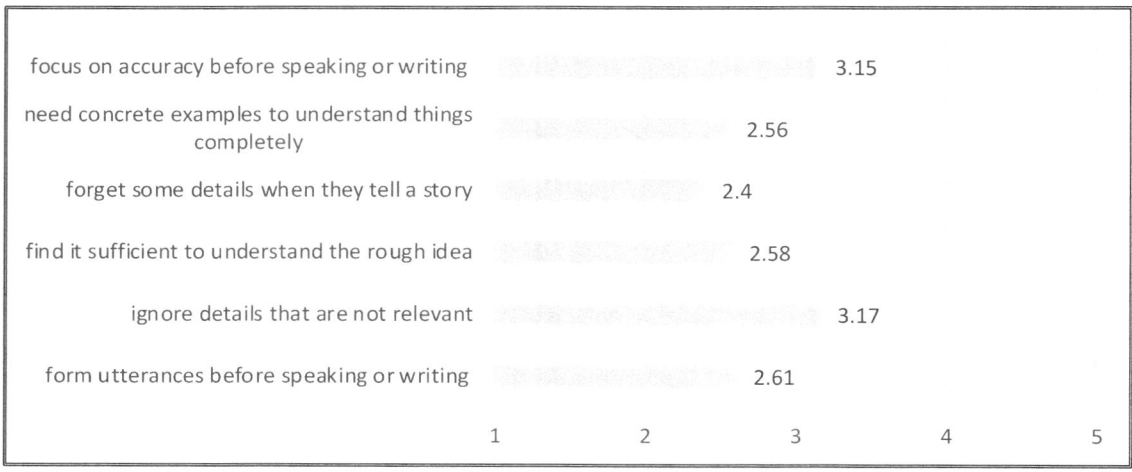

Figure 4. The estimate of how various cognitive styles are representative of "good" learners on a Likert scale (1= "I completely disagree," 2= "I disagree," 3= "I neither disagree nor agree," 4= "I agree," 5= "I completely agree"). Mean scores.

The pre-service FL teachers who took part in the study were also asked to evaluate the extent to which they agreed that various levels of self-organisation and need for structure were characteristic of "good" language learners (Figure 5). Generally, the participants seem to believe that autonomous learners who are well organised (*M*=3.76, *SD*=0.83), have no difficulties with concentration in class (*M*=3.47, *SD*=1.2), can plan their learning well (*M*=3.59, *SD*=1.06), are good problem solvers (*M*=4.0, *SD*=1.2) and show flexibility with respect to the school routines and rules (*M*=3.86, *SD*=1.16) could be considered "good" learners more than the ones who require detailed and clear task descriptions (*M*=2.7, *SD*=0.95) and instructions (*M*=2.89, *SD*=1.13).

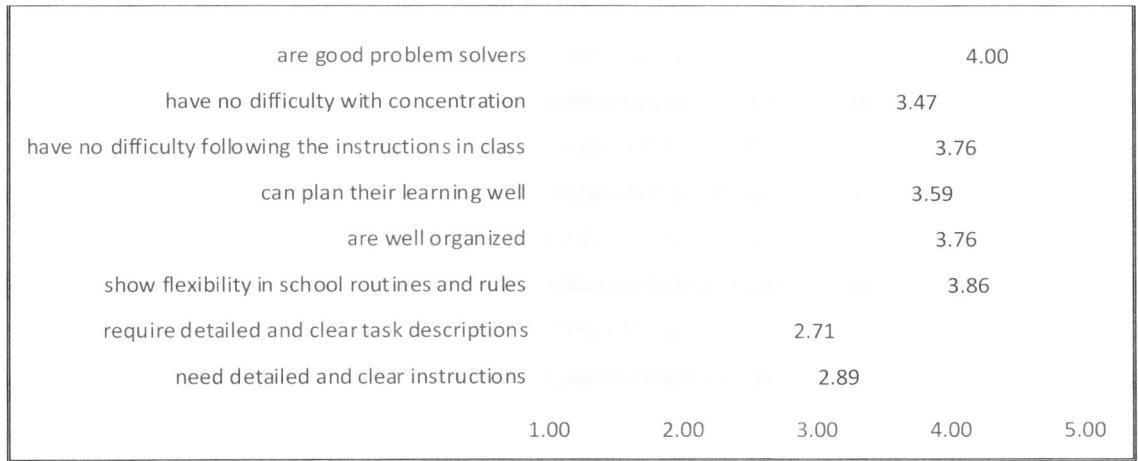

are good problem solvers				4.00	
have no difficulty with concentration				3.47	
have no difficulty following the instructions in class				3.76	
can plan their learning well				3.59	
are well organized				3.76	
show flexibility in school routines and rules				3.86	
require detailed and clear task descriptions			2.71		
need detailed and clear instructions			2.89		
	1.00	2.00	3.00	4.00	5.00

Figure 5. The estimate of how varying degree of organisation and need for structure are representative of "good" learners on a Likert scale (1= "I completely disagree," 2= "I disagree," 3= "I neither disagree nor agree," 4= "I agree," 5= "I completely agree"). Mean scores.

5. DISCUSSION

The main goal of this investigation was to gain insight into the extent to which FL teachers perceive various forms of learner diversity as favourable in the context of the FL classroom. Given that notion of a "good" FL learner was pursued for a significant period of time in the scholarly discourse of the discipline and since the dominant teaching approach of the last 40 years has emphasised the role of communication, interaction, risk-taking and autonomy in the FL classroom, it is sensible to assume that FL teachers do, in fact, rest their professional worldview on the assumption that language learners with certain neurocognitive, affective, linguistic and personality profiles are predisposed to succeed more than others. At the same time, this conviction can be challenged by the basic premise behind inclusive education to increase equity and to recognise and accommodate to the needs of all learners.

The results of the qualitative analysis suggest that German (pre-service) EFL teachers do not reject the notion of a "good" FL learner. In fact, many of them can list several characteristics that they associate with the concept. These are anchored primarily on the affective and dispositional level and encompass learners' motivation, attention, readiness and will to learn, discipline, positive attitudes towards and interest in language learning as well as foreign cultures and mentalities. The quantitative analysis reinforced these findings in that it showed a clear preference among the participants for extrovert learner personality traits over introvert ones. In addition, the analysis revealed that the ability to handle social interactions well and be a successful, risk-taking, flexible communicator, who is not limited by his or her own limited linguistic resources and who does not get hung up on accuracy is associated with the conceptualisation of a "good" FL learner.

191

These results echo what Moyer (2021, p. 28) describes as a "relatively uncontested" assumption that learners "who attain near-native or native-like fluency according to various linguistic skill areas are said to be *gifted, extraordinary,* or *exceptional*". Native-like or near-native skills are believed to be associated with exceptional neurocognitive abilities, positive attitudes, tolerance for risk-taking, motivation, various aspects of personality, consistent experience and L2 use and musical ability (Moyer 2021, p. 44).

Interestingly enough, while some of the participants in this study also operated with the notion of a "poor" learner (and tended to attribute the opposite characteristics to these associated with "good" learners), many pre-service EFL teachers rejected the notion that learners are inherently "poor" and were open to the possibility that external factors (for example, the teacher) influence the success of learning. This scepticism could be a sign that the participants do, in fact, sense that labelling learners as "good" could be interpreted as counterproductive or negative, similarly to Biedron and Pawlak's (2016) description of "giftedness" as an undemocratic designation.

Thus, on a more general level, the results of the study point to the conclusion that pre-service FL teachers are capable of deconstructing the notion of a "good" learner in a relatively complex way, in the sense that they jointly identify a myriad of potential traits that could be associated with the concept. At the same time, it is clear that the demonstrated level of reflection lacks sufficient depth. The participants fail to question some of their (potentially wrong) assumptions or forms of bias, such as believing that "good" learners are extrovert learners or asymmetrically rejecting the notion of a "poor" learner, while accepting the idea of a "good" one. In other words, pre-service FL teachers seem not to realise fully that assigning significance to various learner traits may in fact be problematic, or even wrong, on their part as teachers. In this sense, they seem to be having difficulties navigating between various contradicting assumptions about how FL education should be organised, focusing more on the individual learner rather than socially-constructed barriers produced by the environment.

Yet, there are several reasons why the results of the study should be interpreted with a degree of caution. The relatively small sample consisted of pre-service teachers pursuing their teaching degree in and for the German educational system, more specifically for the northern state of Bremen. Some observations in the field of educational science suggest that teacher beliefs are relatively specific and bound to their local contexts. Tyack and Tobin (1994) demonstrate that institutionalised education generally tends to be stable and robust in terms of its organisation and structure. Bloemert et al. (2016) suggest that such set ways, or curricular heritage(s), are inherited within the local context, at least with respect to teaching certain content aspects. It is thus conceivable that teachers, often being products of the very same educational system that they act within, largely adopt the existing local curricula and teaching approaches, and thereby create their unique teaching contexts and belief systems that may differ across borders. Assuming that different educational systems in Europe have established their robust local traditions and structures in the course of their histories, it is plausible that teachers involved in these systems experience their workings in idiosyncratic ways and would thus express different views with respect to the notion of a "good" FL learner.

6. CONCLUSION

The perception of a "good" FL learner as an autonomous, interactive, motivated and well-organised individual expressed by pre-service teachers involved in the German/Bremen educational system is not that uncommon in FL contexts. In fact, it is frequently channelled in communicative methodologies and materials typically used in English language classrooms. These often promote a learner-centred rather than teacher-orientated and interactive learning environment, which has the potential to nurture learning difficulties rather than to address the needs of all learners (Oxford University Press Experts, n.d.). A similar problem can be seen in the more recent developments in research into learner strategies, which have focused on acknowledging various forms of learner techniques, rather than concentrating on capturing the nature of "good" learners. These accounts encourage FL learners to explore and take on different learning styles that are not necessarily natural for them and call for awareness raising, strategic thinking and being in control of their own learning (Cohen & Weaver, 2006). The question that arises here is whether such an autonomous and proactive approach to learning is attainable and in fact desirable to every student and, more importantly, whether it is compatible with the goal to increase equity in an FL classroom. If the principles of inclusive education are to set foot in the FL classroom for good, communicative language teaching will need to ease on the necessity to organise learning primarily as social interaction, thereby accommodating to the needs of learners who are for example naturally and neurodiversely less inclined to communicate. These learners may benefit from quiet time to work individually and from initially working in smaller groups. FL education may also need to rethink the degree of teacher-led practice and drills of, for example, phonological elements of language, which typically gives way to more interactionist and naturalist ways of acquiring language but can foster the much needed development of phonological awareness among learners who are challenged in that area (Daloiso, 2017). Last but not least, FL education may need to critically reflect on the organisation of teaching in terms of the degree of autonomy, need for structure, range of attitudes, amount of discipline and self-organisation that can and should be expected and/or required of FL students. These are the questions that need to be addressed if hidden contradictions associated with dominant teaching approaches are not to exert a negative impact on the overt teaching practice.

REFERENCES

Allan, J. (2006). Failing to Make Progress? The aporias of responsible inclusion. In E. Brantlinger (Ed.), *Who benefits from special education? Remediating (Fixing) other people's children.* (pp. 27–44). Mahwah, NJ: Lawrence Erlbaum Associates.

American Psychiatric Association. (2013). DSM-5 diagnostic classification. Retrieved from https://doi.org/10.1176/appi.books.9780890425596

Baecco, J. C., & Byram, M. (2007). *From linguistic diversity to plurilingual education: Guide for the development of language education policies in Europe.* Strasbourg: Council of Europe.

Bandura, A. (1986). Fearful expectations and avoidant actions as coeffects of perceived self-inefficacy. *American Psychologist, 41*(12), 1389–1391.

Biedron, A., & Pawlak, M. (2016). New conceptualizations of linguistic giftedness. *Language Teaching, 49*, 151-185.

Bloemert, J., Jansen, E., & van de Grift, W. (2016). Exploring EFL literature approaches in Dutch secondary education. *Language, Culture and Curriculum, 29*(2), 169–188.

Booth, T., & Ainscow, M. (2003). *Index for inclusion: Developing learning and participation in schools.* Bristol: Centre for Studies on Inclusive Education.

Brady, S. A., & Shankweiler, D. P. (Eds.). (1991). *Phonological processes in literacy: A tribute to Isabelle Y. Liberman.* Hillsdale, NJ: Lawrence Erlbaum Associates.

Brown, D. (2001). *Teaching by principle.* White Plains, NY: Addison Wesley Longman.

Canale, M. (1983). On some dimensions of language proficiency. In J. W. Oller (Ed.), *Issues in language testing research* (pp. 333–342). Rowley, MA: Newbury House Publishers.

Canale, M., & Swain, M. (1980). Theoretical bases of communicative approaches to second language teaching and testing. *Applied Linguistics, 1*(1), 1–47.

Celce-Murcia, M. (2007). Rethinking the role of communicative competence in language teaching. In E. A. Soler & M. S. Jorda (Eds.), *Intercultural language use and language learning* (pp. 41–57). Dordrecht: Springer.

Clough, P., & Corbett, J. (2000). *Theories of inclusive education.* London: SAGE.

Cohen, A. D., Oxford, R., & Chi, J. (2006). *Learning style survey: Assessing your own learning styles. Maximizing study abroad: An instructional guide to strategies for language and culture learning and use.* Minneapolis, MN: CARLA, University of Minnesota.

Cohen, A. D., & Weaver, S. J. (2006). *Styles- and strategies-based instruction: A teachers' guide.* Minneapolis, MN: Center for Advanced Research on Language Acquisition.

Council of Europe. (2001). *Common European framework of reference for languages: Learning, teaching, assessment.* Cambridge: Cambridge University Press.

Council of Europe. (2018). *Common European framework of reference for languages: Learning, teaching, assessment. Companion volume with new descriptors.* Strasbourg: Council of Europe.

Daloiso, M. (2017). *Supporting learners with dyslexia in the ELT classroom.* Oxford: Oxford University Press.

Dyson, A. (2001). The Gulliford lecture: Special needs in the twenty-first century: Where we've been and where we're going. *British Journal of Special Education, 28*(1), 24–29.

Emanuelsson, I. (2001). Reactive versus proactive support coordinator roles: An international comparison. *European Journal of Special Needs Education, 16*(2), 133–142.

Experts, O. U. (n.d.). *Inclusive practices in English language teaching.* Retrieved from https://elt.oup.com/feature/global/expert/inclusive?cc=de&selLanguage=de

Eysenck, M. W., & Calvo, M. G. (1992). Anxiety and Performance: The processing efficiency theory. *Cognition and Emotion, 6*(6), 409–434.

Fillmore, C. J., Kempler, D., &. Wang, W. S-Y. (1979). *Individual differences in language ability and language behavior.* New York, NY: Academic Press.

Frederickson, N., & Cline, T. (2002). *Special educational needs inclusion and diversity: A textbook*. Buckingham: Open University Press.

Ganschow, L., & Sparks, R. (1995). Effects of direct instruction in Spanish phonology on the native language skills and foreign language aptitude of at-risk foreign language learners. *Journal of Learning Disabilities, 28*, 107–120.

Hochschulrektorenkonferenz, (HRK) [Conference of rectors of higher education institutions]. (2015). *Lehrerbildung für eine Schule der Vielfalt. Gemeinsame Empfehlung von Hochschulrektorenkonferenz und Kultusministerkonferenz* [*Teacher education for a school of diversity. Joint Recommendation of the German Rectors` Conference and the Standing Conference of the Ministers of Education and Cultural Affairs of the States*]. https://www.hrk.de/fileadmin/_migrated/content_uploads/HRK-KMK-Empfehlung_Inklusion_in_LB_032015.pdf

Howatt, A. P. R., & Smith, R. (2014). The history of teaching English as an FL, from a British and European perspective. *Language and History, 57*(1), 75–95.

Jacobs, G. M., & Farrell, T. S. C. (2003). Understanding and implementing the CLT (Communicative Language Teaching) paradigm. *RELC Journal, 34*(1), 4–30.

Kormos, J., & Smith, A. M. (2012). *Teaching languages to students with specific learning differences.* Bristol: Multilingual Matters.

Masgoret, A. M., & Gardner, R. C. (2003). Attitudes, motivation, and second language learning: A meta-analysis of studies conducted by Gardner and associates. *Language Learning, 53*(1), 123–163.

Moody, R. (1988). Personality preferences and FL learning. *The Modern Language Journal, 72*(4), 389–401.

Moyer, A. (2021). *The gifted language learners. A case of nature or nurture?* Cambridge: Cambridge University Press.

Naiman, N., Fröhlich, M., Stern, H. H., & Todesco, A. (1978). *The good language learner.* Toronto: Ontario Institute for Studies in Education.

Nijakowska, J. (2008). An experiment with direct multisensory instruction in teaching word reading and spelling to Polish dyslexic learners of English. In J. Kormos & E. H. Kontra (Eds.), *Language learners with special needs: An international perspective* (pp. 130–157). Bristol: Multilingual Matters.

Norton, B., & Toohey, K. (2001). Changing perspectives on good language learners. *TESOL Quarterly, 35*(2), 307–322.

Nunan, D. (1995). *Language teaching methodology*. Hemel Hempstead: Phoenix ELT.

Oxford, R. L. (2003). Language learning styles and strategies: An overview. *Proceedings of GALA Conference*. Retrieved from http://web.ntpu.edu.tw/~language/workshop/read2.pdf

Ramus, F., Rosen, S., Dakin, S. C., Day, B. L., Castellote, J. M., White, S., & Frith, U. (2003). Theories of developmental dyslexia: Insights from a multiple case study of dyslexic adults. *Brain, 126*(4), 841–865.

Riddick, B. (2001). Dyslexia and inclusion: Time for a social model of disability perspective? *International Studies in Sociology of Education, 11*(3), 223–236.

Rubin, J. (1975). What the "good language learner" can teach us. *TESOL Quarterly, 47*(4), 549–566.

Smith, A-M. (2008). Teachers' and trainers' perspectives of inclusive education within TEFL certificate courses in Britain. In J. Komos & E. H. Kontra (Eds.), *Language learners with special needs: An international perspective* (pp. 214–233). Clevedon: Multilingual Matters.

Sparks, R., & Ganschow, L. (1991). FL learning differences: Affective or native language aptitude differences? *The Modern Language Journal, 75*(1), 3–16.

Thomas, G., & Loxley, A. (2007). *Deconstructing special education and constructing inclusion.* Buckingham: Open University Press.

Tyack, D., & Tobin, W. (1994). The "grammar" of schooling: Why has it been so hard to change? *American Educational Research Journal, 31*(3), 453–479.

Ushioda, E. (2008). Motivation and good language learners. In C. Griffiths (Ed.), *Lessons from good language learners* (pp. 19–34). Cambridge: Cambridge University Press.

Vislie, L. (2003). From integration to inclusion: Focusing global trends and changes in the Western European societies. *European Journal of Special Needs Education, 18*(1), 17–35.

Wickenden, M. (2019). "Disabled" versus "nondisabled": Another redundant binary? In A. Twum-Danso Imoh, M. Bourdillon, & S. Meichsner (Eds.), *Global childhoods beyond the North-South divide* (pp. 123–144). Cham: Palgrave Studies on Children and Development. Palgrave Macmillan.

Wiseman, R. L. (2002). Intercultural communication competence. In W. B. Gudykunst & B. Mody (Eds.), *Handbook of international and intercultural communication* (pp. 207–224). Thousand Oaks, CA: Sage.

Teaching EFL Online

ISBN 9781911369486

An e-moderator's report
(New edition)

Andrew R. Webster

Socially distanced learning and online lessons are playing an increasingly important role in the teaching of English as a Foreign or Second Language. Face-to-face teaching is being supplemented or even replaced by video platforms and e-learning solutions and by the targeted exploitation of virtual reality environments.

This book explores the role played by the e-moderator in creating and teaching an online course in a virtual world. Combining research and practice, this study details relevant theories of online learning and shows how they are represented through various models, creating a framework to assist the e-moderation process.

The result is highly insightful work which uncovers the e-moderator's beliefs and perceptions, revealing not only the complexities, problems, responsibilities and challenges encountered, but also the tremendous rewards that can be gained from e-moderation.

EFL Communication Strategies in a Virtual World

ISBN 9781911369509

(New edition)

Susan Gowans

This book reports the findings of an exploratory case study examining the communication strategies used between three adult EFL learners and their teacher during meaning-focused conversation tasks in the virtual 3D world of Second Life. The analysis of the session transcript reveals the extent to which the participants employed communication strategies concomitant with face-to-face interactions for effective conversation management.

The data also shows that the participants adapted their communication strategies to suit the virtual world platform, thereby overcoming the conversational ambiguities that arose from the absence of paralinguistic signals.

Discourse analysis of the transcript offers further insight into power relations, politeness and risk taking and provides signs of sociocultural learning and language development in keeping with Second Language Acquisition theory.

Gateway English

ISBN 9781911369097

How to Boost your English Word Power and Unlock New Languages

Dr Michael Arnheim

Dr Arnheim's unique approach shows how English can be used as a gateway to other languages.

Taking you on a rollercoaster ride of linguistic discovery, the author guides you through the origins and interconnections of words you know, words that may be new to you and words you only thought you knew.

Vocabulary is the undisputed key to language learning, and the author draws on a wealth of experience and insight to illustrate that the more you know about English words and their origins, the easier it is to study any related language. More than an academic study, more than mere entertainment and more than a conventional language course, Gateway English enables you to boost your English word power and unlock new languages.

Dr Michael Arnheim is a practising London barrister and author of over twenty published books. Educated in the United Kingdom and South Africa, he is a Sometime Fellow of St John's College, Cambridge, and former Professor of Classics at the University of the Witwatersrand, Johannesburg.

Practice Makes Perfect

ISBN 9781911369523

Partner Grammar Drills for English Language Learners Intermediate (B2)

Andrew Garth

Practice Makes Perfect proves that grammar training can be fun. This innovative classroom resource is ideal for intermediate to advanced learners who want to improve their grammatical accuracy through spoken practice. Taking an experience-driven approach, the activities focus on language points that are known to require extensive practice before learners can begin to use them accurately and with confidence.

What sets this book apart from other grammar books is that structures are practised primarily through interactive pair work. This guided speaking practice incorporates student-to-student partner drills whereby one partner can check the other partner's answers in real time, providing immediate feedback.

The partner drill focus of this book makes it suitable for use in classes of all sizes as well as in multi-level classes, since the framework used enables less advanced students to complete the activities in dialogue with linguistically more advanced members of their peer group.

Artificial Intelligence in Autonomous Language Learning

An Expert Systems Approach to Computer Assisted EFL Self Study

Maurice Claypole

Despite major advances in computer hardware generally and in software development techniques in areas such as engineering troubleshooting and gaming, computer assisted foreign language learning applications have not kept pace with the general trend.

This is as true today as it was when the content of this book was first set out and in a sense we are still waiting for the envisaged breakthrough which will harness the power of artificial intelligence and object-oriented software development in order to create truly effective software solutions specifically designed for the independent language learner.

The third edition of this book presents a snapshot in time outlining the scope of software solutions available for autonomous language learning at an early stage of their development and then goes on to examine the interface between the technology of expert systems and the latest applications in the fields of natural language processing, interactive gaming, online learning and virtual reality.

DEVELOPING LEARNER AUTONOMY THROUGH TASKS

ISBN 9781911369011

THEORY, RESEARCH, PRACTICE

Andrzej Cirocki

At the heart of this study is the fostering of learner autonomy in the language classroom, in particular how learner autonomy can be developed through pedagogical tasks. The work focuses on four different approaches: learner-related, classroom-related, resource-related and technology-related.

Developing Learner Autonomy through Tasks combines classroom theory, research and practice, all of which are immersed in the philosophy of social constructivism, whereby knowledge and learning are seen as both the context for and the result of human interaction.

"This is the book everyone in the field has been waiting for. It is the product of excellent classroom research. . . highly engaging, relevant, readable, and above all, practical in its handling of the issues."

Prof. John McRae, University of Nottingham, UK

"This book is a perfect combination of theoretical and practical proposals that make it possible to implement and foster learner autonomy in the Efl/Esl classroom."

Prof. Wolfgang Hallet, Justus Liebig University, Giessen, Germany

Student's Book
ISBN 9781911369240

Academic Presenting and Presentations

A preparation course for university students

Peter Levrai and Averil Bolster

CEFR Level B2 - C1

This practical training course is designed to help students cultivate academic presentation skills and deal with the variety of presentation tasks they may need to master during their studies.

Teacher's Book
ISBN 9781911369257

The material is suitable for a global audience and can be used in a wide range of academic contexts since the content not only helps learners develop their presentation skills in English but also considers wider topics relevant to English for Academic Purposes, such as principles of research and the dangers of plagiarism.

The accompanying online video presentations enable learners to immerse themselves still further in the material presented and witness first hand the impact of the techniques illustrated.

LinguaBooks Adult Readers

Short stories for adult learners

CEFR Level C1 - C2

Each reader in this series consists of a collection of five original short stories with accompanying explanations, exercises and extension tasks. The focus throughout is on authenticity and originality.

In this approach, the language of the stories has not been simplified for easy reading ; rather, emergent difficulties are explained in the notes with further guidance provided for deeper understanding, creative extension and autonomous learning.

The stories themselves present a varied mix of style and content, ranging from the surprising to the contemplative, with a touch of humour and an occasional hint of pathos.

A Busker on Bow Street
ISBN 9781911369103

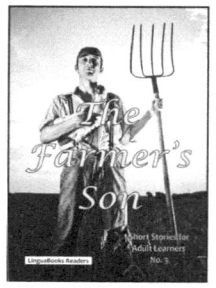

The Farmer's Son
ISBN 9781911369127

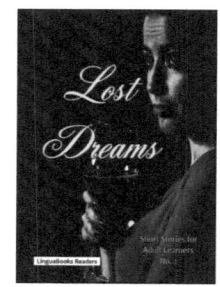

Lost Dreams
ISBN 9781911369110

The Seasonal Visitor
ISBN 9781911369134

www.linguabooks.com